SMYTHE'S MOUNTAINS

SMYTHE'S MOUNTAINS

The Climbs of F. S. Smythe

by

HARRY CALVERT

LONDON
VICTOR GOLLANCZ LTD
1985

First published in Great Britain 1985
by Victor Gollancz Ltd,
14 Henrietta Street, London WC2E 8QJ

British Library Cataloguing in Publication Data
Calvert, Harry
Smythe's mountains.
1. Smythe, F. S. 2. Mountaineers—Great
Britain—Biography
I. Title
796.5′22′0924 GV199.92.S9

ISBN 0-575-03550-1

Photoset in Great Britain by
Rowland Phototypesetting Ltd, Bury St Edmunds, Suffolk
and printed by St Edmundsbury Press
Bury St Edmunds, Suffolk
Illustrations originated and printed by Thomas Campone, Southampton

To Heather

ACKNOWLEDGMENTS

I am very grateful to the Countess of Essex for permission to reproduce a selection of Smythe's photographs and wish to thank the Alpine Club for allowing me to use Ruttledge's photograph of the 1936 Everest expedition team and for their library facilities. I wish to acknowledge the sources upon which I have liberally drawn, the chief of which are listed in the bibliography.

H.C.

CONTENTS

LIST OF ILLUSTRATIONS

following page 64

following page 160

NOTE

All photographs by F. S. Smythe are reproduced by kind permission of the Countess of Essex.

DIAGRAM & MAPS

PREFACE

IT IS IMPOSSIBLE adequately to describe the pleasure Frank Smythe has given me. I had done a little walking in the Lakes and the Yorkshire Dales when I received his photographic album, *Alpine Ways*, as a Christmas present. It opened a window on a whole new aspect of the hills, and I shall be eternally grateful for that. I gradually acquired and read others of his books; increasingly, I found myself covering the same ground and standing on the same summits that Smythe had visited many years earlier. I had not planned this and were it not that the coincidence could easily be explained by Smythe having been just about everywhere where there were mountains, I would have begun to suspect supernatural intervention. The prosaic reality is that I am one of countless thousands whose lives have been enriched by his indirect acquaintance.

For these thousands, to whom this book is offered, the great merit of Smythe's writing is that he says what they want to hear. Smythe had a unique capacity for putting into words and pictures what we want to read and see. If there is a justification for this book, it is as a reminder of the career he describes and as offering another opportunity to relive his adventures and share his vision of mountains.

The book is neither a climbing guide nor a biography except in a most unusual sense. Being a mountaineer of mediocre pretensions, I have followed Smythe's footsteps only over relatively easy ground —much as I would like to, I have never yet ventured on to the Brenva Face and have not been nearer than a hundred miles to the scenes of his Himalayan epics. I cannot therefore comment from first-hand experience upon the hard courses which did much to establish his reputation amongst the aficionados of the day.

Nor have I been concerned to probe amongst the interstices of the personality and character of the flesh-and-blood Smythe. Many of his contemporaries are still alive and much better-placed to write about the man they knew. Vastly more know and love the character that emerges from the literature—what Smythe himself wrote and what others chose to write about him. This book is about that Smythe; I do not know and do not wish to enquire whether there also existed a Secret Smythe who had other and different interests.

First and foremost, this book is intended to be enjoyed by the same sort of audience for which Smythe himself primarily wrote. To them, he told two different types of tale. The stories of his more hardy experiences were for the armchair—few would experience the urge, let alone yield to it, to rush out and relive them. Much of what he wrote, however, expressed a simple delight in mountaineering of an altogether more modest character such as almost anyone might seek to emulate. Smythe has been the inspiration of untold numbers who have done just this and it is as one of them, and in a way as an acknowledgment of a debt which can never be repaid, that I have put pen to paper. If what results savours of eulogy, it is entirely appropriate that it should do so.

I acknowledge, with great gratitude, other debts—to many who have, wittingly or otherwise, contributed to the writing of this book. They include all those brave souls who have tied on to the rope at various times, especially Mike, Alan, Dave and my daughters. I am particularly grateful to Jacqui Jones for bringing order out of a chaotic manuscript and to Livia Gollancz who has been patient, long-suffering and helpful far beyond the call of duty. Lastly, Heather, to whom a two-fold debt is due, firstly and mundanely for wrestling nobly with an otherwise more turgid and impenetrable style and secondly for persisting as the only really serious competitor to Smythe as a source of joy.

H.C.

Blades
December 1984

CHAPTER I

A Brief Life

CASUAL OBSERVATION OF the mountaineering scene in the 1980s, especially as depicted in contemporary sources such as books and journals, might well lead one to conclude that the only British mountaineers today are young and extremely fit men climbing at grades of extreme severity; and it is indeed the case that routes are now being done which baffle not merely the physical capacity but even the imagination of lesser mortals. If, however, instead of merely absorbing the literature, one wanders out on to the hillside, it will be seen that mountaineers, in the broadest sense of the term, come in all shapes, sizes and ages. One common type is the slightly portly, somewhat huffy, grey-haired almost-old codger, pottering about the place with a faded sac and ancient boots. Stop one and talk to him. If, as is likely, the conversation gets round to the question of why he ever went on the hill in the first place, you will be surprised how often the name "Frank Smythe" crops up as part of the explanation. It is some 35 years since Smythe died in an Uxbridge hospital. Had he lived he would undoubtedly now be a respected elder statesman of the sport and might, in his most articulate way, have come to offer us some explanation of the mystery and paradox which surrounded him. As it is, we can only speculate.

In very many respects, Francis Sydney Smythe is an enigma. Sickly throughout childhood and invalided out of the Royal Air Force in his mid-twenties, he became a legend in his own lifetime for his feats of courage and endurance in the most inhospitable of mountain ranges. Almost retarded in his education as a result of this frailty, he became one of the most articulate, popular and prolific of all mountaineering authors. Clearly capable of close and affectionate relationships with some people, he was nevertheless almost despised by others and, indeed, positively hated by one. He began and finished his climbing career alone. Some considered him clumsy and incompetent; others have characterized several of his climbing feats as the greatest they ever witnessed.

This paradoxical note is continued in the personal views and attitudes revealed in his writings. Obsessed in one place with setting the first foot on the summit of Everest, in another he bestows the highest praise on mountain wandering in humble ranges. At one moment he lauds the companionship of the hills; at another it is solitary climbing which is the "grand cognac" of mountaineering. He frequently reveals himself as what can be most kindly (and, appropriately, paradoxically) described as a liberal of limited tolerance, at one moment exhorting the masses to savour the bouquet of the mountain experience and at the next castigating trippers, tourists and even anyone daring to occupy a mattress in the same hut so as to rob him of his solitary enjoyment of the hills.

Whatever contradiction may attend his motivation, skill or personality, however, two facts are indisputable. Firstly, measured against the standards of the day Smythe's record of mountaineering achievement is outstanding, whether as a party to the most significant advances in Alpine climbing between the wars or as leader of what was, in its day, the most successful Himalayan climbing expedition ever. Secondly, and perhaps even more significantly, Smythe was the greatest of all popularizers of the sport, and this in two quite different respects. His accounts of his mountaineering adventures were certainly widely read, and he thus secured for mountaineering literature a popular readership where, previously, it had consisted largely of the cognoscenti. But his books were very often accounts not of the great feats of the most able and accomplished (although these certainly figure) but, on the contrary, descriptions of mountain experiences which were quite unremarkable as feats of physical prowess, couched in terms of simple delight and enjoyment, available to all and calculated to tempt ordinary men and women into sharing them. *Kamet Conquered* and *Camp Six* might well thrill but would likely deter. *Over Tyrolese Hills* and *Again Switzerland*, by contrast, send one rushing for the train in order to emulate.

Smythe's life spanned almost exactly the first half of this century and ended at an age less than that at which men have subsequently set foot on the summit which Everest denied him. He did, however, contrive to spend an extraordinary proportion of this brief life in the mountains. If we are to believe his account, his association with the hills spanned 46 of his 49 years.

He was born, on 6 July 1900, into a fairly well-to-do Kentish rentier family. But he was only two years old when the event occurred which, more than any other, influenced his subsequent career. His father, who owned a timber wharf and other property in and around Maidstone, died and can thus have never exercised any significant influence over the development of his son's character and personality. Had he lived, the response to the ill-health which marked Smythe's early life might well have been different. As it was, it was left to his mother to cope.

There is little doubt that the young Smythe endured repeated illnesses. He suffered from a persistent heart-murmur which, a quarter of a century later, was considered sufficiently serious to warrant his discharge from the RAF. Only when it was detected by Raymond Greene, a surgeon, on the Kamet expedition in 1931, was it found to be of no "sinister significance". Even in later life, most descriptions of Smythe refer to him as "frail", "slightly-built" or "small" (although one, incongruously, refers to him as "robust and well-built"). Whilst the heart-murmur posed no serious threat to his well-being, his mother's response to it did. She considered him to be of a dangerously weak constitution and she behaved over-protectively towards him with the result that his upbringing was unduly impaired.

His physical condition appears not to have been totally inhibiting for, so he tells us, he first felt the pull of the hills at the age of three and was only seven or eight years old when, sent to Switzerland for health reasons, he made his first significant ascent, that of Mont Cray, a very modest 6,000 foot summit overlooking Château d'Oex. The motivation for this adventure came from within himself and the sense of wonder which the ascent awakened in that young imagination in no way differs from that frequently revealed by the mature man on numerous occasions throughout the ensuing decades.

Smythe himself attributes the further development of this interest in mountaineering to Whymper's *Scrambles Amongst the Alps*, presented to him whilst still too young to enthuse and then rediscovered with seminal effect a year or so later. It is, however, doubtful whether Whymper's influence extended beyond crystallizing ideas and ambitions already forming in Smythe's mind.

When thirteen years old, he was sent to Berkhamsted School as a "day-bug", where his career was the very opposite of distinguished. Raymond Greene, also at the school where his father was headmaster, later spoke of Smythe's subsequent achievement as indicating that his education had been beneficial. He considered that it amply vindicated the judgment that Smythe should concentrate in the areas of geography, English literature and electrical mechanics. However, everyone else came to the opposite conclusion. Far from being, as Greene would have it, "testimonials to a brilliant educational experiment", Smythe's subsequent careers were referable to his school experience, if they were so referable at all, only in a wholly different way.

He himself attributed his failure at school to "myself, the system of education and the war". His own contribution consisted, it seems, on the physiological side of contracting "chronic bronchitis, influenza, pneumonia (twice) and an enlarged heart", and on the psychological side of an antipathy towards the exploitation of the competitive instinct as an educational method. His delicate health not only impeded his academic development but was assumed to rule out entirely the physical demands of games and sports. The result was a deprivation of companionship and the nurturing of a bitter resentment not so much against the school and its personnel as against the values which the system endorsed and the fates which conspired to render his schooldays so painful and unrewarding. The English school system has still not overcome its tendency to regard underachievement as morally reprehensible; in Smythe's days at Berkhamsted, the attempt to do so was still some decades off. If, in his later years, he was not always comfortable in society, the germs of that reticence and of the dislike which it seems to have aroused in some others are to be found here; and if his school career was to have any immediate impact upon the development of a great mountaineer, it was neither through the inculcation of team spirit, nor the pseudo-masochistic ideals of a Gordonstoun, but rather through the creation of a sheer necessity to escape, in the life of the imagination at least, from the enduring humiliation, loneliness and alienation which were the education system's legacies to Smythe.

This barren harvest of Smythe's schooldays is the more surprising in view of the later evidence of undeniable talent. He himself confesses to an interest in geography and nothing else. Yet his travel books reveal a literacy, an articulateness and particularly an imagination which must surely have been present in embryo at a much earlier age. Similarly, his outstanding contribution to mountain photography in later life cannot have sprung from nothing but must surely have been the realization of a talent latent in the young Smythe of Berkhamsted School.

In the final analysis, school seems to have had a profound impact on the development of Smythe the mountaineer only in a perverse but nevertheless very seminal way. He was not one of those who, like Andrew Irvine, were embraced and shaped by the public school system to emerge with the ideals manifested by Irvine on his one short sortie into the highest mountains. Smythe was a misfit. School gave him dreams as an escape, and self-sufficiency as a means of survival. Throughout his life, he was as happy with his own company as with almost any other save only his second wife. School seems to have taught him little of the joys of companionship and, although he later learned something of them, social living was rarely unaccompanied by stress. He became, and by disposition remained to the end, a "loner". Nor was this simply a one-way process of Smythe being excluded from the inner circles of first the school and later other establishments. School seems to have offered him little opportunity for social giving as well as taking. Others' opinions of the mature man, although frequently complimentary of his skills and laudatory of his achievements, are less commonly affectionate or kindly-disposed towards the man himself. Those who never came to know him well commonly thought him to be arrogant, taciturn, standoffish and even "infuriatingly self-sufficient". Perhaps significantly, it was more than once remarked that the higher and tougher the going, the more companionable he became; it looks as though hardship evaporated the need for the social niceties and made relationships easier.

Smythe's condition has been diagnosed as "a severe inferiority complex" and his mountaineering achievements explained as a classic case of over-compensation. Whilst this judgment may have some merit as a thumb-nail sketch of the man and what drove him on, it is by no means the whole story. Smythe's schooldays may or may not have left him with a feeling of inferiority—it would be surprising if they had not; but less doubtfully and more relevantly, they left him with a feeling of alienation. They may have made him determined to prove wrong those whose judgment seemed to be that he was a boy of neither talent nor promise; more likely, they failed to interest and absorb him—failed, in other words, to imbue in him any ambition or purpose and left him to generate within himself ideals and standards fostered by experience and the likes of Whymper's *Scrambles* . . .

From the age of fifteen, these ideals were realized in summer holidays, wandering alone amongst the hills of North Wales. There is no evidence that in so doing he was, in any sense, performing for an audience, which one would have expected to be the case had the sole motivation been a sense of inferiority. If his own account is to be believed, and there is no reason to doubt it, the urge was curiosity and self-challenge and the result not at all invariably pleasurable and flattering.

For some years after school, Smythe persisted in a half-hearted attempt to carve out a career as an electrical engineer. He pursued courses at Faraday House Electrical Engineering College and then worked for a year in Bradford, Yorkshire, which at least had the virtue of offering ready access to the Dales and to Almscliff Crag. Prior to this, the nearest Smythe had come to associating with climbers was to gaze in awestruck admiration from the summit of Tryfan at a rope emerging over the lip of the steep East Face. Now, in the immediate post-war years, Almscliff, that insignificant gritstone pimple overlooking Wharfedale, was teeming with great names such as Howard Somervell and Ernest Roberts. Smythe joined this circle and thereafter, sometimes with the Yorkshire Ramblers, frequently alone, made regular visits to the Lakes. He here learned the rudiments of rock-climbing and he seems also to have learned something else for he spoke in later years in uncomplimentary terms about "Northern climbers", regarding them in much the same light as had the Romans, in earlier centuries, the Picts and Scots.

Smythe's professional leanings next inclined him in the direction of hydro-electric power generation and we find him, by the happiest of coincidences, spending two years in Austria and Switzerland, based for most of the time in the areas around Innsbruck and Baden. Almost every spare moment seems to have been spent in the mountains, and in the space of eighteen months he had become a competent skier and had laid the foundations of that brilliant technique on snow and ice which was to be his pre-eminent skill in the years that followed. In all these matters, he was entirely self-taught except for such guidance as might be gleaned from the texts of Whymper,

Mummery and others. Throughout his whole career, Smythe never employed a guide purely as a guide. To what extent this was merely fortuitous, a matter of principle or simply the product of a sense of economy deriving from his earlier days in Yorkshire is not clear. He did not dislike guides; on the contrary, he had great affection and respect for them. He did, on one occasion, flirt with the idea of employing the services of Winthrop Young's great guide, Joseph Knubel, then well into his fifties. He was, it is true, "guided" up his first modest Swiss peak by a lad from the village—and twice teamed up with guides as companions for a particular purpose. It rather seems, though, that he considered to submit to the leadership of a guide would destroy a large part of the purpose of climbing at all and it was that, rather than high principle, which explained his abstinence.

Electrical engineering appears to have been unfulfilling or unrewarding. On completion of his training, Smythe took up an appointment in Buenos Aires but despite the proximity of the Andes (and they had, after all, attracted his great hero Whymper and the Carrels) rapidly tired of it, resigned and returned. Thereafter, he worked at nothing for long. He joined the RAF, surprisingly because he despised his OTC experience at school and came to regard war as the supreme human folly. Why he enlisted remains a mystery unless it was an association with high places! His first and only overseas posting was to Egypt and that was short-lived.

Within months, he was invalided out and cautioned to climb stairs slowly for the rest of his life. This proved doubly ironic, for not only did he proceed to embark immediately upon the remarkable series of mountaineering feats which culminated in his Himalayan expeditions, but when the occasion for serving King and country arose, in the Second World War, Smythe, far from being rejected as unfit, found himself appointed head of a commando-training school where most of his teaching was by example.

Except for a short, though no doubt valuable, spell with Kodak Ltd (from 1926), Smythe made a career out of mountaineering. He never worked as a guide and, indeed, it would never have occurred to an Englishman to do so in those days. He earned his living by producing a series of more than twenty books and photographic albums, as well as at least one film and innumerable shorter articles for *The Times*, leading mountaineering journals and other periodicals.

Strangely, this distanced Smythe even further from full membership of the climbing establishment, on whose fringes he had uncertainly lurked. He had not, after all, been properly introduced into the fraternity. He had not entered via friends nor via the Church, the services, the professions or academic life. He had, rather oddly, simply gone off and learned how to climb mountains on his own. And now, to cap it all, he had become a professional of sorts at a time when the amateur tradition was at its zenith. Whether this later cost him preferment which would otherwise have come his way, is speculative. That his writing attracted an increasingly large and enthusiastic audience prepared to pay for their pleasure, is beyond question.

The following years, 1927–30, were a time of intense activity in the Alps and Corsica. This was the period of the great Alpine routes. But although some companions figured more than once in these exploits, no one found a regular place on Smythe's rope. There followed the Himalayan expeditions of the 1930s, particularly those to Kangchenjunga, the summit of Kamet and the frustrating attempts on Everest which, by 1938, had become almost an obsession. But these expeditions were merely the peaks in a continuous curve of activity. The months between them were occupied in part by his Alpine wanderings, sometimes alone, sometimes with chosen companions, which reveal Smythe at his most fulfilled and contented; and in part by describing them for an increasingly large and voracious readership. The last of these, the tour of the Dauphiné and Mont Blanc described in *Mountaineering Holiday*, was carried through in the shadow of the Second World War when Smythe turned to training troops in mountain warfare with, one suspects, less than wholehearted enthusiasm. In the RAF at first, he later transferred and served on the staff of the Eighth Army in Italy before it was possible to return to his first love.

Not until 1946 did Smythe again visit the Alps. A protracted trip to Switzerland then, described in *Again Switzerland*, shows us a less aggressive, more nostalgic Smythe. It was followed, in 1946 and 1947, by visits to, and highly successful explorations in, the then largely unknown Rocky Mountains of Canada. In 1949, he arranged a Himalayan expedition, the party consisting of himself alone and sherpas. He was taken ill just before he was due to embark on it and flown back to England where he died, still under fifty, on 27 July

1949. At his death, he was President of the Alpine Ski Club and Vice-President of the RAF Mountaineering Association. Although an honorary member of the continental Alpine Clubs, he never attained office in *the* Alpine Club.

He married twice. The first marriage failed. It would have been a remarkable woman who would happily tolerate the time-consuming rivalry of Smythe's first love. Later, he married again and Nona, his second wife, was his partner in a very happy relationship, frequently travelled with him, was an efficient base-camp manager and did little climbing. She was almost the ideal companion.

There is no evidence of Smythe's own assessment of his career as a mountaineer. The student of mountaineering history must conclude, simply on the basis of his record, that he stands in direct line of succession to his heroes, Whymper, Mummery and Mallory, whose mantle he immediately assumed and which, in due course, he handed on to some of "those dreadful Northern climbers" of the post-war era. It is an odd dynasty for, with the partial exception of Mallory, all its figures stood outside and, on occasion, in conflict with, the climbing establishment of the day—they were mainly associated with trade, or worse.

It is doubtful if Smythe would have cared very deeply whether the judgment of experts placed him amongst the greatest of modern mountaineers. His first wish would certainly have been to maximize his delight in mountains, and in this he patently succeeded. In what were to be his last years, spent in his Sussex home, he developed interests in Alpine gardening (particularly rhododendrons), art history and wines, though these never rose above the level of being diversions when he returned home from the mountains that he loved. If, in loving them, he also succeeded in communicating his delight to thousands of ordinary men and women, prompting many of them to seek to share it, he would have regarded this as a far more worthy achievement than the accolades and gold medals awarded by a select few.

CHAPTER II

First Steps

THE LOVE OF mountains is a relatively recent historical phenomenon, and how it emerged is a good topic for a foul day. The earlier prevailing popular view of the ranges now so beloved, was that they were places inspiring terror and therefore to be shunned. All this has now changed, yet the new attitude is by no means universal and it can confidently be predicted that of the generation born into our own times, some few will develop an all-consuming passion for the hills whilst others will remain wholly unmoved by their pretended attractions.

Why, in any individual case, the passion grows, it is hard to say, and evidence the victim has of its first stirrings is not necessarily very cogent. There is photographic and documentary evidence that I myself spent annual holidays in Windermere and Ambleside from the age of four, and I seem to remember first steps on Loughrigg Terrace in those days, but I cannot be certain. Smythe's earliest recollections date from the age of three and seem clear: a slope of the North Downs near Maidstone overlooking the Weald and scented with thyme, a misty horizon and billowing white clouds in a deep blue sky, whispered adventure even then. They also proffered escape to solitude, away from the urban landscape which oppressed even Smythe the toddler. Nor, it appears, was this an exceptional snapshot of an otherwise very different early lifescape. Rather it is a frame in a family film of days in the countryside with picnics, remembered chiefly because they enabled the infant Smythe to escape, briefly, the clutches of family and retainers.

There may be artistic licence in the picture which Smythe paints of these very early years. There seems, however, little reason to doubt the veracity, even in detail, of the next scenes. Smythe's father had died when the son was two, and an over-protective mother was already much concerned about her young offspring's health. There was, indeed, the "heart murmur" finally categorized as unremarkable on the Kamet expedition a quarter of a century later, but its significance at the time was grossly over-exaggerated and it figured as an important element in Mrs Smythe's decision to transport the boy for a protracted stay in Switzerland for health reasons at seven or eight years of age. The journey itself yielded his first view of the Alps from the train as it topped the Jura near Pontarlier. It must have been the famous distant scene with the Oberland wall, which he was later to visit on numerous occasions, in centre stage.

This first journey was destined to end at Château d'Oex where the family stayed for several months. This charming town tends to hit the headlines nowadays only on those rare occasions when a famous ex-Hollywood resident dies. The burgeoning of ski-ing which has spoiled so many Alpine resorts has left it almost untouched and it remains today pretty much the same as it was when Smythe climbed his first Alpine peak in the course of his convalescent sojourn if, that is, it is proper to describe Smythe's "Mont Cray" as an Alpine peak at all. It stands, less than 1,000 metres above the town, its summit stretching a humble 70 metres above the 2,000 metre contour. It is more properly named "La Pointe de Cray" and is the terminal point of a ridge which rises in a series of grassy summits culminating, at the other, north-eastern extreme, in the Vanil Noir, at 2,389 metres. The minuscule massif is reminiscent more of the Brecon Beacons than of the Alps.

This, his first ascent of a true mountain, was the one occasion on which Smythe, hardly more than a toddler, used a guide—a sixteen-year-old village lad—purely as a guide, and even that was at parental insistence. The track which carried the party the first few hundred feet up the easy flank is now asphalted, and passable for jeeps for a further couple of hundred feet up through the forest after that. It then becomes a true hill path, zig-zagging up the breast of an alp before embarking on a long rising traverse to the south-west to where the rounded south ridge falls gently to the valley. There the path turns back on itself, rising now in a northerly direction until it rushes in a series of smaller legs up to the low point of the south-western end of the ridge. The rest, fortunately for the now tiring Smythe, consists of a gently rising track on the crest of the ridge to the pointed summit knoll. This early mountaineering experience would be enhanced by the view of the steeper north ridge, much of it bare limestone, falling to the valley in a series of steps which promise a more interesting scramble.

Extensive views may be had from this humble summit. Smythe was able to look out over range after range of hills to the high Alps and wonder if he would ever have the good fortune to tread their snows. All I had, in the course of re-tracing his steps, was the occasional glimpse of middle-distance craggy limestone, sub-Alpine summits emerging briefly from an early morning mix of swirling mist and haze, but I was rather more than a mere seven years old. Smythe was obviously and understandably impressed. The mountain, which consists in greater part of easy grass slopes down which it is possible to run at no greater risk than that of an occasional undignified slide on the backside, struck him as perilous; the prospect fired a lifelong ambition. Mont Cray is a goodly day out for a sickly seven-year-old and, indeed, probably has much to offer to an impressionable young imagination which it would withhold from an older, more jaded and cynical mind.

This first, family, Alpine season yielded no more adventure. They later moved to Glion and this enabled Smythe to gaze speculatively on the Dents du Midi. A stay in Wengen brought walks with his mother and a closer acquaintance with Eiger, Mönch, Jungfrau and the Lauterbrunnen Peaks which he later trod. This very same scene was my first eyeball-to-eyeball contact with the High Alps and many will testify that its siren-like qualities are undeniable. A further move to Bern irritated and frustrated him, whilst the return to England shortly thereafter deprived him even of the consolatory view of that city's Oberland back-cloth.

The next few years offered no opportunity to renew this fleeting acquaintance with the mountains, at least directly. One Christmas brought a gift of Whymper's *Scrambles* . . ., at first merely dipped into but later voraciously devoured and possibly the source of an infection which, many years later, developed into his biography of Whymper.

The First World War repatriated the Smythe holidays and, on the very day war broke out, they arrived for a stay in Tintagel, scene of such modern-day classic climbs as Littlejohn's terrifying *Il Duce*. Smythe managed to terrify himself by a desperate struggle on unquestionably easier rock on a crag facing King Arthur's castle. It cannot have been more than a few yards high and he eventually hauled himself over the top muttering the vow, as many have done before and since, that he would never again do such a thing. Such vows have a habit of being short-lived, as history records them to have been in Smythe's case. Retrospect yielded only an inexplicable if tearful joy. He was, in a word, addicted. It is a rough wine with a superb aftertaste.

Next summer saw the family at Penrhyn Bay near Llandudno and brought the now adolescent Smythe's introduction to the mountains of North Wales, to which he was to return time and again throughout his life. His first ventures were modest indeed. The map showed a one thousand foot contour line inland from Colwyn Bay, and one thousand feet used to be considered to make a mountain. Smythe cycled to a point near the top, ascended the last grassy rise on foot and beheld the hills of Snowdonia for the first time. A later objective with a similar outcome was humble Penmaenmawr Mountain. Closer acquaintance had to wait.

Back at Berkhamsted School, after bronchitis, influenza and two bouts of pneumonia, mountaineering activity was confined to exhausting the limited potential of the library, amongst other things renewing his acquaintance with Whymper's *Scrambles* . . . and poring over maps of the world's great ranges. Then the family lighted upon Borth-y-Gest, near Portmadoc, as the holiday home and Smythe was at last able to gorge himself on solitary rambles in the Welsh Hills, previously only distantly viewed.

The exact site of his first epic mountain scramble is a mystery. It took place in a gully leading to a summit above Beddgelert identified by him in one place as Moel Hebog and in another as Moel Siabod. The former better suits the location of the scene as "above Beddgelert". There is, on the other hand, cogent evidence that as a small boy he squelched over the bogs of Moel Siabod from the Vale of Gwynant. Smythe's description does not enable this gully to be identified with certainty. The Eastern face of Moel Siabod is craggy and broken and two gullies reach the summit ridge from here. One particularly catches the eye, curving up narrowly and mysteriously out of sight above scree slopes and steepening to a stiffish scramble before being seen to break out on to this ridge. The other one is perhaps less obvious and slightly more difficult though neither is technically anything more than moderate, and it may well have been that the crisis which the young Smythe underwent was as much psychological as anything else. If that were so, it would not be surprising. Although only an hour's easy walking from Capel Curig, this eastern corrie of Moel Siabod, from all usual aspects an innocent looking mountain, can seem a fearsome place. With the lake below obscured by cloud and the crags around soaring up into swirling mists, one is beset by an awesome feeling in the upper reaches of these gullies, and their features can easily be exaggerated. An optical illusion fortifies this impression: the crags around in fact lean back at an easy enough angle but, being crags, tend to appear vertical, and it is easy to assume that the gullies which they contain are consequently very much steeper. It would be wholly unsurprising if this atmosphere "got to" this young and, at that time, inexperienced Smythe.

But so also might the wildness of the gully which cleaves the summit crags of Moel Hebog, Simnai Foel Hebog. It is a gully to which myth attaches, for it is up here, legend informs us, that Owen Glendower fled to escape pursuers, a motivation which the young Smythe might fairly point out was lacking in his case. Still known as Glyndwr's Ladder, this gully just achieves recognition as a rock-climb in the easiest grade. Although technically easy, it is a place by no means free from danger, being loose and frequently wet.

Many climbers will have shared Smythe's experience on this first, solo, encounter with rock-climbing as such: the confident start and the relatively rapid progress over the first few obstacles—then the gradually increasing difficulty and, with it, an increasing consciousness thereof—and finally, the impasse—the apparently equal impossibilities of either advance or retreat. There is, in this situation, a momentary struggle between panic and logic before the latter triumphs and finally compels the realization that there really is no reason why what has been climbed could not be down-climbed. So it was with Smythe on his remote Welsh mountain—easily, at first, up the gully until, after increasing difficulty and steepness, a casual look back informed him of the seriousness of his position, only for a look up to offer no escape in that direction.

It was a timorous but not wholly chastened Smythe who accepted the logic of his position on that occasion and found his way gradually down. If the essence of a good mountaineering decision is to go back whenever you ought not to go on, this may well have been a good introduction to the art and Smythe, as we shall see, learned well.

In the course of this and subsequent visits to North Wales in the following years, Smythe came to know the area well, particularly its popular summits. Most of his exploration he did alone; friends turned out to be inconstant companions. An early expedition to Y Cnicht, the proud but deceptive little peak which stands above Penrhyndeudraeth, set out as a party of two but it was Smythe alone who reached the summit. The classic walk from Pen-y-Gwryd, reached by cycle from Borth-y-Gest, over the Glyders, descending Bristly Ridge and climbing Tryfan by its South Ridge, he did alone, as he did the Snowdon Horseshoe. He did not always lack companionship: one summer he camped for a fortnight with a friend in Cwm Gwynant, amongst other things climbing Snowdon by the tiresome Watkin Path and observing, en route, a massive stonefall from near the summit.

In terms of technical difficulty and arduousness, these forays were all ordinary in the extreme—the early gully incident seems to have dulled the attraction of any rock harder than that to be found on Bristly Ridge. They were the classic days out in the Snowdon massif known and loved by thousands of us. It is not at all unusual to encounter young families negotiating the Crib Goch pinnacles or savouring the fear-thrill of peering over the East Face of Tryfan. The unusual feature of these earlier experiences of the teenage Smythe is that the desire to savour them was entirely self-generated. Most of us learn at the heels of a fond uncle or are initiated by more experienced friends or fellow club members. Because these opportunities did not come his way, Smythe became a moving spirit and a frequent solitary climber from his earliest days. He was to remain so throughout his career, although often criticized for engaging in the practice, not least by himself. What critics frequently overlook is that the alternative to solo-climbing in many cases, as in Smythe's, is no climbing at all.

The gully incident may have sated Smythe's appetite for rock, but only temporarily. Before the end of his initiation in the mountains of North Wales, he was back on rock, this time on Lliwedd, said to be the largest crag in England and Wales, and dominating the southern shore of Llyn Llydaw which nestles in the arms of the Snowdon Horseshoe. During the years before the First World War, the cliffs of Lliwedd were the pre-eminent area of rock-climbing development in Britain and a young devotee can hardly have been ignorant of their challenge. The list of first ascents bristles with the great names of the age: the Abrahams brothers, H. V. Reade, Geoffrey Winthrop Young, the unsavoury but inventive Oscar Eckenstein, G. H. L. Mallory, H. O. Jones and, greatest of all in the exploration of Lliwedd, the Llandudno headmaster, J. M. Archer Thompson.

That Smythe ventured on to this cliff in the early days we only discover incidentally to an occurrence during the course of the climb which he graphically describes. We do not know exactly what route he took, but it was on the West Buttress, and was very likely the scramble which finds its way deviously upwards for a thousand feet to the summit from the left-hand side of the foot of the Buttress, via the Bilberry Terrace and Craig Yr Aderyn. As he neared the top, he pulled himself up on to a grassy ledge where, as it turned out, he was not expected and where, it was learned too late, sheep may not safely graze. His abrupt arrival disturbed such a poor creature; it leapt for another lower ledge but failed to secure a foothold on the sloping rock and sailed out into space where it prescribed a slow and graceful arc before dashing itself on to the rocks a thousand feet below. It must have been a graphic illustration of the danger inevitably attending solo-climbing and it certainly impressed itself on Smythe's memory. Clearly, it did not deter him but it remained a rare occasion, in a crowded career, on which he actually observed the death of any creature in the mountains.

In retrospect it can be seen that these years amongst the hills of North Wales must have been an ideal apprenticeship for a mountaineer. Smythe's expeditions, easy though they were, were carried out in all weathers and always entirely on his own responsibility. "Mountaineering," he found (and some, always reliant on others, never do), "is not something to be bullocked at blindly; it is an art and a craft that demands as much mental as physical energy. It makes a man observant. He must watch the weather, estimate difficulty and danger, study topography, be expert in the use of map and compass, and above all he must always keep a margin of strength to deal with unforeseen emergencies."

Throughout these events, Smythe's utterly undistinguished career at Berkhamsted School was grinding its way to an end. These were the days when distinction at school led to "Greats" at Oxbridge. At the other extreme, Smythe was guided in the direction of electrical engineering—*plus ça change* . . . In 1919 he thus found himself at college in Bradford and before long his forays into the Dales and moors to the north had brought him into contact with that august club, the Yorkshire Ramblers, and initiated him into the mysteries of gritstone. Most weekends saw him at places such as Ilkley and Almscliff, the latter the most common venue for the instruction of junior members such as he. It was here that he met E. E. Roberts, that great mentor of Yorkshire climbers, who took a particular interest in him and with whom he was subsequently to make many expeditions in the Alps. Smythe also met and particularly admired the skills of the great C. D. Frankland, killed on Great Gable in 1927. Another acquaintanceship, in the event detrimental to Smythe, struck here was that with T. H. Somervell; their paths were later to cross in the Dolomites and in the context of selection for the Everest expeditions.

These three, Roberts, Frankland and Somervell, first made Smythe's acquaintance all on the same occasion, on a December day in 1919 when, near Pool-in-Wharfedale, and on their way to Almscliff, they were overtaken by a "fair-haired young man on a cycle" who introduced himself as "F. S. Smythe, a new member". Somervell disliked him on sight. After only a brief experience acquired mainly at Almscliff and in the Lakes, Roberts reported that "a new star has risen".

Few Yorkshire climbers have not spent at least a little time scrambling over Almscliff's humble outcrop which defiantly crowns the moorland between Otley and Harrogate. It is a typically English crag, almost every feature on it housing at least one problem; some, such as Frankland's celebrated *Green Crack*, still very much the preserve of budding "hard men", others, such as *Parson's Chimney*, classics within the capacity of any reasonably able and flexible climber. It is a far cry from the twenty-foot boulder problems of Almscliff to the Brenva face of Mont Blanc or Everest, but the connection is not wholly lacking. It was, after all, Joe Brown's gritstone hand-jamming which overcame the so-conceived last problem on the first ascent of Kangchenjunga.

On longer expeditions, the Yorkshire Ramblers would make for the Lakes, and Smythe was introduced to the famous crags of Langdale, Wasdale and Ennerdale. His first climbs here, under instruction, were first *Little Gully* (Moderate) and then *Great Gully* (Difficult) on Pavey Ark. *Gwynne's Chimney* followed. He graduated from here to his first lead, *Gimmer Chimney* (Very Difficult) on Gimmer Crag under the eye of Roberts.

Either he concluded that this terminated his apprenticeship or the Ramblers' Lakeland meets were insufficient to satisfy his appetite, for he now reverted to solitary ventures. He was off to the Lakes at every opportunity, every holiday, every weekend, fair weather or foul. One such visit saw him alone on the Napes of Great Gable. Never one to rely excessively on guide books, he tended always to climb what he saw, liked and considered feasible. On this occasion, his eye fell first on *Needle Ridge* (Diff.) and *Arrowhead Ridge* (V. Diff.) which he duly ascended. Then between them, he remarked upon a "much more formidable edge, a gigantic prow of rock that projected from the mountainside like the bows of a battle-cruiser" which he recognized as an "exceptionally severe" climb about which he had read in the Abrahams' classic *British Mountain Climbs*. In these days when the route is classified as merely Very Severe, the standard which most young climbers today hope to attain, it is well to remember its reputation in earlier times. This is the Abrahams' description which Smythe recalled: "The direct ascent looks difficult, and it is difficult; the climb is only for the expert of experts, and even then a previous inspection with the rope held from above is advisable."

(This latter recommendation is an interesting reflection on much more modern controversies about the ethics of prior inspection etc.)

Nevertheless, and notwithstanding the existence of a much easier and more attractive variation (*Eagle's Nest Ridge via the West Chimney*, Hard Diff.), Smythe found the direct route irresistible and, removing his boots, he set off up it in stockinged feet. He might well have sought to turn back at the crux but just at that moment he discovered that he had an audience and youthful pride carried him over it and thence, joyously, to the top. In retrospect, he thought it an irresponsible climb to have made. Any conceit which it brought was rapidly deflated. He proceeded from the Ridge to the relatively easy Needle and, his reserves of emotional energy apparently exhausted, froze at the difficult mantelshelf on to the crowning block and had to endure the chastening experience of having a bystander climb by him in order to lend him a top-rope.

Eagle's Nest Ridge Direct remains, however, a seminal achievement, easy to underestimate in these days of specialist gear and rock-boots. When I first read of Smythe's ascent, I took the view that he must have climbed the Ridge via the West Chimney, but another account leaves no room for such doubts. Smythe never attained the very front rank amongst British rock-climbers, but his failure to do so may be attributed rather to disposition than to capacity.

Although his most frequent venue during these years was on the Lakeland crags, he did not totally neglect other areas. One Saturday evening saw him leaving Horton-in-Ribblesdale up Pen-y-Ghent on the first leg of that famous Yorkshire walker's marathon, the Three Peaks. Darkness had fallen by the time he left the summit for Whernside and he spent an extremely uncomfortable couple of hours stumbling through bog and peat-hags—the moon, on which he had relied, perversely refusing to appear. Smythe failed to complete the Three Peaks Walk: it is by no means a severe test, involving about 23 miles and 5,000 feet of ascent, all on easy ground, provided, of course, that the path is not deserted for the bog. Smythe omitted Whernside, slept on Ingleborough and finished the shortened round the following morning.

Another holiday brought him back to the hills of Wales, staying with his fellow Rambler and mentor, E. E. Roberts, at a small inn in Rhyd Ddu. The pair made various "trouser-splitting" ascents on the cliffs of Llechog, and discovered and made several ascents in mist on a small and sound but mysterious crag in Cwm Clogwyn, which ever thereafter thwarted repeated attempts at rediscovery. If it was not part of the Llechog Facet, it remains unknown; but the most significant episode on this tour was the early exploration of Clogwyn du'r Arddu ("Cloggy").

There is a tendency these days to assume that the cliffs of Cloggy were effectively virgin until the start of modern development, first with Pigott's climb and Longland's in the late 1920s and then with the creations of Colin Kirkus in the 1930s. This is true of the two great central buttresses and largely so of the Far East Buttress but the easier-angled Far West Buttress had already undergone development at the hands of climbers such as P. S. Thompson and H. R. C. Carr. Smythe had earlier spent some time in solitary exploration of the Idwal Slabs and the Far West Buttress of Cloggy and in September 1921 spent three days there with E. E. Roberts. The two forged a "worthy little scramble" up rocks between the West and Far West Terrace, evading the steep band, and giving it the name which it still holds, the *Giant's Trod*. *East Wall Climb*, an Abrahams brothers' creation (V. Diff.) was repeated; Smythe thought it detestable. The pair later made the first ascent of the Far East Buttress via a poor route containing only one decent crack pitch, which they named *Nonsuch*. It is not clear exactly which line they took; it does not appear to have merited mention in the next edition of "Abraham" and has faded into oblivion. It was presumably a scramble up the loose and vegetated right-hand side. In view of later developments on the cliff, two other features of this visit assume greater importance. Tempted by the virginity of the central buttresses, the pair made a determined attempt on *Chimney Route* (V. Severe) on East Buttress but failed on the line which repulsed all attempts until it fell, a decade later, to the celebrated rope of Colin Kirkus and J. Menlove Edwards. They also searched the West Buttress for possible weaknesses, but although faint possibilities were detected, such that Smythe later regretted not having adopted a bolder approach, no attempt was made.

Shortly after these last events, Smythe's career took him abroad and the next few years were occupied largely with his Alpine apprenticeships and the problems of earning a living. These developments did not, however, mark the end of his association with, and love for the British hills. He was to return to them with gratitude and affection throughout the rest of his life.

CHAPTER III

Further Climbs in Britain

AFTER 1920, SMYTHE'S mountaineering career divides neatly into three decades. The 1920s were pre-eminently the years of his Alpine climbing; the 1930s was the era of his Himalayan experience and the 1940s are marked first by his war-time activities and later by his pioneering in the Canadian Rocky Mountains. However, these are crude divisions. He did not by any means utterly neglect the Alps in the 30s and 40s and, throughout, he returned to the British hills, not, it would seem, for deeds of daring (although there were notable achievements) but rather for refreshment and a renovation of the spirit.

In the 1920s, he came to know something of the mountains of Scotland; though his visits were neither lengthy nor frequent, he clearly developed an affection for them and they drew him back on a number of occasions. His introduction to the Scottish hills was entirely at the hands of J. H. B. Bell whom he had met in Wasdale during his Yorkshire Rambler days. They climbed together on Pillar and Scafell and struck up a relationship which survived for many years and led to some notable expeditions in the Alps. Each was at the start of an outstanding career, Bell being four years the elder, and each would have recognized in the other a kindred spirit.

Their Scottish forays concentrated on the classic routes in classic areas. An assault in winter conditions on Tower Ridge on Ben Nevis in April 1925 ended in a cautious retreat from Tower Gap with time running short. Neither had climbed the ridge previously, even in summer conditions, and Bell later considered that had he known the ground ahead, they would have been better advised to continue. It took Bell a further four attempts before he finally completed the route in 1932. They were more successful in Skye, completing the entire Cuillin ridge in a day and putting up a new route, *West Trap Route* (V.Diff.), one of the longest on the island. Smythe considered the Cuillins to be the truest mountains and the ridge to be "the grandest day's scrambling" in Britain. This opinion quite remarkably survived a camping holiday in June 1939 notable for the most malignant and prolonged downpour in his experience, the sun being visible for a total of only two and a half hours in a fortnight.

Smythe's ventures were not confined to climbing. In *The Mountain Vision*, he describes a walk in the Highlands over the hills from Morvich on Loch Duich to the Falls of Glomach, vividly recalling an odd experience in a narrow defile dropping down to Glen Glomach where he claims to have observed the bloody massacre of a crowd of men, women and children. Glencoe was presumably not far from his mind. Another visit to Ben Nevis in winter brought hours of hacking away at snow and ice on the steep side and culminated in the party crawling on hands and knees across the summit plateau. Not surprisingly, he chose the Scottish mountains as one of the venues for training commandos in mountain warfare in World War Two.

The English hills never tempted him in the same way. He did revisit the Yorkshire Fells and later undertook a fifty-mile walk across the Surrey hills with Hugh Slingsby with whom he climbed in Corsica. More exotically, he introduced skiing to Tring and describes how he later, with P. H. H. Unna and J. D. Waler, made a ski ascent of Leith Hill near Dorking. The planned assault "was to be made by the great east face . . . Crossing a bergschrund (ditch) the party started up a steep couloir (narrow lane)" and so to the top.

Catholic though these tastes were, the hills to which he always returned were those of Wales though not, it appears, for any obvious quality which they peculiarly possessed. The Lakeland hills he always found "cheerful and colourful". Scotland's mountains were not only extensive but also mysterious. About the Welsh hills he found it more difficult to explain his feelings. They were sombre; they lacked the gaiety and colour of the Lakes. It was not the people; he developed no excessive liking for the Welsh, though there may have been some fellow-feeling for the loneliness and solitude, even the sadness of the mountains of Wales. They were, after all, the hills he climbed as a boy, and a childhood sweetheart often retains a cherished place no matter what heights of passion are reached in later life.

He walked and scrambled many times over the old ground. One August, with an Army friend, he trudged across the southern fells, wild and rugged and dotted with small lakes, to the Vale of Ffestiniog.

On a number of occasions, he visited the Carneddau in winter, once starting for Carnedd Dafydd from Pont Rhyd Goch over Craig Llugwy and continuing over Pen yr Oleu Wen; and later traversing the whole via Pen Llithrig y Wrach, Pen Helyg, Craig yr Ysfa, Carnedd Llewelyn, Carnedd Dafydd and Pen yr Oleu Wen, on a January day, a grand course indeed.

Most commonly, however, it was to the Snowdon range that he resorted. He climbed on the Parson's Nose and Clogwyn y Ddysgl which contains a plethora of now unfashionable but delightful, easy, long routes. On Lliwedd, he returned to *Route Two* (Severe) and *Avalanche* (V. Diff.) and, having on another occasion strung together bits of different routes in disdainful disregard of the guide book, was chastised by a purist for "not having done a route at all". His activities here in later years embraced rescue work, bringing down an injured tourist from the Llyn Llydaw face of Crib Goch, and training commandos, once combining the two in organizing the troops in a search for a woman lost in the area of Llanberis Pass. Two features of the Snowdon range held particular attraction for him, each in a quite different way, but together epitomizing the dual appeal of the mountains and his whole experience of them. These were the Horseshoe Ridge and Cloggy.

The attraction of the Snowdon Horseshoe is obvious to thousands of Britain's mountain-lovers. It is rightly popular. I made my first acquaintance with it as a schoolboy during the Second World War when money, clothing and transport were all in short supply. We had cycled in, and camped off the road between Capel Curig and Pen-y-Gwryd, arranging for ourselves the luxury of a bath and loo in a nearby stream. Our diet, as I recall, consisted largely of potato sandwiches and I do remember that at great family clothing-coupon sacrifice, I had been kitted out with a brand-new pair of hob-nailed boots. They did not last long; a seam split on one of them on the slopes of Crib Goch, the other soon followed suit and the heels of both disappeared amongst scree descending Lliwedd. It was, in the event, nearly four decades before I came again to the Horseshoe, this time alone and in March in perfect winter conditions, with the light but well-crusted snow that one normally merely dreams about, beneath a crystal clear sky. It is, in a sense, a pity that it is necessary in the literature to warn the reader that the mountains in winter are not nearly so innocent as they look, for it must deter many and deny them an unsurpassable experience. One can, after all, die of exposure on the Thames Embankment. On such a day as I had, the ridge was about as dangerous as an anaesthetized hamster and the going was as perfectly Alpine as it is possible for any hill south of the Border to offer. It may well have been because, in its various moods, it can be reminiscent of all the different types of easy mountaineering that it appealed to Smythe, and caused him to escape to it whenever opportunity offered, especially one April during the Second World War when he found it in much this same condition. It emphasizes the pluralism of Smythe's approach to the mountains, for repeated visits must clearly have left the Horseshoe entirely without challenge for him and there can have been no fear of the "conquest" which he came to deride. His passion for it is wholly understandable; no doubt spiritual and mystical, an attitude which tended to make Smythe a slightly suspicious character (except to the French), and which is today regarded as rather passé. So be it; there is something to be said for the old values yet.

The Horseshoe contrasts strikingly with Cloggy, yet there is no doubt that that side of Smythe's character to which the challenge of Cloggy appealed was equally genuine.

Clogwyn du'r Arddu, superbly described in Crew's *The Black Cliff*, is not the highest, but is surely the most demanding cliff in Wales. It buttresses the northern flanks of the West ridge of Snowdon and rises 600 feet above Llyn du'r Arddu in five buttresses, three of which consist in part, or in whole, of intimidatingly steep and apparently holdless rock, the two grandest being East and West buttresses in the centre. It is best-known nowadays as the chief scene of the great advances made in British rock-climbing in the 1950s, particularly by the *Rock and Ice* group of Brown, Whillans and company, before the circus moved on eventually to venues such as Gogarth. But the story began in the 1920s.

Such climbing as had been done on Cloggy prior to the 1920s, had been largely confined to the easier Far West Buttress, although the Abrahams's East Wall Climb is an exception. The hard challenge of the East and West Buttresses had not been met; they remained virgin. Smythe's interest dates from the early 1920s. His visits with J. H. B. Bell were not his only ones. There were at least two earlier occasions when he visited the crag alone, to probe its possibilities, climbing the Far West Buttress and girdling the crag via the terraces.

The breakthrough came on 1 May 1927, when the Rucksack Club rope of A. S. Pigott, M. Wood, L. Henshaw and J. E. Burton forced a way up the East Buttress known, in honour of its leader, as Pigott's Climb (V. Severe). Rather oddly, however, the event most celebrated was the first ascent of Longland's Climb at Whitsuntide 1928, "oddly" because Pigott's Climb seems to be somewhat the harder route, came first in time, and broke the ice; it seems to have lacked only the imprimatur of the Climbers' Club on the rope. Crew, in *The Black Cliff*, refers the awakening of Smythe's interest in Cloggy to Pigott's success in 1927 but, as has been seen, it occurred some years before that event and Smythe's attendance on the cliff in 1928 (he had been abroad for much of the intervening period) showed, at the most, a reawakening.

The occasion was the Climbers' Club meet at the Pen-y-Pass Hotel at Easter, 1928. The party included such illustrious names in British mountaineering as Longland himself, and the doyen, Geoffrey Winthrop Young. Smythe and Professor Thomas Graham Brown had made names for themselves the previous year with the first of their Brenva Face climbs and seem to have earned an entrée into the climbing establishment as a consequence. It was Smythe's first Easter Meet at Pen-y-Pass; it was also his last. Of those gathered there, only Smythe had previously visited Cloggy and his express intention in attending the meet was to renew the acquaintance.

The Easter Meet was devoted at first to reconnaissance. Winthrop Young, Longland and Smythe paid a first visit and possibilities were bandied about. Two days later, Longland, Smythe and Wakefield returned to gather further and better particulars of the West Buttress; a contemporary photograph records the presence also, on some occasion at this time, of Ivan Waller and Thomas Graham Brown. The line which became Longland's was fixed upon, following for the most part a long, slender slab towards the left-hand side of the Buttress, and issue was joined. Longland led out the first 60 feet, cleaning the rock as he went; Smythe then took over for the next 30 feet and, after gardening, unearthed a much needed belay before rain forced a retreat. Strange as it may sound to those familiar with the proprietorial attitudes towards new routes which prevail today, there the matter rested until Whitsuntide when Longland, Smythe and others were again in the area. So also, however, were Pigott and the Rucksackers, and whilst Longland and Smythe were busying themselves on Lliwedd, Pigott and the Rucksackers, apparently initially unaware of any previous attempts, had selected the same narrow slab on the West Buttress of Cloggy for their endeavours. If they were initially unaware, they cannot have remained so for long; if it lasted until then, their ignorance cannot have survived the discovery of Smythe's sling at the Easter high-point. Pigott pushed out the route a further 20 feet before retiring after three and a half hours on the rock. Next day, news reached Longland and Smythe that a party of three was taking an active interest in their West Buttress line and they rushed to the crag. The two teams met at the foot, but the outcome was not the race to be first on the rock which might well be expected today, but rather an agreement for a combined assault by a rope consisting of Longland, Pigott, Smythe, W. Eversden and M. Wood.

Although Smythe and Pigott had each played a part in opening up the route thus far, it was Longland, then twenty-two years old and already recognized as one of the most brilliant climbers of his day, who was selected to lead the rope. He did so throughout, beautifully by all accounts. A judicially-placed chockstone gave some protection for the difficult step and, horror of horrors, a piton was employed on the stance above the slab section which Smythe named "Faith and Friction". Longland then had to negotiate a turf barrier before emerging at the quartz-crowned ledge. Above, the face overhung—just as well since the weather had now turned and the shelter was welcome. A difficult fifteen feet up an overhanging arête remained but posed no insuperable problems for Longland and soon he was on easier ground to the top where he was left to sit in the rain whilst the others smoked contemplative pipes in the shelter of the overhang.

Pigott's Climb started it all and Longland's was the "last great problem" of its day. Together they were seminal, ushering in the great advances of Kirkus and Menlove Edwards in the 1930s. Longland's Climb is rightly named, for it was Longland's talented lead which opened the way for the rest of the party and all who came after, notwithstanding the contributions of Smythe and Pigott in leading sections of it on earlier attempts. Pigott, perhaps, could have led it; it is doubtful if anyone else could. Nevertheless, although the execution was Longland's, the most substantial contribution in terms of planning, persistence and encouragement was Smythe's. In addition to the part which he played in these final endeavours, he had twice, between the Easter attempt and the Whitsun success, revisited the crag and explored the upper reaches of the route on a top-rope and established that, if the section immediately above the quartz-topped ledge could be passed, no insuperable difficulties would remain. He had identified it as "the last great problem" with Bell in 1921 and had rubbed his nose up against it. It was he who introduced the others to it in 1928 and persevered with different parties until success eventually crowned their efforts.

Longland's probably marks the high-point of Smythe's career on British rock in terms of technical difficulty. Even in its day, it was not the hardest climb on British rock, and today the advance in standards which has accompanied the vast strides that have been made in the realms of safety and equipment has reduced it to being a route of merely medium severity. It is now somewhat neglected and climbed sufficiently rarely for the vegetation painstakingly removed by the pioneers to be returning. For Smythe personally, its chief significance lies in relation to the opinion, not infrequently voiced, that he was essentially a "snow-and-ice man" . . . "no good on rock". Whether he is to be regarded as being in the front rank of British climbers of the period is entirely a matter of how many one cares to admit to it. If it be confined to half-a-dozen or so of the names that stand out in British rock-climbing in the 1920s, he is no doubt rightly excluded, although his part in the first ascent of Longland's on Cloggy surely entitles him to stand alongside some pretty illustrious colleagues in the second rank. This is, however, to miss the point. In a sense, Longland's was, for him, an aberration. Once his apprenticeship was over, he was always, first and foremost, a mountaineer and only incidentally did he normally bother with rock at all. He was never what, in modern parlance and somewhat unfairly, might be called a "crag-rat". After his apprenticeship, his ventures on to British rock tended to be more a nostalgic diversion than anything else. Hard rock was never an end in itself and he would have been the first to disclaim any title to rank amongst the great exponents of the art.

CHAPTER IV

Alpine Apprenticeship

IN DECEMBER, 1921, Smythe boarded the boat-train at Victoria, bound for Innsbruck. Ostensibly, engineering studies were to preoccupy him in Austria and Switzerland for the next two years. Actually, for Smythe, it represented a return to the high mountains after an interval of over twelve years. His previous acquaintanceship, however, had been confined to the very modest Mont Cray and to admiring, gazing from the Wengenalp. Now he was to come to know them much more intimately and from a different perspective.

From the time of his arrival in Innsbruck he spent almost every weekend and much of his holidays, no matter what the time of year, in the mountains, on ski or on foot. Of particular importance for his later career were his winter expeditions; by the end of his apprenticeship, he had an experience, unparalleled in Britain, of mountain snow and ice.

What period one cares to characterize as an apprenticeship is, to some extent, arbitrary. Like the rest of us, Smythe continued to learn throughout his life. It is abundantly clear that, by the time the period of his great climbs arrived, from 1927 onwards, he was a fully-fledged alpinist, therefore the years before 1926 can conveniently be treated as the qualifying period. There are likewise convenient limits of space. By reason of being based in Innsbruck, most of Smythe's time was spent in the mountains round about, and his first Alpine love was his last. Although the great deeds were performed in the Bernese Oberland and the Mont Blanc range, it was to the Tyrol that he returned time and time again, and which he came to regard, after savouring all the delights of other areas, as his favourite. His experience was first in and around the Stubai and Zillertal Alps, the Hohe Tauern and the Arlberg, then, into Switzerland, the Silvretta and Glarus Alps. From this central area of activity he made forays into the Dolomites and, perhaps most seminally, the Bernese Oberland.

Probably for no reason other than the time of year, Smythe sampled *ski alpin* before *alpinisme* proper. He had hardly arrived before he was off on his first ski-tour. He had never skied before but, then, he had yet to cut a step in ice. He crossed the Solstein Sattel to Scharnay and next to Fulpmes (easy of access from Innsbruck) which became his favourite centre. An early venture from here saw him setting out to cross the Schlecker Schartl but retreating in the face of what he considered to be an avalanche threat. He had done his homework well—he was already an avid reader of mountaineering literature—and recognized, when he reached the Schlecker Alp, that the way ahead led through a narrow, steep sided valley, a likely place for hundreds of picnicking families in summer but a death trap in the conditions which confronted him. A later ski-ing expedition from Fulpmes took him up to the Waldrastjoch and along the ridge to the north-east.

Between these two trips he had made his first winter ascent, that of a very modest outlier of the Stubai Alps south of Innsbruck, the Saïle. The ascent posed no problems; a glissading descent started a small avalanche which no doubt added to his increasing stock of knowledge.

These early expeditions were all solitary and guideless, not as a matter of principle but for want of companions and funds. They probably gave rise to the "self-sufficiency" which so irritated Somervell. They certainly became the habit of a lifetime, and although Smythe never hesitated to emphasize the dangers of solitary climbing, he was frequently unable to resist the temptation to allude to its attraction, describing it on one occasion as "the Grand Cognac of mountaineering".

Such a solitary journey on ski in the nearby Kitzbühel Alps, the hills of which he found ideal for ski-touring, gave him his first glimpse of the Gross Venediger. He determined straight away to climb it and eventually succeeded in doing so, although not at the first attempt, which he made on ski with a fellow engineering student, G. N. Hewett, and Hewett's sister. Leaving Kitzbühel, they went to Neukirchen in the Pinzgau valley where they spent the night. Next day, they set out for the Kürsinger Hut, but, hoping that the summer route would be safely passable and afford them a short-cut, sought to make their way over the Ober Sulzbach Glacier, Smythe's first glacier-footing. When they eventually reached the hut on the following day, they were forced to admit that they had insufficient food to press the attempt further and had to descend. Smythe erased the failure in July when the Gross Venediger's north-west ridge yielded the only ascent made with J. H. B. Bell (who distinguished himself by breakfasting on sardine and honey sandwiches) in the first half of a summer season beset by foul weather.

Lesson number one in ice-craft came on a minor peak in the Stubai Alps. Smythe had spent the night at the Franz Senn hut on the north side of the Stubaital, where he spent a good proportion of his early days on ski and foot. His objective the following morning seems to have been the Kraulspitze, an easy summit in summer readily reached from the climber's traverse between Franz Senn and Regensburger Huts. Smythe ascended by the straightforward *voie normale* and then succumbed to the temptation to descend by a different and unknown route.

There is always something hard to resist about a traverse of a mountain as opposed to doing the presumptively correct thing and descending by the known route of ascent. Perhaps it enables one to believe that one is undertaking a journey as opposed to pointlessly going up and down; perhaps two different routes offer better value than a single one repeated. Whatever the reason, Smythe conceived the idea of scrambling along a rock ridge in order to descend a slope of several hundred feet to the glacier below. All went well for the first 300 feet down broken rocks, but then an icy flank led down to a bergschrund several hundred feet below. Until then, he had never cut a step in his life; but he had devoured the manuals and, learning by doing, gradually made his way down. Half-way down, and with a gathering storm, he hesitated like a poor man's Hamlet and considered re-tracing his steps but decided to press on. He eventually reached the bergschrund to discover that what had appeared from above to be a mere fissure now assumed the proportions of a bottomless ravine in the ice, vulnerable to a bold leap though with the bottom edge some ten feet lower than the top. Cutting for himself a good base from which to take off, he made to thrust himself forward, but a fair bit of the propulsion went only to drive his feet back, and instead of landing well clear of the gaping schrund he found himself merely breasting its far lip, his legs in space. A quick placement with the pick of his axe enabled him to drag himself clear and recover his breath to the tinkle of ice-fragments gradually fading into the depths below.

It would be an unusual apprentice who was not chastened by such an experience, and Smythe still had to negotiate the unknown glacier. Thoroughly probing with his axe before every step, he crossed it like a blind man on an obstacle course and finally reached a moraine down which he made his way back to the Hut. Not long thereafter, it seemed, momentarily, that he had cheated one bergschrund only to fall victim to another, on the Olperer.

The Olperer is the highest point of the Tuxer Hauptkamm in the north-western sector of the Zillertal Alps. It is a fairly heavily glaciated mountain of about 11,500 feet but is easily ascended from the Innsbruck side by the north ridge route, so liberally bestrewn with metal stanchions that it is hardly necessary, any longer, to touch rock. If you set off to climb the north ridge from the Geraer Hut, as did Smythe and a companion, the route to the Wildlahnerscharte (from immediately below the crest of which the north ridge route starts) passes beneath the western flanks of the north ridge; but it clearly seemed to Smythe, ignorant of the details of the route, a good idea to ascend this flank bristling with ice-cliffs and thus reach more quickly a point high on the ridge. It was some time after crossing the bergschrund that Smythe came to the conclusion that they were off route. The slope had steepened and the strengthening sun was loosening the snow from the glassy ice beneath; the correct mountaineering decision was obviously to retreat, and they set off down. The sun, however, had also worked on the ice holding the cliff above together, and as they neared the bergschrund the morning silence was disrupted by a shattering roar and they looked up to see an enormous mass of rock and ice crashing down on them. There was no time to escape: it seemed that it must brush them away and entomb them in the bergschrund when suddenly the bulk of it disappeared, engulfed by a hidden crevasse above. Not all of it was contained by the chasm in the slope above, but the rogue fragments, including many large enough to crush them, missed them and they were able to make their way nervously down. They did not complete the climb; the companion, indeed, never climbed again.

In spite of all the frenzied activity in the Tyrol, it was in the Glarus in Switzerland that Smythe climbed his first high peaks. The Glarus are unfashionable and little frequented by British mountaineers these days. Their highest peak, the Tödi, is known to the Swiss as the "king of the little mountains" in the Alps. Smythe's first ascent in the Glarus was not the Tödi but the Claridenstock, 10,722 feet, to the north which he climbed alone on ski. It introduced him to the Tödi and on 31 May 1922, he and Hewett set out to make the ascent.

Little the Tödi may be to some, but at almost 12,000 feet it ranks as a substantial mountain to lesser mortals, and height alone is not an accurate indicator of its stature. It stands about 1,500 feet above any other top for miles around; it is as though Ben Nevis, which in some ways it resembles, had been planted down in the middle of the Pennine fells. Smythe and Hewett planned to climb it via the *voie normale* from the Grünhorn Hut to the east, and spent the first night in a chalet at Sand Alp having arrived at Linthal by train in the afternoon. The path from Linthal to the Grünhorn Hut follows the valley to the south as far as Hinterersand, and then takes to subsidary slopes on the left, past the Fridolins Hut and up the hillside. They arrived here early the next afternoon, after encountering difficulties on a "short-cut" and spending two hours drying out in the Fridolins Hut, with only the vaguest idea about the route to be taken. It is, in fact, easy, but to the uninitiated, exaggerated descriptions of the difficulties of the Gelb Wand, via which the summit is reached, sounded horrifying. The Gelb Wand turned out to be a series of broad terraces along and between which it was possible to scramble with ease and thus reach the summit snow slopes. They had allowed themselves ample time; the summit was reached before 7 a.m., five hours after starting.

Much as he enjoyed it, climbing on a rope of two was untypical of Smythe's activities at this time. He preferred his own company—he was not just making a virtue of necessity and was at his most contented in exploring on ski and foot the delights of modest and easily accessible peaks, ideally, although not invariably, by taking them in in the course of extended traverses. His interests were now extended to the Arlberg and Silvretta and, as the winter of 1922–3 approached its end, he seized the opportunity to spend some days amongst their delights.

Leaving St Anton at mid-morning, he made his way up the Moostal and, in the later afternoon, and in deteriorating weather, took occupancy of the Darmstädter Hut, alone save for a colony of mice. For the next five days he skied and climbed on the delightful and virtually unknown peaks forming the broad cirque in which the hut stands. He first ascended the Faselfadspitze by a scramble over the mixed ground of the south ridge, and varying his route of descent took in a subsidiary summit on the way back to the hut. Next day, ascending to the Kuchen Joch, he followed the southern slopes of the Scheibler to the summit and sat there, imbibing the near and distant scene, until a gathering storm drove him down to his ski and back to the hut. Then it was the Küchel Spitze from the Raute Joch via the east ridge, which, with rock verglassed from the overnight storms, turned out to be more problematical than he had thought. He was eventually brought up against a 30 foot wall draped in ice, and set off to try and turn it by a ledge, on the southern side, which eventually petered out without offering a return to the ridge. No matter—it was a good place for a pipe, if not for a doze, and by the time he was ready for a reconsideration of the wall the sun had already set about its work, and the ice yielded to his axe sufficiently for the wall to be passed more readily than he had expected. Tea, another pipe and now a doze on the summit completed the morning's work. Hours later, finding a suitable couloir (which in fact would have offered a much easier line of ascent), a glissade and a short walk brought him once again to the hut.

Shortly thereafter, Smythe was in the Silvretta, a delightful small group with simple glaciers and an ample supply of easy short routes up beautiful peaks: a miniature Oberland. Leaving Klosters, now noticeably more fashionable than in his day but still spared the devastation which "development" has visited on nearby Davos, he headed in the later afternoons up the Sardasca Valley, passed the night in a chalet and arrived at the Silvretta Haus, devoting the remainder of the day to an ascent of the Tällispitze, in summer an easy rock peak, standing about 1,600 feet above the hut. He followed this with a round trip: up the Silvretta Glacier and over the gentle Silvretta Pass, then the Fuorcla dal Cunfin and the Piz Buin via the West Ridge before traversing the Signalhorn back to the hut. This was followed by a traverse of the Silvrettahorn to the Wiesbadener Hut and, the day after that, by the Vermunt Glacier to the Ochsenscharte, then the traverse of the Dreiländerspitz by the north and east ridges, on to the Vorderer Jamspitz, before descending to the Jamtal Glacier and running down to the Jamtal Hut. The penultimate day saw him up the Hinterer Augstenberg and he ended by ascending the

Fluchthorn on ski and foot and crossing the Schnee Joch to the Heidelberger Hut. The Silvretta are not big in stature—the highest point, the Fluchthorn, is little over 11,000 feet—the summits often stand above the glaciers by a mere thousand feet or so, and there is no club-night-kudos to be gained from setting foot on them. The obsessive younger climber of today who could describe in intimate detail every hold on Cemetery Gates will not even have heard of the Silvretta. They are not the material out of which reputations are made; they are merely the stuff of unsullied mountain joy. That was why Smythe went and later returned to them and that is what he found there and, indeed, in all the modest mountain wandering which became the first love of the more mature mountaineer. A young man, however, could hardly be expected to avoid the challenge of more difficult peaks and even, although Smythe denied the lure, the scent of danger which hovered round them. Although he was ever sensitive to the attractions of the welcoming peaks of the Tyrol and central Switzerland, the more celebrated areas also had their allure.

On days in the mountains of the Tyrol, Smythe had frequently gazed to the south and seen the improbable spires of the Dolomites. No description can do them justice. They resemble nothing so much as a child's drawing of mountains he has never seen—or the background of a well-known painting by Breughel, the Flemish painter whose visit to the Alps must have taken in the Dolomites.

Smythe's first "normal" season (winter soloing usually comes at a fairly late stage in an apprenticeship) was the summer of 1922 when he teamed up with J. H. B. Bell whom he had met in the Lakes. Though they started in the Austrian Alps, after the ascent of the Gross Venediger they were baulked at every turn by the weather and eventually turned to the Dolomites. Smythe was intrigued and Bell, probably the outstanding Scottish rock-climber between the wars, would not have been averse, for the Dolomites are essentially rock peaks; they boast of only one or two relatively small glaciers.

So it was that a day in July 1922 saw them heading across the Brenner Pass for Chiusa, then Santa Cristina, and finally to the Langkofel Hut which the recent war had left in a somewhat dilapidated state. With a whole afternoon ahead of them, and briefed, as they thought, by Baedeker which described the Langkofel as being an easy half-hour's walk from the hut and as easily ascended on the far, western side, they set out to stretch their legs on the traverse.

These names can confuse: from the Langkofel Hut, and armed with Baedeker's description of the route to the Langkofelkar, a rocky cwm, Smythe and Bell unwittingly set out to climb the Langkofelkarspitze. How they would have coped today I cannot imagine; the Langkofel has become the Sasso Lungo, the hut is now the Vicenza Hut. The Langkofelkarspitze, however, remains a relatively minor peak rising about 2,000 feet above the hut to the south, but, tackled from that side, quite a testing initiation to the Dolomites for young men in their first full season.

Bell did most of the leading. Three hours' climbing led them on to an airy summit but separated, to their dismay, from the main summit 300 feet higher by a deep gap. It was already 6 p.m. Somewhat awed by the difficulties of their ascent, they settled on Baedeker's "easy" way down to the west and thus began Smythe's first real epic.

Later, of course, they discovered their error; and with hindsight Smythe chastised himself for setting off down an unknown Dolomite mountainside just as the daylight started to disappear, but the first few hundred feet were deceptively easy and enough to give them a commitment to continuing the descent even when the going had obviously become perceptibly harder. What now confronted them was a sheer precipice falling several hundred feet to scree slopes, with only one fierce gash of a gully as a relative weakness which might be exploited. Bell led off down the almost vertical gully side but one rope-length was far too little to reach the gully bed. Smythe joined him and Bell set off down again, this time on even steeper rock until he reached a small ledge, still short of the gully bed, where he untied in order to inch sideways out of harm's way of any loose rock which Smythe might dislodge, and in order to enable Smythe to abseil down on the double rope. Almost predictably, when Smythe sought to pull down the doubled rope, it refused to budge and then, to compound a serious enough predicament, in trying to tug the rope clear, Smythe brought down loose rock on his head and, stunned, swayed out over the void.

There is probably, somewhere, the grave of an unknown young mountaineer who, had he survived such an incident, might well have gone on to enjoy a career as illustrious as Smythe's. Smythe did survive, just. Instinctively, he hung on and gradually returned to his senses; but the problem of the jammed rope remained. They could not descend without it; and Bell, unconcussed and the better rock-technician of the two, could not pass Smythe in order to climb up and get it, so there was no choice but for Smythe to do so. Apart from indirect light from a newly-risen moon, it was now completely dark but, strangely detached in the way one becomes when all other options are closed, and concentrating on the climb in such a way that he was subsequently able to recall every detail of it, he slowly inched his way up the 50 feet of rock, freed the rope and then eased his way, equally painstakingly, back down to Bell.

This was by no means the end of their troubles. With the gully bed only 50 feet below and a convenient spike around which to loop the rope, they first made sure, as they thought, that the rope would this time run free and then abseiled down. But again it jammed and resisted all their efforts to pull it clear. Nor had either of them the bottle, this time, to climb up and free it, so there it stayed and they faced the remaining 300 feet unroped. Although the worst of the climbing was over, what remained was not easy, and parts of it could only be negotiated in stockinged feet. Eventually they reached névé on the scree below and made their way back to the hut, where their afternoon stroll ended at midnight. It was almost a premature end to two very fruitful careers. However, the Dolomites had not yet finished with Smythe, although they reserved their next epic for another season.

Undeterred by the episode of the Langkofelkarspitze, Smythe and Bell went on to the Fünffingerspitze which flanks the Langkofel Joch on the south-west side. They had in their sights the series of chimneys on the east face which present the classic line of the Schmitt Kamin, for many years one of the hardest climbs in the Dolomites, but were stopped by a jammed boulder and had to descend and follow an easier line, seemingly the 1907 "Ramp" route.

The following summer, Smythe was back in the Dolomites again. Still fascinated by the Langkofel, he met up with T. H. and Leslie Somervell and together they climbed on the Kahnkofel and ascended the Langkofelkarspitze by the east face, where Leslie succeeded on the crucial pitch after both T. H. Somervell and Smythe had failed. Then with E. E. Roberts, his mentor from the Yorkshire Rambler days and companion in Snowdonia, he set out for the Grohmannspitze, which they planned to climb from the gap between it and the Fünffingerspitze, via the east-north-east ridge. Except for one pitch of Grade IV, this is one of the easier of the classic Dolomite routes and had they stuck to it they would, no doubt, have enjoyed a pleasant but uneventful day. But they were seduced by a couloir which seemed to offer a more direct route up on to the summit ridge and although it gave pleasant easy climbing for some way they eventually found themselves up against a 150 foot wall which presented no obvious line of weakness. The only possibility seemed to be to take to an adjoining wall on the left which, although also steep, was more broken, provided that an initial overhanging bulge immediately above the stance could be turned. Smythe, leading, managed this and eased his way delicately upwards, the last twenty feet on tiny nicks and rugosities until a "thank God!" jug enabled him to haul himself over the top.

Those who have made a similar mistake and lived to tell the tale, will find it possible to forgive Smythe what he did next; no one else would. The only belay he could find was a small flake, sufficient to take one turn of the rope and no more. This would not have mattered if he had done the sensible thing and tied himself close up to it, taking in the rope round his waist as Roberts climbed, but he did not. The rock which Roberts had to climb was difficult, but it was well supplied with holds, albeit rather small, and Roberts was one of the best rock-climbers of his day. It is easy to assume in such circumstances that any belay is purely theoretical and this is just what Smythe did. He took in about twenty feet of slack, tied a bight in it and passed the bight over the flake. Then, making himself as firm as possible, he took Roberts's rope over his shoulders and called Roberts up. The rope came up slowly and steadily; all was going well. Then, suddenly, came a cry from Roberts and, simultaneously, the rope which Smythe had taken in whipped away and, in an instant, tautened and wrenched him sideways off the stance. He used what fleeting chance he had to try and stop himself by any means, but failed, and in no time was jerked over the edge of the precipice and into space.

Smythe's next recollection, after some hasty speculation about the after life, was of finding himself hanging some distance below the edge, his waist bruised by the rope. Hastily, he secured holds on the rock and heard an assurance floating up from Roberts. As Roberts had stepped across the overhanging bulge on his way up, relying only on his footholds, it had parted company from the mountainside and collapsed completely beneath him, depositing him uninjured on the ledge below. The rope had held and, somewhat surprisingly, had stayed on the belay.

They duly recovered the situation, climbed back to the ridge and from there scrambled easily to the summit. They then descended uneventfully and proceeded to make good use of the rest of the season without exposing themselves to undue excitement.

Although they were, for a time, one of Smythe's favourite stomping grounds, he never spoke with affection of the Dolomites, but rather with awe. I wonder why? They were, after all, very kind to him.

In 1923, he first visited the Bernese Oberland as a mountaineer. As a boy, he had gazed longingly at the Lauterbrunnen peaks from below, but in April 1923 came his first chance to go up amongst them and build a more familiar acquaintance. His companion on this first exploration was Colonel P. Neame with whom he had walked the hills of North Wales. It was their intention to spend two weeks in the high Oberland, and two porters, laden with supplies, accompanied them on the first leg of the journey from Fiesch up to the Hotel. Although still sometimes used as a descent route from the Konkordia Hut, it is a measure of changing standards that you are today thought of as slightly mad if you prefer this walk-in to the Jungfraujoch railway, or at least the Eggishorn cableway.

On this occasion, the gods were not smiling on Smythe's enterprises. They awoke the following morning to a blizzard. Twice in the course of the next three days, breaks in the weather tempted them to set out for Konkordia via the Tälligrat and Marjelensee path and twice they were driven stumbling back down the slopes. They had to return to Fiesch for more supplies and a replacement ice-axe for the one Smythe had broken over his knee in boredom. Eventually they were able to go back up and, this time, reach Konkordia, the last five miles over the great Aletsch Glacier, before the weather closed in yet again, for another three days, which yielded only one short expedition to the Grünhornlücke. The first fine day which followed had to be devoted to a descent to the Hotel to bring up more stores, and half the tour was over before they were able to set foot in earnest upon a mountainside.

At last, however, things improved sufficiently to allow an ascent of the Mönch by the south-east ridge, a trade route in the summers of today, but a rather different proposition after a week of foul April weather. The ridge was covered in loose powdery snow and, towards the summit, massive cornices overhanging to the north made it necessary to traverse out on to the steep south face in order to progress. Eventually the summit was reached, although the bitter cold precluded any leisurely sojourn there, and before long they were running on ski the five miles back to Konkordia.

After a morning basking on the rocks, the following afternoon saw them traversing the Grünhornlücke, en route for the Finsteraarhorn Hut which in those days was a tiny primitive shack. The next day gave them an ascent of the Finsteraarhorn via the breakfast place and the Hugisattel although cornices on the summit ridge again forced them out on to the western face before they were able to ascend ice slopes to the summit to complete the last route of a tour which, in spite of its disappointment, had its compensations. To some extent, the deficiencies were made good that very summer when, as a member of T. H. Somervell's party which, amongst other things, was testing oxygen equipment for the forthcoming Everest expedition, Smythe made the ascent of the Eiger via the south-west flank and west ridge, descending via the south ridge to the north Eiger Joch and thence traversing the ridge to the south Eiger Joch, a passage which seems today to have gone completely out of fashion. Somervell's party also included in its programme the ascent of the Schreckhorn via the Schrecksattel and east-south-east ridge which prompted Smythe to add to his list the traverse of the Schreckhorn and Lauteraarhorn, an item which was placed on the agenda when Smythe returned to the Oberland with J. H. B. Bell in July 1925.

On this occasion, the pair left Grindelwald to arrive at the Strahlegg Hut on 25 July which, as it happened, coincided with the start of yet another of those three-day spells of forced inertia which so often accompanied Smythe's Oberland ventures. It was 2.50 a.m. on the morning of 28 July when they eventually left on their way for the traverse of the Schreckhorn. Ascending the Gaagg Valley behind the hut, they encountered no difficulty at the bergschrund and, in spite of dubious weather signs, were soon mounting the south-west ridge, and arrived at the summit at 9.15 a.m. They were quickly down the east-south-east ridge of the Schreckhorn and by ten o'clock had started to surmount the series of pinnacles which constitute the north-west ridge of the Lauteraarhorn, the Lauteraargrat.

The numbing east wind duped them into supposing that one

particularly obstructive pinnacle would be best turned by traversing out on to the west (lee) face and considerable time was lost, with the result that it was well after five o'clock before they reached the summit of the Lauteraarhorn. Poor snow conditions delayed them further on the descent and they finally returned to the hut by the light of the moon after nearly twenty hours on the move. In spite of its imperfections, however, it was a vastly more enjoyable experience for Smythe than was his next venture on the Schreckhorn.

Bell and Smythe had planned, after a day's rest, to try a new route on the Klein Fiescherhorn, or Ochs, a route which Smythe later accomplished. But immediate plans for the attempt had to be postponed owing to a foot injury of Bell's. Staying at the hut at the same time were Alexander Harrison and C. M. K. Douglas, intent on the Schreckhorn via the Schrecksattel, but Smythe prevailed upon them to try the south-west ridge which he considered to be a superior climb. A calm fine morning saw them on their way easily across the Schreckfirn and negotiating the avalanche-choked bergschrund without difficulty. By now, the sun had risen, and in an extraordinary sky which was suffused with a "weird greenish glow"—a sign of which none of them knew the meaning. They pressed on up the thousand foot ramp/gully which leads to the notch on the south-west ridge, reached it within the hour and set off up the steep rocks of the ridge proper, the air remaining still warm. Concentrating on the rock, they did not look about them until, 500 feet below the summit, they were distracted by a long roll of thunder and, looking to the north west, saw a solid-looking mass of slate-grey cloud decorated with the flicker of lightning approaching the Oberland Wall. It overwhelmed Jungfrau, Mönch and Eiger and, within ten minutes of them first noticing it, was upon them.

It was suicidal to stay on the ridge a second longer than necessary and, leaving axes, which would attract the lightning, they made their way down to a sheltered ledge on the lee side there to sit out the storm. The fury of hail, thunder and lightning continued for an hour before they were able to return, stiff with cold, to their axes. The ridge above was now plastered with ice and hail and the sole objective had now become escape from the mountain and the blizzard which was likely to follow the storm. One possibility was to traverse the summit and descend, over easier ground, via the Schrecksattel at the far side. The rocks above, however, would take too long to climb, and the preferred alternative was to descend by the way they had come up. They set off immediately but far from quickly for the rock was now wet and the holds filled with melting hail. By the time they had reached the head of the ramp/couloir, thunder again drew their attention to gathering storm clouds and before they had progressed any great distance down the couloir, a second storm, if anything more intense than the first, was upon them. They had no priority now but to descend with maximum haste: Douglas and Harrison moved on down; Smythe had stopped to protect them over a short section when suddenly he received a stunning blow on the head. Dazed, he slipped from his holds and came on the rope, then, instinctively regaining a hold on the rock and crouching to recover, he called down to the others that he had been struck. Fortunately, they were sound and competent mountaineers, and Harrison effectively took over responsibility for the party. Smythe was, for a while, unable to continue and even then, was given to fits of trembling. The delay turned out to be their salvation; they had descended, painstakingly slowly, only a short way down the couloir (at one point, the rate was a mere 200 feet per hour), when their attention was distracted by a new roar, over and above that of the storm, and a massive stone-fall crashed into the gully just ahead of them and roared off down the route which they would have been descending had they not been held up. By now, their slow rate of progress in the freezing gale was numbing hands and feet and they were weakened almost to the point where it was impossible to continue, when at last the storm relented. They were able to rest and recover and restore enough energy by eating some chocolate to be able to complete the extremely hazardous descent without further incident.

In later years, Smythe became something of a specialist in hazardous descents—his solo descent from high on Everest and his negotiation of the passage down from the Aiguille Blanche de Peuterey (with Dr Graham MacPhee) over new ground come to mind. It is doubtful, though, if any subsequent struggle with the elements brought him as close to death on a mountain. The blow of the lightning or the fall which it prompted could each have killed him; the stone-fall could easily have wiped out the party. Had it not been a strong one, and had Harrison in particular not been able to supply the drive which it lost when Smythe was struck, they could not have continued. And notwithstanding all this, had the storm not relented just in time, another tragic chapter would have been written in the history of the Alps.

As it was, the season with Bell continued, fruitfully if less eventfully. They started by reconnoitring the route on the north-east face of the Klein Fiescherhorn—today much more fashionable and, better known as the Ochs, the scene of a number of modern hard routes. The Smythe route took a more classic line, following a subsidiary ridge running up from the Ober Grindelwald Glacier to the terrace which nestles about one thousand feet below the summit of the Ochs to the north east. Smythe and Bell pressed the route up an initial buttress with about 30 feet of very steep climbing and were then forced left up sound slabs before encountering easier going over broken rocks to the crest of the buttress from which the rest of the route was visible. There was not on that occasion sufficient time to finish the route and after lazing in the sun, they retreated and Bell returned home. Some ten days later Smythe returned with J. V. Hazard and together they covered the same ground and then, following the ridge to the terrace, mounted steep snow slopes to the north-east ridge proper which they followed to the top by kicking steps in steep, well consolidated snow.

Before Bell went home, they plucked the prize of their season, the Guggi route on the Jungfrau. This, again, is one of those old-style classic routes first done as long ago as 1865 but very variable from season to season and generally tending to become harder over the years. It is, they say, impossible for years at a time. Bell's description suggests that, in 1925, they found it in very challenging condition. It consists, in effect, of the ascent of the Jungfrau via a tour of all the famous features of the north side of the mountain. It starts up the Guggi Glacier, access to which itself involves quite a tour, and a necessary climb at the head to the ice-fall leading on to the Kühlauenen Glacier. The classic line then takes in the Schneehorn, Klein Silberhorn and Silberhorn (although this latter can be omitted) before following the Silber ridge route from the Silberlücke to the summit. It is a long route, bristling with variations the relative attractions of which differ according to conditions. It is, therefore, a test as much of route-finding as of anything else, although it requires snow and ice work of a fairly high technical standard—very much a Smythe route. They overcame its difficulties without error and went on to complete the traverse of the mountain in a very long and exhausting day. Bell remembered it 25 years later as illustrating Smythe's "amazing capacity for route-finding especially in the classic tradition of snow and ice routes."

The last outstanding landmark in a highly successful first season in the Oberland was the traverse of the Bietschhorn, again a mountain to which Smythe was to return. Were it not for foreign surveyors who insist that their science establishes it to be some 60 or so metres short of being a "Viertausender", the Bietschhorn would be accepted by all as being one of the greatest mountains in the Alps. Even British surveyors would leave it a hundred feet short of 13,000. The important fact is that it is an awesome peak. It looks immense and fierce, dominating the Lötschental and outstanding on that valley's otherwise overpowering south-east wall. It is one of those few peaks in the Alps which lack any easy route of ascent. Eiger and Matterhorn have their north walls and Mont Blanc has its Brenva face, but these mountains can also be climbed by routes markedly easier than anything on offer on the Bietschhorn. It ranks with La Meije in this respect—to find significant mountains with a more difficult easiest route up, one is compelled to resort to such obscure summits as the Corno Stella in the Italian Maritime Alps; although the *voies normales* on such mountains as the Dent Blanche and Weisshorn, while technically less difficult than anything on the Bietschhorn, are serious.

Smythe's route of ascent was the west-south-west ridge, the easiest route of ascent from the Lötschental side. Viewed from the south west, foreshortening makes it look a formidable proposition. It falls from the north-western end of the summit ridge, where it joins the north ridge, bounding the enormous névé which clothes the west face of the mountain, and falling to the Bietsch Glacier plateau about 2,500 feet below. It is a long route, but then so are they all on the Bietschhorn, including the east ridge by which Smythe descended to the Baltschiederklause Hut.

The tours and climbs detailed here were but some of those undertaken by Smythe during the years of his apprenticeship. Infant classes in the Tyrol and Central Switzerland were followed by junior school in the Oberland. He later moved on to the Pennine Alps and Mont Blanc, then to even greater routes and ranges. This graduation to higher things was by no means the end of his association with the scenes of his early schooldays. He made several returns to the Oberland to savour more of its *grandes courses*; he never lost his affection for the more modest and simple mountain wandering to which the less celebrated ranges so admirably lend themselves and which, for all the great deeds, remain peculiarly characteristic of Smythe's attitude towards the mountain scene.

CHAPTER V

Corsican Interlude

NOWADAYS, ONE HARDLY thinks of Corsica as an Alpine country: its mountains lack the height, the routes, and the seriousness and grandeur of the more demanding Alpine courses. Nevertheless, it was early recognized that the Corsican uplands offered suitable sport for a member of the Alpine Club and such eminent mountaineers as Freshfield and Tuckett were associated with their exploration. Later, the Finch brothers continued the work before it was left to further generations of continental climbers to bring it up to date.

Corsica's early popularity amongst British climbers did not last. When those in the van of Alpine climbing turned to the great routes on the north faces, Corsica ceased to have anything to offer them, though the headline-makers were totally untypical of the general run of European climbers with whom it has always been popular. It remains today well worth a visit, especially since it has, in effect, a more extended season than can reasonably be expected of the higher Alpine ranges.

British climbers know little about Corsica. The literature tends to concentrate upon the more heavily-trafficked areas, no doubt for the very good reason that they are heavily trafficked because they have most to offer. Nevertheless, Corsica is not merely an island that has some mountains. Except for a narrow coastal strip on the eastern side, Corsica *is* mountains and quite apart from those on or near the beaten track, where there are several peaks of over 8,000 feet culminating at Cinto at nearly 9,000 feet, the island contains hundreds of summits of between 4,000 and 7,000 feet. I am constantly astonished that mountaineers, who are genuinely an anarchic and adventurous lot, behave so conservatively about the areas they visit and the climbs they undertake. Crete, for example, has a 6,000 foot mountain, Gingolos, with a quite splendid 4,000 foot north face, but I have yet to meet a fellow mountaineer (other than the one whom I dragged there) who has heard of it.

Smythe, like any young climber in the mid-1920s, would have heard of the mountains of Corsica. Even if the exploits of Freshfield and Tuckett were not immediately to mind, George Finch had published the account of their climbs as recently as 1924 in *The Making of a Mountaineer* and that is why, late in May 1926, Smythe found himself on board ship *en route* from Marseilles to Ajaccio in the company of F. H. Slingsby. From Ajaccio, they proceeded by train to Vizzavona on the far, eastern side of the pass of that name and were in position to attempt the climb of Monte d'Oro the following day.

The most favoured routes on the mountain today approach its summit either from the col to the west or via the north ridge. There is, however, a more direct if steeper and more complex way up the mountain from Vizzavona and this, the south-east ridge, is the route taken by Smythe and Slingsby. Via this route, although not entirely without difficulty, they duly arrived at the summit, descending to the east, initially by a glissade down a couloir, later through forest and field back to Vizzavona, and an entire day's rest on the morrow.

The following morning saw them resolved to make the ascent of Monte Renoso but insufficiently well-informed to carry out this plan. A combination of an inadequate map and unclear instructions from the locals led them to the summit not of Monte Renoso but to that of the Punta Dell'Oriente a mile or two along the ridge to the north. Not surprisingly, they settled for that and eventually made their way back, again with the assistance of a glissade.

A train to Corte and a motor diligence thence took them to Calacuccia next day. The Hotel des Touristes there can hardly have changed at all since their visit and remains today a rare surviving example of the early climbers' hotel, the walls still decorated with sepia prints celebrating the first explorations. Its function has changed little—practically the first question I was asked, on arrival, was whether I was there for "la montagne"—Monte Cinto.

Monte Cinto is by no means the only mountain worth reconnoitring in the Calacuccia area and Smythe and Slingsby had several other worthwhile encounters before they confronted "la montagne". Rising at 5 a.m., at which time little is happening in Calacuccia, they set out up the broken ridge, broad at first, which slants up from

Lozzi, above Calacuccia. This culminates, eventually, in the summit of the Capa Falu which is to Monte Cinto as Lliwedd is to Crib-y-Ddysgl. Stopped by a steep tower where the ridge narrows, they moved out on to the north face along ledges and eventually managed to find a way up excellent rock to the summit.

Fit at last, they then loaded up with supplies and set off, through Albertacce and Calasima to the Grotte des Anges from a bivouac near which (not, for sanitary reasons, *in* which) they climbed for the following few days.

Setting off at four the next morning, they made their way towards the Col Foggiale but, immensely impressed by the Paglia Orba (known, for little good reason, as the Matterhorn of Corsica) and presented with the prospect of its east ridge, they decided to mount an assault. It availed them nought. The east ridge repulsed all their efforts and such variations as they could conjure took them no closer than 600 feet from the summit. They should have searched a bit harder for there is a short and easy but rather obscure way up to the summit plateau from here, via the Foggiale chimneys.

Somewhat chastened, they returned to the attack two days later, traversed the Punta Costeluccia, descended to the Col Foggiale and then made the ascent of the Paglia Orba by its relatively easy south face route.

Slingsby's stay was almost at an end but, before he departed, the pair made the obligatory ascent of Monte Cinto by its Calacuccia *voie normale*. This seemed to excite them not at all, but is by no means lacking in merit in its upper reaches if one incorporates some wholly unnecessary but interesting scrambling, as one can. Nowadays, the ascent from Calacuccia is much facilitated by comparison with half a century ago. A new hut serves those who wish to make use of it. Those who prefer the somewhat austere and by no means inexpensive comfort of the hotel can now drive along a rough road from Lozzi, preferably in a hired car. This road climbs to about 1,500 metres and a couple of miles short of the hut and the foot of the flank of the mountain, although those who prefer arriving there to wallowing interminably in the maquis are advised to wait at least for the first streaks of dawn.

Smythe and Slingsby had to do it in the old style. They might have been more excited by the experience had their arrival at the summit been otherwise than in rain-soaked mist. On a clear dawn one can gaze over the whole mountainous mass of the island and beyond. Nevertheless, the attainment of Corsica's highest point must, in some respect, have sounded a pleasant note on which to end Slingsby's tour.

Left to his own devices, and unimpressed by such information as his enquiries about local guides yielded, Smythe initially headed back to the Grotte des Anges bivvy and scrambled on the pinnacles of the Grande Barrière, north of the Paglia Orba, for a couple of days. He then crossed the Col Foggiale, traversed round the foot of the Tafonata and then followed its east face route to the famous hole which penetrates right through the entire mountain some hundreds of feet below the summit. He then traversed round and over the north ridge to the west side and, after steep snow and a scramble, attained the north summit.

Now, his time too was up, and Chamonix beckoned.

In a very real sense, the Corsica interlude marks the end of Smythe's apprenticeship. It was perhaps a rather specialized apprenticeship—a preparation particularly apt for the sort of exploratory wandering which he later undertook in the Bhyundar Valley and the Lloyd George mountains. At all events, it marked the watershed. What lay ahead could in no wise be considered to be mere preparation or training. It was mountaineering of the highest order and fit to be undertaken only by one whose ability and experience had been thoroughly tested and established beyond all doubt.

CHAPTER VI

*The Great Alpine Routes**

THE 1927 SEASON could hardly have started less auspiciously. Much of 1926 and the first months of 1927 had been devoted to trying to establish a career. Smythe had first gone to Buenos Aires, though, strangely for him, he never penetrated as far as the Andes. Then he had joined the fledgling Royal Air Force and been posted to Egypt —no new routes appeared on the Pyramids. The circumstances of his quitting the RAF did not augur well for a future amongst the mountains, for he was invalided out and cautioned to "take it easy up stairs" for the rest of his life.

Why Smythe responded to this advice as he did, it is hard to say. Perhaps, having been repeatedly told, as a boy, that he was weak and sickly, he had become case-hardened to such diagnoses and simply ignored them; perhaps, feeling that he had little to lose, he acquired a sense of immortality. Whatever the reason, his response was to embark upon the most remarkable season yet, included in which were some of the most striking advances of the era in Alpine climbing. The venue chosen for these performances was the Mont Blanc range which Smythe had not previously visited.

Today, the Mont Blanc range is the most popular part of the Alps by far, and it is easy to understand why. Within a small compass it offers a plethora of superb routes of all kinds—rock, snow and ice, and mixed; easy, medium-grade and hard. Itself easy of access, it is also easy to get away from, in the event of foul weather, to alternatives less likely to be affected. Were it not so attractive as to attract the hordes (which really only means too many others of one's own ilk), it would remain the most attractive part of the Alps. Today, however, although it is still possible to get away on one's own in the less well known parts of the range, solitude is practically unobtainable, during the season, on the best routes which have established its reputation. Smythe and his contemporaries of the 1920s and 1930s enjoyed the

*See p.211 for Smythe's routes on the Brenva Face

now unobtainable experience of savouring the range before it was swamped by the post-war boom in Alpine climbing.

At that time, and for some decades previously, attention in the Mont Blanc range had been focused chiefly on the Chamonix Aiguilles, the chain of sharply pointed rock peaks extending for four miles from the precocious little Aiguille de l'M to the Aiguille du Midi and forming the north-western ramparts of the southern half of the range. The great Mont Blanc summits had all fallen to a variety of classic routes in the course of the latter half of the nineteenth century and the challenge which had replaced them, and to which the likes of Mummery had responded, was that of the long steep rock routes of the Aiguilles. As early as 1881, the Grépon fell to Mummery, Burgener and Venetz via the north ridge, a route which has remained a classic prize ever since, and it is arguable that the first of the "modern" routes was that put up on the same mountain in 1911 by a party including Winthrop Young and Joseph Knubel who climbed it via the Mer de Glace face.

Early in the 1927 season, Smythe met up with G. S. Bower and set off for the Grépon. They chose a route which incorporated the crux section of the Mer de Glace route, the "Knubel Crack", a 60 foot chimney leading out on to the summit and at that time one of the hardest known pitches of rock-climbing anywhere in the Alps. It is not at all the sort of route one associates with Smythe, who never claimed to be in the very front rank of rock-climbers, and that they succeeded was, according to him, largely due to Bower who led the crux. A few days later, Smythe was to return to the Aiguilles but, before doing so, he set off with Dr Graham MacPhee, ascended the Col Maudit from the Géant Glacier, by no means a "doddle", and turned north with "absurd peak-bagging instinct" to claim Mont Blanc du Tacul before traversing Mont Maudit to make the ascent of Mont Blanc, the first among many.

The route in the Aiguilles which particularly interested Smythe was the traverse of the Col du Pain de Sucre, which he had reconnoitred and attempted with T. S. Blakeney. The south-west side, by which they intended to descend, is unproblematical. The ascent by the north-east face is a different proposition, and although Blakeney and Smythe made several hundred feet of progress they were eventually driven off by a storm. Technically a very difficult ice route, it was eventually ascended by a party led by G. and M. Charlet in 1931 and received its first British ascent only in 1954.

On 21 July, Smythe arrived at Montenvers with J. H. B. Bell with a view to mounting another attempt on the Col du Pain de Sucre. They were first of all delayed by bad weather and then, when they were able to get out to reconnoitre a route to the start, they discovered that the bergschrund had become impassable and the slopes above icy and dangerous. It was at this juncture, and only as an alternative to a frustrating retreat to Montenvers, that they considered other plans and set their sights on the east ridge of the Aiguille du Plan. The collective memory yielded the information that the ridge had been climbed many years previously, by J. V. Ryan with the Lochmatters, but beyond that nothing. They decided to give it a go.

It was, in fact, 21 years previously that Ryan and the Lochmatters first climbed the ridge and that remained the only ascent. They were a formidable team; a good case can be made for the proposition that they were, measured against the prevailing standards of any age, the strongest ever. Some of their routes, such as the South West Face of the Täschhorn, climbed in 1906, are rarely attempted even today. Many years later, Smythe met the "incomparable" Franz Lochmatter at Montenvers where a number of young tigers were struggling unsuccessfully with a boulder problem and recounts how "a tall thin man, who was standing nearby, quietly watching, strolled across and, without preamble, without fuss or bother, without it appeared the slightest effort, leisurely climbed the steep and apparently holdless slab. It was Franz Lochmatter." Recalling the climb on the Plan years later, Ryan and Franz Lochmatter considered that notwithstanding the perfect conditions they had for the expedition it was the most difficult climb they ever did; and the great Swiss, André Roch, writing in 1949, counselled the aspirant alpinist that "before venturing to climb any very special faces, such as the Ryan-Lochmatter route on the Aiguille du Plan, the mountaineer should first scale . . . the most difficult of the classical ascents."

Whether Smythe and Bell would have embarked on the route at all had they researched it better, it is hard to tell. Quite apart from anything else, Ryan and the Lochmatters had found the ridge in excellent condition for their attempt in 1906, whilst that was far from being the case as Smythe and Bell approached it.

Although technically no longer in the hardest class (it is graded

D+ and the hardest pitch is V and avoidable) the east ridge of the Plan remains a testing and serious proposition. Conditions permitting, the ridge can be followed from toe to summit. Such conditions did not greet Smythe and Bell and it was not until 3 p.m., after an eventful encounter with the lower reaches of the Plan/Crocodile couloir followed by five hours of step-cutting by Smythe, that the ridge was attained, at a point still some 1,200 feet below the summit. Smythe had experienced a rare slip, with a fall of some 40 to 50 feet into the ice-runnel in the couloir, after which a tough ice-slope that Smythe "conservatively" estimated at in excess of 60 degrees had offered the only and timely means of escape from the couloir—raked with stonefall under the mid-day sun.

Bell's turn came with the rock. Snow and verglas polluted the holds; a shifting chockstone imprisoned Smythe's knee and Bell descended to the rescue just in time. Smythe was "little more than a passenger for the rest of the day" which ended at 7 p.m. with the inevitable bivouac. It seems to have been a long, cold and lonely wait and it was not until two hours after dawn that circulations were sufficiently restored to continue. Bell still led, except for one or two short stretches, and more than one blind alley was desperately explored before the pair emerged, apparently via the right-hand branch of the final chimney, on the ridge of the *voie normale* just below the summit.

Bell's role during the latter half of this climb was a *tour de force*. The rock was in appalling condition. Bell was in the very van of rock-climbing in Scotland and, indeed, Britain, between the wars, and the Plan route stretched him continuously to his limit. Yet he sustained the effort, coolly except for the occasional monotonously muttered string of oaths, for the better part of two days. Each of the pair eventually endorsed Franz Lochmatter's opinion. Of the rock, Bell opined it was the hardest he had ever encountered; of the ice, Smythe avows "never before had I climbed a slope of such continuous steepness"; and of the route as a whole, concludes, "for length, interest, excitement and standard of difficulty, the ascent of the Aiguille du Plan by the east ridge was the finest and most difficult rock climb I have ever accomplished."

For the record, and to be strictly accurate, Smythe and Bell did not so much repeat the Ryan/Lochmatter route as add a substantial, new, difficult and emphatically unrecommended variation to it. The original route, a much more classic line, gains the arête at the "épaule inférieur",

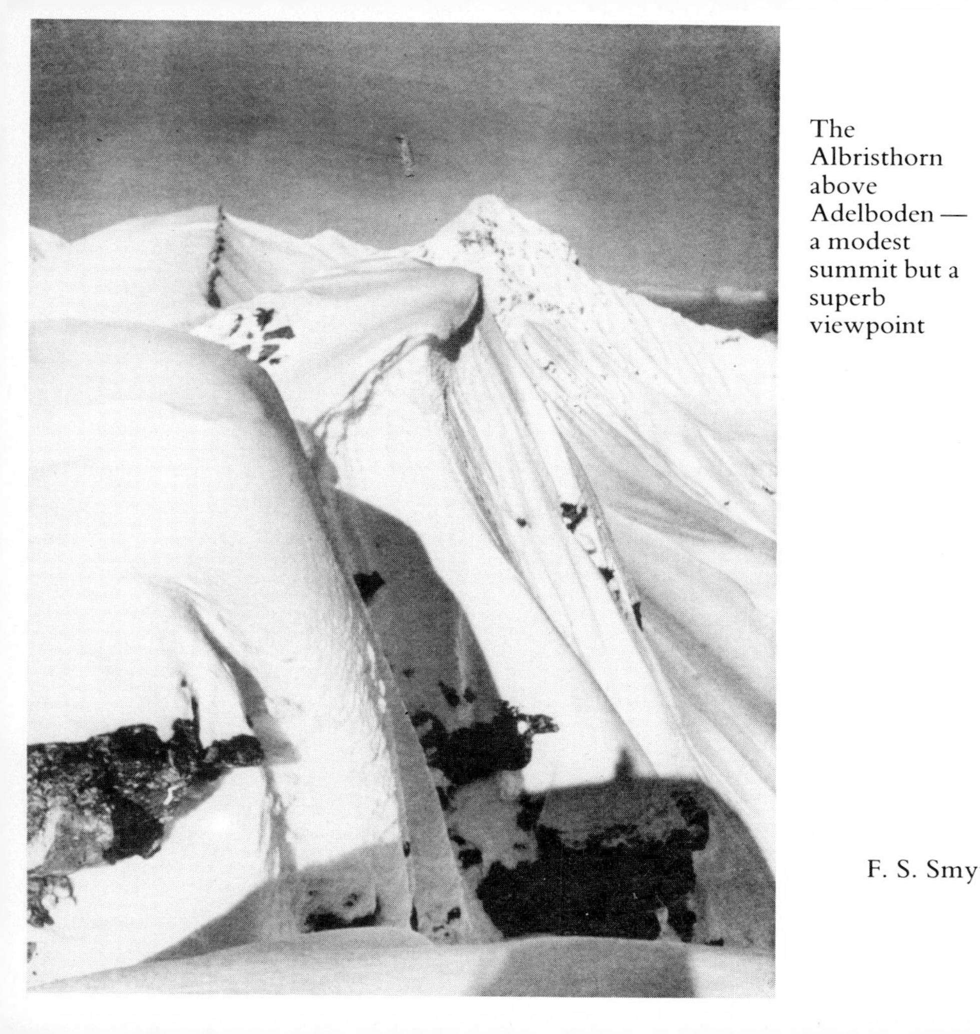

The Albristhorn above Adelboden — a modest summit but a superb viewpoint

F. S. Smythe

Snowdon

Sunrise on the Riffelalp

Les Bans. The route takes the left-hand sky-line ridge

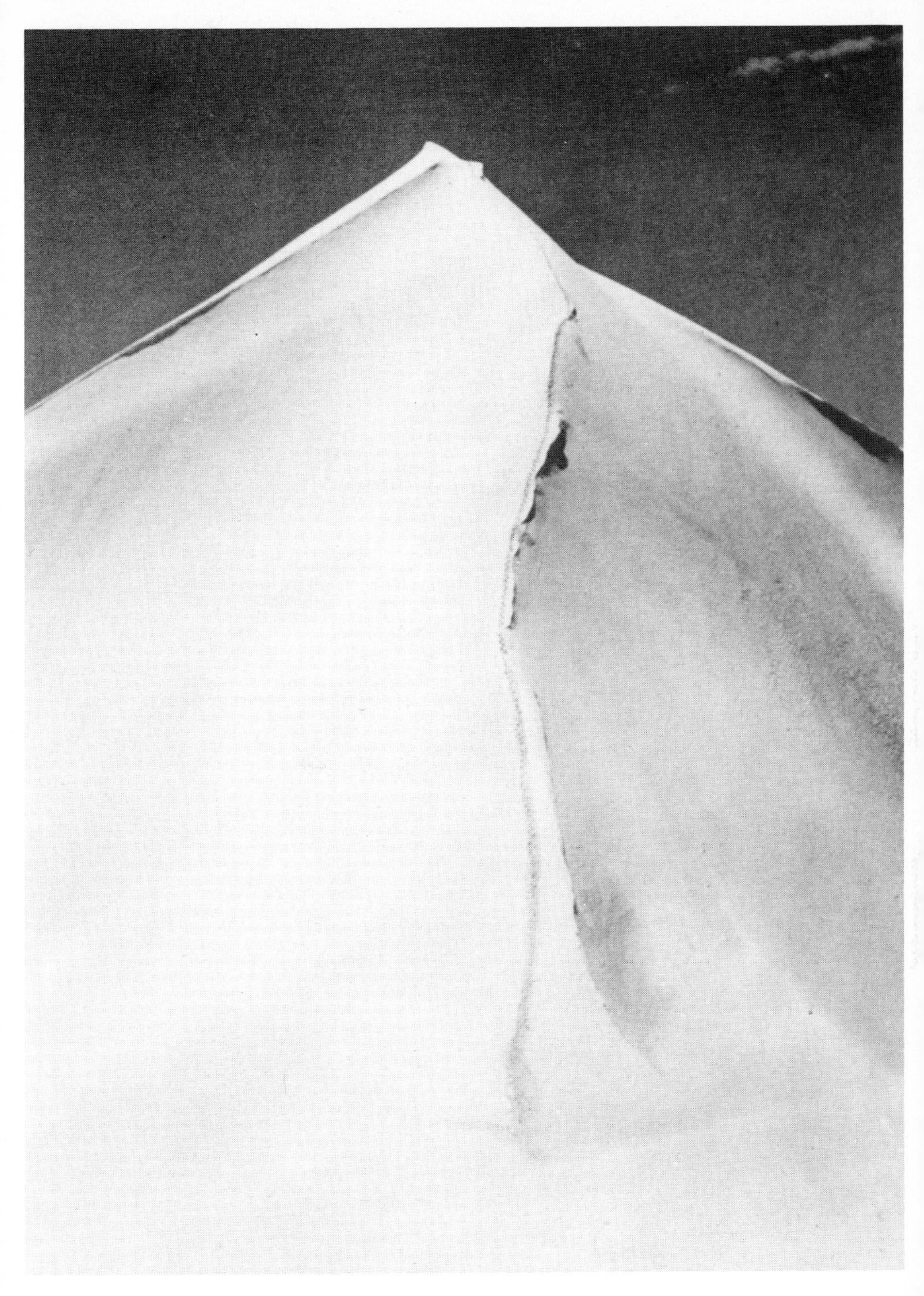

Dômes de Miage

The Schreckhorn — scene of a near disaster

Aiguilles Noires and Dames Anglaises — Peuterey Ridge of Mont Blanc

Avalanche on Kangchenjunga. It was such an avalanche which killed Chettan and put an end to the attempt on this face.

about a quarter of the way up the ridge. Smythe and Bell felt obliged to continue in the extremely steep couloir, traversing out on to the ridge only with great difficulty, some hundreds of feet above.

The Grépon and the Plan may have temporarily blunted Smythe's appetite for hard Alpine rock, for he now turned to the south side of the range and the great mixed routes which abound there. By the opening of the 1927 season, all the great ridges of Mont Blanc had been traversed, save one. That one was the greatest and most demanding of all, the Peuterey Ridge, which retains to this day the reputation of offering the most challenging and sustained route in the Alps. Its challenge resides not so much in its technical difficulty for that is surpassed on many lesser routes. Rather, it is its length and seriousness (for it is given to bad weather and escape is difficult once committed) and the fact that it leads inexorably to the highest summit in the Alps that lend it its character.

The entire ridge, the route following which is known as the Peuterey Ridge Intégrale, is a range in itself. It rises out of the Val Veni via what is in substance the south ridge of the Aiguille Noire de Peuterey, descending thence to the Brèche des Dames Anglaises before rising again over the Aiguille Blanche and down to the Col de Peuterey, rising from there for the last time to the eastern summit of Mont Blanc, Mont Blanc de Courmayeur. Not until 1953 was this route successfully engaged for the first time. It was, anomalously, the upper part of the ridge which was first climbed—as early as 1877 by James Eccles with the Payots who followed a long couloir from the upper Frêney Glacier to join the ridge well above the Col de Peuterey. The Col itself was first reached, from the Frêney side, in 1880. By the 1920s, though, the "received version" of the Peuterey Ridge, and that which was receiving attention as the current *grande problème*, involved gaining access to the ridge at the Brèche des Dames Anglaises, thence traversing the Aiguille Blanche and Col de Peuterey, and following it to the summit. I find it very hard to appreciate the scale of such an undertaking, let alone the Intégrale. The Aiguille Blanche, which one tends to think of as a rather large gendarme on this route, is itself a very significant mountain. Its summit stands 2,000 feet above the Brèche des Dames Anglaises to reach which requires an ascent of some 3,000 feet from the Monzino Hut. Once on its 13,500 foot summit, one then has to descend to the Col and climb a further 3,000 feet to the summit of Mont Blanc.

Until the start of the 1927 season, this version of the Peuterey Ridge had resisted all attempts. It finally fell, at the end of July in that year, to Obersteiner and Schreiner and was repeated four days later. When Smythe set out for it with MacPhee on 10 August they were bent on the third, and first British, ascent.

Today, the usual base for the Peuterey Ridge is the Monzino Hut which stands on a spur between the snouts of the Brouillard and Frêney Glaciers, near the site of the old Gamba Hut which, in the 1920s, constituted the last habitation before embarking on the route. MacPhee and Smythe set out thence at 5.15 p.m. intending to bivouac on the Brèche des Dames Anglaises (the route is today rendered marginally less serious by the establishment of a bivouac hut here). By 6.30 they stood on the Col de L'Innominata and began the descent, down a crumbling rock face and icy gully, to the Frêney Glacier, the crossing of which was time-consuming and, apparently, frustrating, particularly to Smythe who demonstrated his opinion that the sacs were over heavy for the job by hurling a large morsel of MacPhee's cheese into the maw of the glacier. A bivouac site was settled upon only at 2 a.m., after ascending the Isolée Couloir under the Brèche by its left upper branch by moonlight to just below the Brèche.

The ascent was resumed at 5.30 a.m. after a coldly uncomfortable few hours. Dawn presented them with a canvas of lenticular cloud auguring ill for the day as they crested the Brèche and embarked upon the south-west ridge of the Aiguille Blanche. They were already thinking in terms of a possible retreat but were not keen to reverse the route to the Brèche and settled for descent to the Frêney Glacier from the Col de Peuterey as a way of escape, should it become necessary. It did become necessary; the view from the summit of the Aiguille Blanche at which they arrived only at 1 p.m. was of "the undisciplined armies of the storm marshalling to the attack". After two hours of hazardous descent to the Col de Peuterey, the wind had risen to hurricane force—it was, apparently, recorded as highly exceptional on that day in both Montreux and Piedmont. Descent was imperative.

Some idea of the dangerous situation in which they now found themselves is given by the history of the Col de Peuterey as it stood in 1927. Its north-east side was known as a death-trap and was first climbed eventually only in 1944 by the Herzogs with Rebuffat and

Terray. The south-west side had been climbed via the Rochers Gruber in 1880 but had not been repeated and a descent had never been successfully negotiated. MacPhee and Smythe knew only that Balfour and his guide Johannes Petrus had died in the attempt. Nevertheless, it was this side which logic and instinct dictated, rightly as events turned out. It is now recognized as the best bad weather descent from the ridge, in spite of the line being hard to find.

Bombarded by rocks blown off the col and by enormous hailstones, the pair inched downwards, abseiling where necessary, finally reaching the Frêney Glacier four hours later and the Gamba Hut two hours after that. The whole escapade had occupied 28 hours' absence from the hut, including the three and a half of the bivouac. Smythe's account concentrates on the conditions which they endured. It was left to MacPhee to publish the opinion that in leading this first descent, in appalling conditions, Smythe was never once at fault in negotiating the unknown route: it was mountaineering of the highest order.

Smythe never, before or since, found himself in positions of such seriousness as those he encountered on the Plan and the Aiguille Blanche. Each involved encountering adverse conditions on long routes which were amongst the hardest of their day. The zenith of his Alpine career was, however, yet to be reached. The great routes which followed were significant and seminal; they remain amongst the classic greats and one of them, the Route Major, has not been and cannot be excelled.

In any survey of developments in Alpine climbing between the two world wars, a small number of landmarks stand out. The most notorious events were those of the 1930s, concerning the then-current "last great problems" of the Alps, particularly the north faces of the Grandes Jorasses and the Eiger. But the greatest face of all is the Brenva Face of Mont Blanc and at the commencement of the inter-war era, it was unclimbed.

The south-eastern slopes of Mont Blanc rise out of the Val Veni to the summit of the mountain 12,000 feet above Courmayeur. They extend from the frontier or Brenva arête, linking the Tour Ronde to Mont Maudit, round to the Miage face in a continuous series of enormous precipices broken up by soaring ridges and buttresses that contain much of the most testing climbing in the Alps. The earliest ascents of Mont Blanc were first from the Chamonix side, later, on the Italian side, from the north along the frontier ridge and also from the south west. Then, one by one, the great southern ridges fell, the last of them, the Peuterey, during Smythe's 1927 season. What remained was the great headwall rising from the upper part of the Brenva Glacier to the summit ridge of Mont Blanc and the upper section of its north ridge. The one point of relative weakness to the right of this wall, the Brenva Spur, had been exploited by Moore's party in putting up the "Old Brenva" route in 1865, an historic route and ahead of its time, much to the chagrin of the Italian climbing establishment which has been trying ever since to prove that the men of Courmayeur pioneered the route in 1854. Between it and the crest of the Peuterey Ridge lies the Brenva Face.

From the highest point of Mont Blanc, its summit ridge snakes down to Mont Blanc de Courmayeur to the south east and distant a thousand yards or so, whilst to the north, the Brenva Ridge slopes down to Mont Maudit. The eastern flank of the crest thus formed falls relatively gently for a few hundred feet and then terminates abruptly in ice-cliffs extending, with few weaknesses, for about a mile and dominating a precipice of rock and ice of a scale unparalleled in the Alps. This precipice falls, without any break offering access or escape, to the Brenva Glacier over 5,000 feet below the summit, at an average angle in excess of 45 degrees.

Its very inaccessibility had lent to the Brenva Face an air of mystery. Prior to 1927, few had any intimate knowledge of it; even getting to its foot involves quite a respectable expedition. A few hardy souls had allowed themselves to consider the question whether or not a way might be found up it. A strong and famous party had launched an attack at the northern end of the face, but the line of attack they chose really amounted to nothing more than a variation start to the Brenva Spur route and they were, in any case, repulsed by impassable ice-cliffs. At the start of the 1927 season it thus stood inviolate. By the end of the 1928 season, it had been climbed twice, on each occasion by a different route, but by the same pair. These two were Smythe and Professor Thomas Graham Brown.

Smythe and Graham Brown enjoyed a fruitful relationship. For two seasons it was fruitful of climbs; thereafter it was fruitful of controversy. Graham Brown was a Scot and a physiologist. He had climbed but little, mostly in the Lake District before the First World War broke out and he joined the Army Medical Corps. His channel of escape from the horrors of the Salonika front was to dream about the mountains and, in particular, about the great south-eastern side of Mont Blanc which, at this stage, he knew only, and that imperfectly, from maps and the accounts of others. He conceived in his imagination making a route up this face before ever setting eyes upon it, and it is as well that he did not proceed straight away to put plans into execution for, by his own account, he laboured at this stage under a misapprehension about the geography and structure of the eastern side of the mountain, confusing the Brenva Spur with the frontier ridge of Mont Maudit.

After the war, these dreams seem to have receded and he devoted himself to his profession, occupying the chair of physiology in University College, Cardiff, and achieving at an early age the distinction of being made a Fellow of the Royal Society. Only in 1926, at the age of 43, did he embark upon a serious Alpine career which, thereafter, claimed an increasing proportion of his time to such an extent that his employer sought several times to get rid of his services. He went on to build up a formidable record in the Alps and visited the Himalayas on the Nanda Devi expedition of 1936, and Masherbrum in 1938. In the Alps, although he himself sought to make the point that he often climbed guideless, he nevertheless relied upon guides for most of his major expeditions and has been fairly described as "the last representative of an earlier epoch when the amateur planned the expedition and guides supplied much of the technical expertise."

Smythe was, at that time, twenty-seven years old and basking in the limelight after his recent successes in the Aiguilles; Graham Brown was forty-five, virtually unknown and limited in experience. Graham Brown was the last of the old guard, Smythe in the van of new, semi-professional young turks. Graham Brown used guides; Smythe abhorred their use. They nevertheless had some things in common. Oddly, for a pair about to embark on one of the most serious and strenuous expeditions the Alps had to offer, both were invalided out of the services. Each contrived, in the course of a distinguished Alpine career, to establish a reputation for being difficult to get on with. More relevant for immediate purposes, each found himself at the Montenvers in August 1927 deserted by companions who had had to return home; and each professed an interest in the Brenva Face.

Smythe's interest stemmed from the previous year when he had discussed the possibilities with T. S. Blakeney. When viewed face on, from the Tour Ronde, the Brenva Face is seen, by reason of its sheer steepness, to be relatively simple. It consists largely of ridges and couloirs perpendicular to the glacier beneath. The most obvious of these are the great rib in the centre of the face and, reaching from top to bottom on its northern side, the Great Couloir originating in the ice-cliffs at the top and falling, through fine narrows at one point, the entire length of the face. At about half-height, this couloir forks and the space between the two arms of the Y thus formed is occupied by a "twisting" rib whilst another long rib, "Mummery's Rib", reaches down the face to the north, or right, of the Great Couloir and its north branch. Just to the right of the toe of this latter rib, and some 1,500 feet above the glacier, stands a prominent buttress of red granite to which Smythe gave the name "Sentinelle Rouge".

The most striking line of all was undoubtedly that of the great rib in the centre of the face. It was a line which, on the better view (though this is part of the later controversy), each independently had in mind; but the weather had other plans for them, and they inaugurated their partnership with a climb which could hardly be more different: the Petite Aiguille Verte. It was, in those days, a little more exacting than it is now, since the construction of the Grands Montets téléférique. In 1927 it could still offer the solitude which Smythe so prized. He was, no doubt, anxious to get some impression of Graham Brown's capabilities and none of the higher peaks was in condition. A further deterioration in the weather drove them away from the Mont Blanc range entirely and they spent some days walking near Mégève before a sufficient improvement prompted their return to the Montenvers.

They left Montenvers on 30 August for the Torino Hut on the Col du Géant, stopping overnight at the Requin Hut en route. Their first sighting—of the upper part of the Face over the Tour Ronde ridge, from the rocks of La Vierge—was encouraging. The ice-wall at the top of the face was not continuous throughout its length; at one point it petered out into a smooth unbroken ice-slope. Graham Brown entertained reservations, quite rightly; the lower slopes had yet to be examined. Smythe was more optimistic but it seems, in retrospect, that the two were not seeking to answer the same question. Graham Brown was almost certainly concentrating his attention on the great rib, specifically—he had never conducted a close examination of the lower slopes. Smythe's main anxiety had been about the ice-cliff at the top. He had had the opportunity, on the Old Brenva, of taking a look at the lower slopes and believed that if the ice-cliff could be breached, a route could be forced somehow.

The exact line which it was to take was not settled until they had had the opportunity to study the face in more minute detail through the telescope at the Torino Hut. Smythe vetoed the line via the great rib, ostensibly because there was no obvious exit through the impending ice-cliffs at its top, and they agreed on the line which came to bear the name of the buttress at its foot, the Sentinelle Rouge. It would involve using the twisting rib between the arms of the Y of the Great Couloir as a means of gaining access, through the ice-cliffs, to the summit ridge. In order to reach the foot of the twisting rib, the right-hand branch of the Great Couloir would have to be crossed, an undertaking which would become dangerous once the morning sun had loosened the rock and ice above, which used the couloir as an avalanche chute. That in turn would need a bivouac somewhere lower down the face, and the obvious place was beneath the shelter of the Sentinelle Rouge which would divert any debris coming down. It was not possible to fix upon a way to the Sentinelle Rouge until they could view the bottom part of the face at closer quarters. The one obvious option was to make a rising traverse from the vicinity of the Col Moore which links the Brenva Spur to the peaklet at its foot, the Pic Moore, which would necessitate crossing some mixed ground, including four couloirs seaming the face at this point.

On what was half-intended to be merely a reconnaissance, Smythe and Graham Brown left the Torino Hut at 3.30 a.m. the following day and headed over the Col des Flambeaux for the Col du Trident, descent from which is the usual means of access to the Brenva Glacier. The snow on the slopes leading up to it was discouragingly soft and at that point the attempt was almost postponed. They set off, instead, to seek a better viewpoint for the foot of the face, making first for the Aiguille de Toule and then, when that proved inadequate, the Tour Ronde. Following a couloir, they arrived at the ridge near the summit at 10 a.m., hopes revived by much improved snow conditions, and decided to press the reconnaissance further. Making a descending traverse across the southern face they reached the Col Oriental de la Tour Ronde and made their way down to the glacier and across it to the Col Moore. This they were able to negotiate only with difficulty—the slopes leading up to it were steep and the Col consisted of a blade of ice along which they proceeded, "à cheval" according to Graham Brown, worming their way "inch by inch, on our bellies" according to Smythe.

Here, at last, they were able to stop and observe the lower face below the Sentinelle Rouge. It was immediately apparent that there existed no realistic option but the rising traverse line across the couloirs and that would have to await the sinking of the sun and the freezing into place of loose material. It was, accordingly, 4.50 p.m. and several pipes later before they set out for the Sentinelle Rouge where they arrived, after running the gauntlet of the couloirs, just after 7 p.m. Thus far, they had encountered no great difficulties, the only technical demands on Smythe being cutting up to the Col Moore and across the second couloir, the one place where they had been unable to move together. They hacked out a platform for the Zdarsky bivouac sac underneath an overhanging flake of rock, heated up some soup and settled in for what turned out to be a cold and uncomfortable night.

They were off at 5.30 the following morning, turning the Sentinelle on its left, eastern side, crossing a couloir and the foot of "Mummery's Rib" to the near side of the Great Couloir, the edge of which they followed, beneath the shelter of a projecting crag above, until they were able to set off, in good snow, across the right-hand branch of the Great Couloir to the foot of the twisting rib. Here they arrived, all serious danger from rock and ice fall now past, at 7.10 a.m., for a leisurely second breakfast. All had again gone well—they had moved together all the way on good snow and easy rock; it might have been wiser to have been on the twisting rib before the sun got to work, but luck was with them.

After an hour, they set off again up what they had rather expected to be easier ground but which they soon discovered to be otherwise. They were still moving together, but that was now to become the exception, rather than the rule. They first of all encountered the rock wall, about 150 feet high, which they had seen from the Torino Hut, and managed to turn it on the right, regaining the now snowy crest of the rib by its steep icy flank. The crest became an ice-blade which had to be blunted for a passage to another rock barrier around which it was necessary to cut hand- as well as foot-holds before the crest could be regained. An easier section now followed—shallow rocks leading to an almost horizontal section where they were able to take a break, at about 10.30 a.m., before setting off again about an hour later for the final and most intimidating section of the climb. Above them stretched a one hundred foot wall of rock through which a slanting chimney fortuitously provided a way on to the "staircase" above: a long section of short rock steps separated by snow and ice-slopes, over much of which they were obliged to move one at a time, Smythe cutting ladders of steps over two sections and occasional ones elsewhere. As the ice-cliff above came gradually into close-up view, they were able to follow its course to the left and confirm that at one point it petered out into an ice-slope. By traversing across steep ice, they could reach an ice-rib up which they were able, with difficulty, to cut steps until reaching well-consolidated snow which led them up between bulges to the breach in the ice-cliff. Climbing on through it, they eventually reached a low cornice, hacked it down and, at about 3 p.m., nearly 36 hours after leaving the Torino Hut, stepped out on to the easy slopes of the summit ridge, freed at last from the continuous tension and uncertainty of the climb. Forty-five minutes later, they stood in sole occupation of the summit of Mont Blanc and then made their way down to the Vallot Hut where, after a meal, and in spite of the cold and filth, they smoked, talked and at last slept the sleep of the just.

In some respects, they had been lucky. They had found just a sufficient break in the weather for the ascent—as they slept in the Vallot Hut, Mont Blanc was beset by another furious torment. They seem, as measured against later experience, to have found the route in good condition and relatively free from difficulty. The face had, however, been there, beckoning, since the Alps became the playground of Europe and nothing could detract from the fact that they had been the first to respond and ascend it.

After the Sentinelle Rouge, anything else was bound to be anti-climax. The Sentinelle Rouge is a route for the gods; what followed was for mere mortals, but worthwhile nonetheless. From the Vallot Hut, Smythe and Graham Brown descended via the Aiguille du Goûter to the Tête Rousse and made their way back to Chamonix for a rest. It did not last long and as soon as the weather permitted—they were now well into September—they made the ascent of the Grands Charmoz and then went back to the Montenvers, about to set off for the Couvercle and an ascent of Les Courtes by the Talèfre face.

The great east-south-east ridge of the Aiguille Verte extends for four miles before rising to the Aiguille de Triolet. It passes over the Aiguille du Jardin and Les Droites and then Les Courtes before descending over a remarkable series of pinnacles to the Triolet Plateau. The Courtes is an undistinguished summit, standing a mere 500 feet above the height of the lowest point of the ridge between it and the Aiguille Verte. Leaving it, the ridge descends no more than 1,000 feet before rising again to the Aiguille de Triolet. However, the entire ridge presents an impressive wall to the observer from the famous Jardin du Talèfre below. This face of the Courtes rises in three or four parallel ribs about 2,500 feet in half a mile. The climbing is not technically hard and two or three routes already existed on the left-hand side of this face. The most distinctive rib of all, the south-south-west buttress, rising to the ridge just east of the summit, remained unclimbed and this was their objective.

The route starts up the couloir to the right of the rib and moves up to the crest of the rib at the bergschrund which it follows to the summit, save for a tower which is best turned on the right. The rock is only mediocre but the line is classic and, fortunately, easy. The harder, more modern routes all lie on the other flank of the ridge and the south-south-west buttress route still offers enjoyment and solitude of a character no longer associated with the heart of the Mont Blanc range.

Smythe and Graham Brown descended via the Col de la Tour des Courtes and so ended the season of 1927. It had been Smythe's greatest season and appeared to have forged a promising partnership. There was, indeed, more to come in 1928 before their association finally disintegrated into petty and unbecoming bickering.

In the winter of 1927–8, Smythe visited the Engadine for skiing and climbing. The high point was a winter ascent of the Piz Bernina, the other members of the team being Bentley Beetham, who would become Everest companion of Smythe, and Warren Homer, an American. From the Boval Hut, reached via the Morteratsch Glacier, they set off, first on ski, then crampons, up through the Labyrinth (the glacier ice-fall) to the Crastaguzza Pass and thence to the Marco e Rosa Hut, at about 12,000 feet. From there, next day, they followed the Spallagrat or South East Ridge to the summit, following in the steps of Tuckett on the first summer ascent, some 70 years previously. A speedy descent to Pontresina completed the expedition.

In the Vallot Hut, after the Sentinelle Rouge climb, Graham Brown had again urged upon Smythe an attempt on the Brenva Face via the

Great Rib and they had agreed to meet the following summer with this possibility in mind. They duly rendezvoused and set about getting themselves into condition. A spell in Kandersteg savouring the delights of the Blümlisalp peaks set them on the way. Moving then to the Mont Blanc range, they were led on the Grépon by Ivan Waller, with Smythe in poor form. An attempt on the Droites was frustrated by storm, but they succeeded in climbing the Aiguille Verte by the Moine Ridge, being compelled to bivouac on the descent. It was Smythe's view that if the Great Rib was to be attempted, it should be by a party of four and it had therefore been agreed to invite Ogier Ward and T. S. Blakeney to join. In the event, Ward was unable to do so but Blakeney, whose interest in the Face was longstanding, went out and joined them at the Montenvers. But his time was limited and the only training climb that the tight schedule permitted was the traverse of the Petits Charmoz, a very modest peak at the northern end of the Chamonix Aiguilles. The traverse is a delightful little route—a series of fairly easy rock problems negotiating the Etala Chimneys up to and along a lovely little summit crest overlooking the Mer de Glace face. It is today very popular but, as Graham Brown opined, it was somewhat inadequate as preparation for the Great Rib. Nevertheless, towards the end of July, on the day after the Petits Charmoz, the three set off up the Mer de Glace for the Col du Géant. Next day, they scaled the Trident de Brenva in order to survey the Face, but the prevailing view was that it would be too icy after several days of continual sun and they descended to Courmayeur where, however, encouraging reports of conditions on the Old Brenva resolved them to embark upon the attempt. On 27 July, therefore, they set off for a first bivouac on the Brenva Glacier, intending from there to proceed to a second bivouac at the Sentinelle Rouge before setting out.

Exactly what they intended to do was never agreed. Graham Brown had his own idea: that of traversing the highest col in Europe, by which he meant the lowest point on the ridge between the two summits of Mont Blanc. He already had a name for it—the Col Major. It involved climbing the Brenva Face via the Great Rib, bivouacking near the summit ridge and descending via the south-west face of Mont Blanc early the following morning when it was presumed that good snow conditions would permit it. Since it was his intention to traverse the Col Major, the route via the Great Rib was to become the Route Major.

This reads to me like the project of a megalomaniac although when it comes to planning expeditions, no doubt many of us have that tendency. Nevertheless, many would think the Route Major itself to be a sufficiently demanding undertaking without imposing the added burdens of carrying food and gear for three days, enduring a bivouac for the third successive night, this time at the top of Mont Blanc, and topping it off with a descent of the south-west face direct, still rightly untried. Smythe and Blakeney were clearly after the Route Major—they had a long-standing interest in it—but there is no clear evidence that they ever enthused about the complete traverse, and probably simply humoured Graham Brown on the point. Quite apart from anything else, the Route Major is a natural and classic line which would appeal to anyone, whilst the Col and its traverse seem phoney and artificial in the extreme.

At the Brenva bivouac, the party was reduced from three to two. Blakeney was unwell and had to descend to Courmayeur, a harsh blow for one who had, as will be seen, played no small part in the Brenva Face enterprise. Then a violent storm caused the remaining two to abort and for a few days it was touch-and-go whether any attempt at all would be made that season. By 6 August, however, conditions were again promising and Graham Brown and Smythe were able to set out. They intended, this time, to follow the route of the previous year as far as the Sentinelle Rouge and left the Torino Hut at about 8.15 a.m. Each carried a 30 pound sack and Smythe pressed early on for loads to be lightened but Graham Brown would not have it—no doubt he had the traverse of the Col Major at the forefront of his mind. With some little incident, they arrived at the bivouac site under the Sentinelle Rouge at 6.50 p.m. and settled down for the night.

At five o'clock the following morning they set out. Crossing a small couloir to the left of the Sentinelle Rouge as before, they reached the edge of the Great Couloir—at this point relatively easy-angled and narrow—and made their way with difficulty across to the foot of the first buttress. The steep section of this they turned by descending again to the edge of the Great Couloir and following it until they were able to make their way first up ice, then up steep broken rocks to the crest. Following the crest, they were soon on the first, and shortest, of the four ice arêtes which grace the Route Major, and negotiating the short rock section which separates it from the second ice arête which almost merges into a third and very sharp arête. Here, they had to leave the crest and cut steps along its icy flank before attaining the rocks which separate it from the fourth and last ice arête leading up to the long, final buttress. Time was now pressing—they had gone slowly over the unknown ground and found the going heavy. Signs possibly indicative of bad weather were beginning to appear and unknown difficulties lay ahead. Smythe raised the question of retreat but it was not welcomed. Instead, they pressed on up the 80 foot rock pitch and so reached the fourth ice arête which they traversed to the foot of the final great buttress. It was 1.10 p.m.

The first short wall of the buttress, today usually climbed by a chimney, they turned on ice slopes to the east and found themselves on a broad, snowy shelf. Traversing right along it, a tongue of snow led up to a short overhanging corner which neither of them could get up, and they were obliged to traverse back round the base of the rocks to the right of the corner and up steep slopes on its far side. This manoeuvre consumed a great deal of valuable time and Smythe now pressed the case for retreat much more forcefully. But Graham Brown insisted upon exploring the ground ahead to see what problems immediately confronted them, and Smythe acquiesced. Steep rocks led to the start of a large chimney which they followed until they were able to emerge on a shelf to the right, on good snow, and thence make their way to the top of the buttress. Relatively easy slopes now led them up to and through the final ice-cliff without difficulty and the Route Major was theirs. They made their way to the summit of Mont Blanc de Courmayeur—Smythe vetoed completing the traverse of the Col Major—and then went back over the main summit of Mont Blanc, which they crossed at 8.20 p.m., to the Vallot Hut, reached in the dark at 9 p.m.

These are the bare, bland and uncontroversial facts of the first ascent of the Route Major. It is impossible to ascertain the detail of the ascent with greater accuracy because each man subsequently published an account (indeed, more than one) and the various accounts are discrepant in a number of respects. Sadly, a great climb degenerated into a sordid controversy, the exhaustive treatment of which is meat for a book in itself. The nub of the controversy was, however, the significance of the part played by Graham Brown in the concept and execution of the Brenva Face climbs.

It was Graham Brown who joined issue on these points and he was prompted to do so by the appearance of Smythe's published accounts of the climbs. He clearly considered that in relation to both climbs, but particularly so far as the Route Major was concerned, Smythe had exaggerated his own contributions both to their concept and execution and, conversely, had understated Graham Brown's part.

As Blakeney pointed out after both men were dead, any dispute over the concept of a climb is by definition a petty one, especially in contrast with its execution, although it might be claimed that a dispute about the authorship of such a magnificent route as the Route Major is less petty than most. It might also be said that the notion of conceiving of a climb is a vague one. In what does it consist? In glancing and speculating that it might go? or in studying it in detail and, concluding that it will go, proposing it? . . . Much, anyway, was made of it by Graham Brown and it is possible to arrive at a sensible conclusion on the merits of his objections so far as authorship of the routes goes. It is, however, important to state the issue accurately. Smythe claimed to have had the routes in mind without any prompting from Graham Brown. He did not claim that Graham Brown did not think of the routes himself; he may have assumed that to be the case, but he never made anything of it. Graham Brown claimed not merely to be the discoverer of the routes; he claimed to be their sole author—he had conceived them; Smythe had not—and he went to quite extraordinary lengths in his attempt to prove this to be the case.

Smythe maintained that he had wondered previously about the Face and in April 1927 had discussed it and studied photographs with T. S. Blakeney, noting the Route Major as a possible line. On his ascent of the old Brenva route later in 1927 he had satisfied himself that the Sentinelle Rouge line merited serious consideration. Although, when they first met, Graham Brown had suggested the Great Rib, Smythe had discouraged him partly because he was not happy about the exit but also, and particularly, because he considered it too serious a proposition to tackle with an inexperienced companion.

The issues—who thought of the climbs and the significance of the parts played by each in their execution—simmered for a long time without final resolution. After the death of Graham Brown, who survived Smythe by many years, these issues surfaced again when

Lord Tangley stated it as his view that prior to embarking on the Sentinelle Rouge, Smythe had no ideas about the Brenva Face beyond the old-established Old Brenva route via the Brenva Spur. This in turn prompted the intervention of Blakeney. Smythe had indeed considered climbs on the Brenva Face and had discussed the matter at length with Blakeney before Graham Brown appeared on the scene. It was Blakeney's view (almost certainly an over-modest one since he had played no small part in planning possibilities) that whilst Smythe and Graham Brown had each independently fixed upon the Great Rib as a line, the Sentinelle Rouge was Smythe's idea and his alone.

As far at least as the Sentinelle Rouge is concerned, this seems likely, and Graham Brown's version of events unlikely. By his own account, Graham Brown had not thought of the Sentinelle Rouge until the pair arrived at the Torino Hut immediately prior to the attempt. He, Graham Brown, was bent upon the Great Rib and the Route Major; Smythe would not have it but suggested instead, according to Graham Brown, a somewhat vaguely described line to the left of the Old Brenva—vaguely described because Graham Brown at one point suggests that the proposal was to follow the snow slopes to the left, whilst at another it seems, he suggests, that Smythe had in mind "Mummery's Rib". According to Graham Brown, he rejected this proposal, Smythe disappeared for an hour, and Graham Brown then spotted the Sentinelle Rouge and Smythe accepted it as a *via media*. Graham Brown sought subsequently to substantiate this version of events: Smythe cannot have meant the Sentinelle Rouge as the route he had looked at from the Old Brenva because it is not visible from there, occupying a recessed part of the face and being obscured by Mummery's Rib; and Blakeney had denied to Graham Brown that he, Blakeney, and Smythe had ever discussed the Sentinelle Rouge.

The first of these points falls on the simple fact that the Sentinelle Rouge line is not invisible from the Old Brenva route. It is not wholly visible; but the upper part, the crest of the twisting rib, is, and it is also possible to obtain a reasonably close view of the state of the exit area. The rest of the route can be more readily assessed from below; the main doubts concerned those parts visible from the Old Brenva. So far as the Blakeney discussions were concerned, Graham Brown's attitude is again odd. Smythe never claimed to have discussed the Sentinelle Rouge with Blakeney so it is hardly to the point that Blakeney denied any such discussions. They had discussed climbing the face generally and were expressly interested in the Route Major via the Great Rib, information which Graham Brown would no doubt have obtained had he tried, but which would rather have knocked the stuffing out of his claim for sole authorship of the Route Major.

The crucial issue, so far as the Sentinelle Rouge line is concerned, is whether Graham Brown is to be believed in his assertion that the line which Smythe proposed at the Torino Hut was not the Sentinelle Rouge but lay somewhere to the left of the Old Brenva, on or to the right of Mummery's Rib. This is unlikely. Smythe knew the history of this area and particularly the difficulties of exit. They were still very apparent on inspection at the time and it is extremely unlikely that Smythe would have proposed such a line with no alternative when inspection from the Old Brenva and from the rocks of the Vierge on the ascent had revealed the possibility that exit was feasible further to the left, above the twisting rib. The most charitable interpretation one can put on events is that Graham Brown misunderstood Smythe's proposal, perhaps because Smythe described it inadequately. I find it more likely that Graham Brown continued to the last to hope for the Route Major and paid little or no attention to Smythe's suggestions until Smythe made it abundantly clear that he would not attempt the Route Major, as was indeed the case, although Smythe did not state the true reason: that he was not prepared to venture on to such an obviously serious route with Graham Brown. Success on the Sentinelle Rouge did not prompt Smythe wholly to abandon this view of Graham Brown: when it came to the crunch in 1928 Smythe pressed for a party of four.

Smythe's doubts about Graham Brown's abilities explains why Graham Brown came to see himself as the guiding spirit so far as the Route Major was concerned. He had, independently, come to dream of climbing it. He proposed it to Smythe, who, although he himself had fixed upon it (he had discussed it with Blakeney and others as the "hush hush" route), responded negatively, rather than bluntly saying to Graham Brown, "Yes, I have it in mind, but not with you." If and when Graham Brown came to hear the truth, it would not be the sort of truth that such as Graham Brown would happily accept. For it is in the character and personality of Graham Brown that a true understanding of the causes of the dispute are to be found.

As far as the dispute concerned the significance of the roles played by the two men in the execution of the climbs it is impossible finally to resolve it and I am personally very doubtful if it is desirable. It would have been vastly more edifying if history had transmitted simply the information that both men did both routes, but unfortunately that was not to be. The only witnesses are the two parties to the dispute. That it arose in the first place seems to be because Smythe, in his accounts which appeared first, failed expressly to give to Graham Brown the credit which he, Graham Brown, considered was due to him, particularly in relation to the Route Major. Smythe's accounts are not as detailed as Graham Brown's in his book *Brenva*, published in 1944. They are somewhat abbreviated, written largely in the first person plural but from time to time indicating to the reader Smythe's singular role whilst rarely mentioning that, if any, of Graham Brown. They certainly allow one to retain the impression that Smythe's was the chief role throughout both climbs without ever saying as much.

The clue to the difference so far as the Route Major is concerned lies in Smythe's failure, in Graham Brown's eyes, to do justice to Graham Brown's role in negotiating the upper part of the route, and this centres particularly upon Smythe's proposals, particularly the second of them, for retreat. The two seem, on this occasion, to have reached an impasse, Smythe thinking it folly to continue up unknown ground at such a late and threatening stage in the day, Graham Brown refusing to retreat. Graham Brown resolved the impasse by continuing and may well have played a significant role, possibly even the major role, in completing the climb, and Smythe gave him insufficient credit for this. Subsequently and privately Graham Brown claimed that he had had to "take over" in order to ensure completion of the route.

Given their state of knowledge about the remainder of the route, the correct mountaineering decision may well have been to retreat. The continuation and eventual success do not vindicate the decision to advance; if it was an unjustifiable gamble it remains so, notwithstanding the fact that they won. Graham Brown's accusation of cowardice seems to imply that Smythe's insistence on retreat was due to fear of, rather than a rational appreciation of the folly of, continuing. There is no evidence of irrational fear; it is easy to make a case for folly.

Graham Brown could, nevertheless, claim that if Smythe had had his way, the Route Major would not have been completed: the puzzle is why Graham Brown should have made such a meal out of the controversy until, that is, one turns to the nature of the man himself for an explanation.

Graham Brown was a self-opinionated man with a positively proprietorial attitude towards the Brenva Face. Not all his colleagues disliked him—some found him impish and amusing. Most found him to be an eccentric, cantankerous, difficult intellectual snob with a strong sense of his own importance, and his humour tended to be confined to his own jokes. There are many indications of his nature in *Brenva* where he makes sure the reader appreciates the merits of his contribution. His pursuit of what he conceived to be vindication over the Brenva Face affair soon assumed the proportions of paranoia: he became obsessive about it to the point of giving up his physiology almost entirely, and his battle to retain his university appointment provokes quizzical smiles and shudders to this day.

The sum of it, then, is that Smythe, almost certainly inadvertently, did Graham Brown an injustice in the sense that he did not spell out in detail the contribution which Graham Brown made to the completion of the Route Major, putting on one side for the moment the question of the wisdom of continuing at all. A more balanced person might well have taken exception to this, but would hardly have allowed it to become meat for a crusade extending over decades. Graham Brown did so—he was writing sixty page letters to the Alpine Club and boring any willing listener well over twenty years later. This was a disservice to Smythe, to mountaineering and, most of all, to himself: he deserves pity rather than condemnation.

It is hard to measure the impact on Smythe's career. Almost certainly it formed part of the backcloth to selection for the Everest expeditions of the 1930s. Equally, there were those in mountaineering circles who disapproved of Smythe and who would have been ready to believe the worst. But it did not put a stop to the Alpine career of either man. Graham Brown went on to compile an impressive record of first ascents, chiefly with his guide Graven, varying from the very good, such as the traverse of the summits of the Ailefroide, to the pointless and inept, such as the Chamonix face of Mont Blanc.

In the winter of 1928–9, Smythe found himself in the Oberland with Dr Graham MacPhee. Together with another companion, the two of them had planned to make the high-level traverse through the high Oberland from the Jungfraujoch to the Grimsel Pass and down to Meiringen. Bad weather prompted the abandonment of this plan and the departure of the third man. Smythe and MacPhee got up to the Jungfraujoch and passed several days interspersing expeditions with carousing at the hotel. In such intervals as the weather permitted, they ascended the Gespensterhorn on ski and attempted the south ridge of the Jungfrau only to be driven off. They managed the south-east ridge of the Mönch and one or two runs down from the Obermönchjoch and to Konkordia before going down to the valley. So far, the season had yielded little of great moment; MacPhee had to return home and Smythe was just about to follow when he ran across the Japanese climber, T. Y. Kagami, and the two decided to attempt the Eiger from the north Eigerjoch via the south ridge. Smythe was already familiar with the ground, for he had descended this way when testing oxygen with Howard Somervell in preparation for Everest in 1923, but the route had not previously been traversed in winter.

From the train at Eigergletscher, they spent the first day reconnoitring the route, realizing that it would be necessary to pass beneath the obvious wall of impending seracs, but deciding to proceed anyway. They set out in earnest, next day, running the gauntlet of the seracs traversing under the cliffs of the Klein Eiger and then heading south west until they were beneath the north face of the Mönch, from where they were able to ascend to the north Eigerjoch. The ridge looked and proved discouraging; it was impossible to pass it directly because of verglas and cornices and they found it necessary to traverse out on to the face, hoping to gain access to the summit via a long steep snow slope. When extensive step-cutting consumed the time it became apparent, as the going got even more difficult, that retreat was imperative. A mere 400 feet from the summit they set off down, eventually managing to regain the *voie normale* and so descend to Kleine Scheidegg.

In the summer of 1929, Mont Blanc beckoned, but this time the attraction was the south-east face of Mont Maudit, at that time unclimbed although not for long, after Smythe's attempt. Smythe had proposed the expedition to A. Harrison and C. Parry and they had set out on one of the few apparently good days in a season of variable and unpredictable weather.

The south-east face of Mont Maudit rises 3,000 feet above the terrace of the Upper Brenva Glacier. The first thousand of these feet are gained by climbing snow slopes of ever increasing steepness, negotiating the bergschrund, until one arrives at the foot of the rock-and-ice precipice which rises intimidatingly to the summit. Smythe and his companions deemed a bivouac advisable and progressed some way up this wall before hacking a shelf out of ice and settling in for the night. That was as far as they got. The weather became progressively worse as the night wore on and the first light of dawn revealed at least six inches of fresh-fallen snow which promised to make retreat treacherous. Particular danger attached to crossing a broad couloir, innocent enough in the good conditions they had enjoyed during the ascent but now a main highway for the innumerable tons of snow only loosely held in place higher up the face. Their worst fears almost materialized. Harrison was engulfed as he cut steps about half-way across, but managed to hold on, although the effort to do so exhausted him. Smythe then went at it and just managed to get across when another fall occurred, even larger than the first and which would undoubtedly have carried him away. Continuing the descent as quickly as they possibly could, they got sufficiently far down to the glacier plateau before the new covering started to disintegrate in a series of avalanches which would have swept a party off practically any part of the face.

In better conditions, a French party forced a way up in August of the same year, apparently by a different route, with fairly continuous difficulties, producing a route considered to be substantially harder than either of the Brenva Face routes. It was not until 1973 that a British party made the ascent.

A chance meeting in the Alps with Professor G. O. Dyhrenfurth during the winter of 1929–30 sharpened Smythe's already keen interest in the Himalaya and for much of the next two years he was preoccupied with the Kangchenjunga and Kamet expeditions. In the summer of 1932, however, abandoning Zermatt because of the weather, he returned to the Oberland with H. B. Thompson and visited the little-known sector to the south east of the Lötschental Wall. Here, they made the first British ascent of the south-east ridge of the Jägihorn, still recognized as a middle grade classic today and possessed of the all-too-rare virtue of a walk-in to the start of the route of about ten seconds from the Baltschiederklause Hut.

Thus fortified by success, Smythe and Thompson set off for the Bietschhorn which Smythe had traversed with J. V. Hazard in 1925. On the east face of the mountain, and to the north of the east spur, the north ridge presents a series of broken ribs and couloirs, none of which provides a continuous line from bergschrund to summit ridge. One of them, however, reaches down to the bergschrund and, by following this, it is possible, at about mid-height, to cross a couloir at about 55 degrees, thus gaining access to the flank of another rib which leads directly up to the north summit some 50 feet or so below the main summit. It was this line which Smythe and Thompson chose to follow, completing a novel ascent and traverse of the mountain by descending the east spur. The east rib of the north summit is, like all the Smythe routes, a quality climb, not excessively difficult and on excellent rock.

For one who spent so much of each year in the Alps over such a lengthy period, Smythe was responsible for relatively few first ascents. The opportunity to seek out obscure untrodden lines was there and Smythe had the capability to follow them. A lack of inclination to do so seems the obvious explanation and is entirely consistent with his whole attitude towards the mountaineering experience.

In spite of his attitude, it is not difficult to make out a case for Smythe as one of the most significant Alpine mountaineers of the era and certainly in a sparsely populated front rank so far as British alpinists are concerned. The peak of the achievement was, of course, the Brenva Face climbs and they alone secure him a safe place in the history of mountaineering; no other Alpine exploit of the 1920s approaches their stature. At the same time, it has to be said that Smythe's pleasure in such achievement would not be undiluted. The interminable and rancorous imbroglio with Graham Brown would by itself ensure that. But there was a more fundamental reason: Smythe could never escape from the notion that to climb mountains for achievement, repute or fame was in some sense an abuse of the opportunities which they gave. It was to use them for an alien purpose, rather than to be amongst them and, in a sense, unified with them for the purpose of an experience which was an end in itself. For Smythe, "true" mountaineering, in this sense, did not require the plaudits of an audience, or danger, or difficulty or even, necessarily, novelty.

CHAPTER VII

*Kangchenjunga Adventure**

FRANK SMYTHE'S PASSION for the Himalaya reaches back at least to his schooldays and a youthful imagination kindled by the purple and white of the roof of the world on the relief map of the Indian sub-continent. Once kindled, it was fuelled by the accounts of the early explorers. As a Yorkshire Rambler, he at last became immersed in a strong Himalayan tradition to which Howard Somervell, amongst others, was a contributor.

It was a full decade before he himself became a participant. Although, as will be seen, his name was considered by the early Everest Committees, his only role in those days was as a willing and perhaps hopeful workhorse on training and experimental outings in the Alps. Then, as a result of a chance encounter in 1929, he was selected for Kangchenjunga.

Kangchenjunga is probably the third highest mountain in the world. Most surveys have ranked it after Everest and K2 in elevation, although some calculations have placed it in second place. This fetish with relative heights, which abates the actual problems of any particular mountain not one whit, is ubiquitous. Swiss survey teams have recently "established" that the Lauterbrunnen Briethorn, contrary to prior belief which placed it some metres lower, now overtops its Lötschentaler namesake by one tenth of a metre. When such accuracy reaches the Himalaya, and putting aside the problem of differential snowfall, we may finally settle the pecking order. Even then, Kangchenjunga will remain what it has always been, and was in 1930, one of the very highest mountains posing one of the most serious challenges in the world and most recently measured at 28,146 feet.

Like Mont Blanc and Annapurna, and unlike either Everest or K2, Kangchenjunga is a massif or range rather than a single mountain. Translated, its name is said to mean "the five treasures of the snow"

*See p.212 for a map of the Kangchenjunga area

—a reference to its alleged five summits. It is one of the most photographed of the Himalayan peaks and also one of the most commonly subjected to direct observation for it lies a mere 45 miles north of Darjeeling and is readily visible from there. It does not lie on the main Himalayan chain. A massive spur thrusts south, eventually petering out as the Singalila Ridge west of Darjeeling. On this ridge stand summits such as the highest point of Kangchenjunga and, to the north, The Twins, Tent Peak and Jonsong Peak; and, to the south, Talung Peak and Kabru. From the highest summit, shorter spurs fall roughly in an easterly and a westerly direction, the former from the south-west summit, at 27,820 feet, the latter passing over Kangbachen and Madonna or Ramthang Peak, with Wedge Peak to the north and Jannu to the south. The main spur serves as the boundary between Nepal and Sikkim. Access is also geographically (as opposed to politically) possible from Tibet, the boundary of which reaches south to within ten miles of the highest point.

For practical purposes, there is a simple choice of approaching the massif from east or west. From the east, via Sikkim, the approaches are into the Zemu Glacier sector to the north or that of the Talung Glacier in the south. From the western, Nepal, side entry is into the Yalung Glacier sector in the south or those of the Ramthang or Kangchenjunga Glaciers in the north. These facts and a great deal more were the fruits of early exploration of the area by a few hardy souls amongst whom were Sir Douglas Freshfield and the ubiquitous Kellas who died on the first Everest expedition. Kellas succeeded in climbing a number of lesser peaks in the area but made no attempt specifically on Kangchenjunga itself. The first expedition to do so was that of Aleister Crowley. He chose to attack the Yalung face of the mountain but aborted at 21,000 feet after the loss of four lives which he callously ignored. This face claimed another life in 1929 when a lone American, E. F. Farmer, went up, never to come down, in what bears a strange resemblance to Maurice Wilson's effort on Everest five years later. That same year also witnessed another and altogether more serious attempt. In one of the most stoical and tenacious attempts ever made by any party on any mountain, a group of Bavarian climbers, under the leadership of Dr Paul Bauer, approached the mountain via the Zemu Glacier and laid siege to a spur falling to the east from the north ridge of the mountain via which they hoped to end their journey to the summit. They laboured for weeks in all sorts of conditions, most of the time engaged in technical ice-climbing of a high order, before foul weather finally drove them down from just over 24,000 feet. They did not reach the north ridge.

At this time, Smythe was skiing in the Alps when he made the acquaintance of Professor Gunter Oscar Dyhrenfurth, a geologist and a mediocre, autocratic and megalomaniacal mountaineer engaged at that time in trying to mount an international expedition to attempt Kangchenjunga. Smythe had by now established himself as one of the really bright young men of Alpine climbing, and it was not at all surprising that Dyhrenfurth should invite him to join the expedition. We may reasonably surmise that, at that stage in his career, Smythe would jump at the chance to extend his experience to the Himalaya which had attracted him even as a schoolboy.

He found himself in some very good climbing company. His colleagues included four of the leading alpinists of the day: the Austrians Schneider and Hoerlin, the German, Wieland, who was to die on the catastrophic Nanga Parbat expedition four years later, and Kurz, the Swiss deputy leader. Compatriots associated with the expedition included G. W. Wood Johnson who, after developing an expertise on British rock, had gone straight out to the Himalaya and acquired his "Alpine" experience there. H. W. Tobin, the local secretary of the Himalayan Club, undertook to assist with transport.

Dyhrenfurth seems to have been a leader of the old teutonic school type who believed that the will was everything. That the attempt to climb Kangchenjunga eventually failed, and failed rather clearly, was due in large part to his inability to acknowledge the actualities of the real world and to admit that it might be possible for good advice and sensible ideas to emanate from some source other than his own head. The mere mortals of the expedition, for example, were simply provided with the equipment which Dyhrenfurth thought suitable; there was no consultation, no attempt to benefit from the experience of a team which included practically all the leading winter Alpine mountaineers of the day. Sometimes, he got it right: Smythe approved, for example, of the tents; but the boots provided weighed over eight pounds and most of the climbing members consequently provided and wore their own. They were in a position to choose; most of the porters were not. It was the same with the rest of the clothing; the gloves alone passed muster.

It was a very large expedition. Some 400 porters were required, about 50 for photographic equipment! The logistics were therefore important; but even though he had, in Tobin and Wood Johnson, a wealth of local knowledge and contacts, Dyhrenfurth neither delegated nor confided sufficiently for transport to be efficiently arranged, and a series of crises resulted, some with dire consequences. The dietary planning also seems to have been poor. The expedition suffered more than most from irritating ill-health of a minor kind, which Smythe was inclined to blame on this inadequate diet. It was not necessary for Dyhrenfurth to turn his expedition into a workers' co-operative in order to avoid some, if not all, of these evils: that philosophy of major expeditions was to develop only much later. But if he had been prepared to ask questions and listen to answers, he might have heard something to his, and particularly his team's, advantage. As it was, the will turned out to have its limitations. It was not sufficient simply for Dyhrenfurth to decide that Kangchenjunga be climbed. It had actually to be climbed by flesh and blood human beings, and it was not until the expedition was well under way that the party even knew what approaches were open to it, and therefore what possible routes were available.

So far as Smythe was concerned, however, the entire expedition was most valuable. He left Europe in February with the Dyhrenfurths (Frau Dyhrenfurth accompanied the expedition and discharged various administrative duties) having arranged to meet Wood Johnson in Siliguri prior to the walk-in. The journey from Siliguri to Wood Johnson's plantation at Rangli Rangliot was not uneventful. They travelled via the latter's motor-cycle and it is hard to say from Smythe's account whether this machine, or the tiger which he encountered during a walk following a breakdown, was the more dangerous. Wood Johnson had told him that a man-eater was at large in the area but fortunately the beast which Smythe encountered failed on this occasion to manifest that particular appetite and Smythe and Wood Johnson duly assembled in Darjeeling at the end of March for the preliminaries.

It turned out that Dyhrenfurth had not informed the authorities in Darjeeling of the expedition's plans and so on arrival he was confronted by a total absence of porters. It proved possible, at short notice, to secure the services of a nucleus of good men. These included four sirdars, Naspati, Gyaljen, Narsang and Lobsang, whom Smythe considered to be "incomparably the best". Smythe's personal servant was Nemu and Smythe never for a moment had cause to regret selecting him. Others included "Satan" Chettan who had distinguished himself on the Everest expeditions of the 1920s but whose last adventure this was sadly to be; and Lewa, later to render sterling service on Smythe's Kamet expedition. In order to complete the complement of 400 porters it was necessary to scrape the barrel, and the need to rely upon many of the poorer examples of Darjeeling "market men" created serious problems later.

At this stage, the expedition still did not know where it was going. Permission from Kathmandu was necessary if the expedition wished to approach the mountain from the west and it had not been sought prior to the party's arrival in India. There, the advice was that, because of friction between Nepal and Tibet, it was not politic to apply for permission immediately, and it was left to the discretion of the diplomats to decide when to forward a request. In the meantime, therefore, the plan had to be to attempt the mountain from the Sikkim side and this effectively meant using the Zemu Glacier approach and following in the footsteps of Bauer's powerful Munich party. Perhaps "plan" is the wrong word, for it rather implies the selection of a specific end and the adoption of a systematic means of attaining it, and Dyhrenfurth's mental processes seem never to have progressed thus far. He did not want to try Bauer's route but knew of no better option from the Sikkim side; in defence of his pragmatism, as events turned out, Bauer's route only fell as late as 1977 to a strong Indian party. Nevertheless, Dyhrenfurth's strategy did not go beyond arranging to send out Smythe and Wood Johnson as a vanguard to break the trail to the Zemu Glacier, on the north bank of which it was intended to establish a base camp, with three camps en route.

On the very eve of their departure, permission to enter Nepal unexpectedly arrived and Dyhrenfurth immediately decided to switch the attack to the western side. Here, two approaches were feasible. One, the best-known, was the southern entry, via the Yalung Glacier with its unfortunate history, which many, and particularly Smythe, considered to be unjustifiably dangerous. The Yalung Face looks to the south and receives the first and worst of the precipitation which falls on the Himalaya. Research had suggested that there was no route on that face that was not liable to be swept continuously by ice avalanches from hanging glaciers above. A quarter of a century on,

Sir Charles Evans would radically reassess this conclusion and lead a triumphant and exemplary expedition to success via this face. In 1930, however, it was still possible to hope that something better would turn up if the northerly approach via the Kangchenjunga Glacier were adopted. Freshfield had not ruled it out and Dyhrenfurth went for it.

The northerly approach had three disadvantages: the journey in was much longer and more complex; it would take more time, and time was of the essence; extra porters and supplies would be needed and it was not at all clear where they were to come from. Dyhrenfurth's initial strategy seems to have been to assume or at least hope that something would turn up. Strangely, his attitude may well have paid Smythe enormous dividends: many of Dyhrenfurth's decisions seemed so arbitrary and ill-founded that any intelligent follower would be forced into continual critical reassessment of them and would, in the process, probably learn more about leading an expedition than could possibly be yielded by blindly observing the commands of an able and confident exemplar. Smythe probably learned, from Dyhrenfurth's mistakes, a great deal which he was able to put to good use on Kamet the following year.

Smythe was sceptical about the western approach. Starting from the south, it involved crossing a series of passes, in particular the Kang La, well over 16,000 feet, with an enormous team of porters, some of very dubious quality indeed, less than well-equipped and, by reason of failure of communication on Dyhrenfurth's part, badly organized, this in April—a time of year when it was still quite likely that foul weather would be encountered. Further human and material resources would be required en route and there was no guarantee that they would be forthcoming. It was thoroughly predictable that a price would have to be paid for these shortcomings and that turned out to be the case. Even had it not been so, little was known about the north-west flanks of the mountain up which a route would have to be found. It was not until 1977 that success greeted any approach via these flanks: in that year a Polish-Yugoslavian team forced a route up the north-west face and even then not to the main summit but to that of Kangbachen Peak. Only as late as 1979 did Boardman, Scott and Tasker finally forge the way on to the north ridge from the west and follow it to the highest summit.

Nevertheless, the walk-in proceeded. Smythe was ill and had a rough time for a couple of days. The stages were demanding and almost more than he could cope with in the condition in which he found himself. They were demanding, too, for the porters, many of whom were unfit. This did not deter Dyhrenfurth from suggesting impossible double marches—his suggestions fell on deaf ears. The party was proceeding in three groups. The first of them arrived at the Kang La to find it still covered in winter snow. The porters were ill-shod and some suffered frost-bite. The position would have been even more serious had not Wood Johnson striven heroically to restore some semblance of morale and driven the stragglers in. It was dark and cold by the time the last of them arrived, and due to another failure of logistics or communication by Dyhrenfurth no one knew how the porters were to be fed, and urgent measures had to be taken to try to ensure that the expedition did not grind to a halt for this reason alone.

The second party fared even worse. The weather had deteriorated and, travelling one day behind, many of the porters refused, not unreasonably, to attempt the pass in bare feet. Boots had to be collected from the first party and ferried back across the pass for the second party. That the expedition reached Base Camp at all was a triumph not of organization, but over adversity.

A few days' rest at Base Camp waiting for the expedition to regroup provided Smythe and Wood Johnson with an opportunity to stretch themselves on a peak nearby. They got to about 20,000 feet, within 150 feet of the summit, before being forced to retreat by a fierce, cold wind. This was by no means the last occasion on which Smythe was to taste defeat before his Himalayan career was to succeed. How soon that would be depended immediately upon the possibilities of the north-west face.

They were not immediately obvious. Beneath the face and 11,000 feet below the summit, the Kangchenjunga Glacier is fed by two tributaries, the eastern and western tributary glaciers, the eastern leading up to the north ridge and the western to the north-west ridge and the Kangbachen summit. Between these two ridges, the face falls in three enormous terraces separated by ice-cliffs of terrific proportions. The hope was to make a way up the eastern tributary glacier to the north ridge and thence negotiate the ridge to the summit. From base camp, however, this was a mere hope rather than a prospect, for the terrain was hidden behind a shoulder of The Twins and it was not until Wieland and Smythe were on the way from Camp One on the upper glacier to establish Camp Two that it was possible to observe the entire face and assess the possibilities. They were negligible; there was nothing to discuss. In Smythe's words, "Optimism's flower was already withered as we trudged up the snow slopes".

The first hope, that it would prove possible to mount the eastern tributary glacier and gain access thence to the north ridge, was obviously unrealistic. The way above the glacier consisted of "sheer ice-armoured precipices" and was out of the question. The only alternative, and nothing then established it to be a practical possibility, was to attack the terraces across the face. If access could be gained to the first of these (which involved scaling an ice-wall of 600 to 800 feet) a way might be found in a northerly direction along the first terrace on to the north ridge, and thence to the summit. Smythe and Wood Johnson found the way through a maze of crevasses and seracs to a suitable site for Camp Two, at what appeared to be a safe distance from the ice avalanches threatened by the cliffs. Camp was made, and such members of the climbing party as were fit to do so duly assembled. Smythe was distinctly pessimistic about the prospects; no one was at all optimistic with the possible exception of Dyhrenfurth who went straight back down to base camp with an inflamed throat —not, however, before instructing Smythe, Wood Johnson and Wieland to make every effort to overcome the ice-wall blocking the way to the only possible route.

Next day, they set about the wall. Smythe took the first stint, laboriously hacking a staircase in the steep ice. After a while, Wieland took over. For a lengthy period, they were cutting underneath an enormous semi-detached flake of ice; Smythe subsequently looked back upon it as the most dangerous work he ever undertook. Nevertheless, some cognizable progress was made before they retreated to Camp Two for the night. There they heard the bad news about the transport arrangements, a sirdar's death and the looting of stores. There was not enough reliable manpower to get the rest through. Dyhrenfurth had confided the arrangements to no one and Tobin, by this time ill and suffering from an arm injury received in a fall on the pass, retired in disgust to Darjeeling as soon as he was able to hand over. Wood Johnson was obliged to go down and sort things out. For the time being, the remaining effective climbing party was Smythe, Wieland and Duvanel whose primary function on the expedition was as photographer and reporter.

This was the group which, next day, embarked upon the crux section of the ice-cliff, a wall of about 275 feet, the first 25 feet of which were overhanging. Smythe set about it from Wieland's shoulders but progress was extraordinarily slow and they were still not over it at the end of the day. Next day, they returned to the attack, strengthened by Schneider, now fit and freshly up from base. He took over but the pace remained excruciatingly slow, and before the end of the day progress had been further complicated by bad weather. A series of frightening incidents on the descent served only further to underline the folly of the attempt. Five days had been lavished on 500 feet of ice and neither difficulty nor danger had abated one whit. Smythe by this time had confirmed his opinion of the undertaking. At the very least, it was unjustifiable to abuse the trust of porters by committing them to such an enterprise—and it was not merely wisdom after the event which enabled him to arrive at this view. A despatch to *The Times*, sent before tragedy struck, clearly heralds it. Possibly it is a view which he might have sought more forcibly to impress upon his companions; possibly, indeed, they shared it. But there was no change of plan and dire consequences followed.

Hoerlin was by now fit and had joined them. Smythe and Wieland had been at the wall for six straight days and Hoerlin now teamed up with his regular partner Schneider for a spell at the sharp end. After a day's progress, they returned with the news that the problem now confronting them was which to choose from two possible lines of attack on the top section of the cliff immediately below the first terrace. One possibility was to confront it directly; the other was to seek to make use of a crack separating the ice of the terrace proper from a section of it to the right. They considered that they would probably get up one way or another, although they were suspicious of the crack, and arrangements were made for the establishment of Camp Three on the terrace.

Next day, Smythe was scheduled to stay at Camp Two. Those going up set off in three parties, Schneider and Chettan first; then Duvanel and three porters on filming duties; finally Hoerlin, Wieland and eight porters with loads for Camp Three. They had gone for only half an hour when the tremendous roar of yet another ice avalanche reached the camp; this time it was close at hand and immediately above. Looking up, Smythe saw an enormous portion of the cliff collapsing; it was, in fact, the entire section, separated from the rest by the crack of which Schneider and Hoerlin had been suspicious. Briefly, Smythe observed his colleagues at the foot of the wall frantically trying to escape and then the scene was obliterated. The avalanche eventually came to a halt a mere 200 yards from the Camp, the ice clouds were quickly cleared by the wind and those in Camp were able to search the scene. With some relief, they saw first one, then other figures moving. Grabbing axes and mounting the slope as quickly as they could, they were soon able to ascertain that all but two had escaped, but there was no sign of Chettan nor, at first, of Schneider. Some minutes later, the latter appeared: he had had the narrowest of escapes when the mass of countless tons of ice passed within five yards of him. Chettan was not so lucky. He was soon found buried and crushed and although attempts to revive him were continued for an hour they were ineffectual.

Reading later accounts, it seems astonishingly reckless of them to have persisted to this point, for all the signs of catastrophe were present. Now events had denied them further choice in the matter for, in addition to taking Chettan's life (and he was a climber of stature and reputation), the avalanche had obliterated entirely the work of the previous eight days and also threatened to be the first of a series. The Camp Two survivors accordingly descended to Camp One and sent a request down to base for those there to join them for a conference. The following day the entire party convened at Camp One.

The only item to be discussed was what to do next. The Base Camp proposal was, incredibly, to resume the attack on the ice-wall, presumably with increased will and determination. It was, not surprisingly, rejected unanimously by all those who had participated in the first attempt. On alternatives, there were two schools of thought. Smythe's suggestion, surely with benefit of hindsight the correct one, was to retire from Kangchenjunga altogether, cross the Jonsong La and mount an attempt on the Jonsong Peak, a significant mountain in its own right, 24,344 feet high, and a worthy objective; it would be the highest peak ever climbed. But the majority had not yet done with Kangchenjunga and favoured investigation of the north-west ridge at the head of the western tributary glacier. It appears, in the light of history, to have been a rather desperate proposal, for it would carry the party to the ridge to the east of the Kangbachen summit which it would be necessary to traverse before tackling the long ridge that separated that peak from the main summit of Kangchenjunga—an extraordinary undertaking. One suspects that the proponents of the scheme recognized this in their heart of hearts, for Madonna or Ramthang Peak, which would be accessible from the same sector, was adopted as a "consolation objective" in the event of failure.

Over the next few days, Camps One and Two were evacuated and a new Camp One established in an altogether safer position nearer to the north-west ridge on the western tributary glacier. Not long thereafter, another avalanche from the face overwhelmed the now evacuated site of the old Camp Two.

The assault on the north-west ridge began with an inspection. Smythe, who, although he had been consistently right throughout, must by now have been sounding a bit like Jeremiah, pronounced it hopeless. Events proved him right again, but not before the rest of the party had been forced to the same conclusion by experience. It appeared that it might be possible to reach the ridge by a 600 foot couloir; Smythe's doubts attached not to the couloir, but to the feasibility of traversing the ridge itself.

Hoerlin led the couloir. Although it presented ice at up to 60 degrees and was corniced at the ridge, it went. The ridge, which consisted of ice teeth and flakes in its upper section, was rocky, loose and steep below. It demanding climbing of a high standard on treacherous rock pinnacles at a height well in excess of 20,000 feet. Wieland and Hoerlin nevertheless made a determined attempt and progressed some little way up before they were brought to a halt. Smythe stayed on the ridge above the couloir and satisfied himself an ascent via the Ramthang face was impossible. Wieland and Hoerlin discovered little to encourage optimism in their reconnaissance of the first part of the ridge. Smythe's description reminds me vividly of a rock rib in the Blümlisalp, on which I once had the misfortune to trespass, where everything under one's feet shifted every time one moved and one began to wonder just where the solid mountain actually began if, indeed, it was there at all. They so reported in camp that night to Dyhrenfurth who had gone up from base. Presumably having access to sources of information or evidence denied to those who had actually been along the ridge, he did not agree with this opinion and considered that the attack should be continued.

For once, Dyhrenfurth seems not to have entirely won the day. Poor weather intervened and the party ascended point 20,800 on the south ridge of Ramthang Peak in order to get a better view of the ridge, but although this prospect offered no encouragement, the attack was eventually resumed, this time with two ropes, one of which included Smythe and Dyhrenfurth. It was, however, Schneider and Wieland who actually put the treacherous ridge to the test. The others watched their hesitant progress and observed what Smythe later described as "probably the finest piece of rock climbing ever done at such an altitude". It may even have impressed Dyhrenfurth. Eventually, the others retired and left Schneider and Wieland to get on with it. When they arrived back in camp late that night, it was to report that the ridge was impracticable. If laden porters were to have any chance of negotiating the first great pinnacle, it would have to be equipped with fixed ropes, and even then it was doubtful if they would be able to climb up and over it. Beyond, it would be necessary to bludgeon an icy edge into submission, and if that were done, another pinnacle, even more problematical than the first, would present itself—and that was just the start of the ridge.

Were all these obstacles overcome, the party would then find itself along a ridge from which escape would be virtually impossible in the not unlikely event of bad weather. And even if the good weather held, there would be insufficient time to reach the summit. Clearly, the attempt on Kangchenjunga was over, and not even Dyhrenfurth dissented.

There was one consolation, the Ramthang Peak. On the day after Kangchenjunga was finally abandoned, Smythe and Schneider set out to establish a camp from which the attempt could be made. The site eventually chosen was just below point 20,800 which the party had ascended earlier in order to examine the north-west ridge. Most of the party were paying the price of an unbalanced diet owing to the earlier defects in the transport arrangements; only Smythe and Schneider were near peak fitness, and even Smythe was feeling the effects, psychologically, of having been on the mountain the whole time during the attempts on Kangchenjunga. None of the others was up to the attempt, and so it was that Smythe and Schneider set off for the top at 9 a.m. the following day. In addition to the mental weariness from which he was suffering, Smythe had a further handicap as he was wearing, experimentally, the eight-pound expedition boots which Dyhrenfurth had provided. It was the only occasion on which he climbed in them and he regretted even that. Schneider seems to have been in excellent form and it was he who bore the brunt of the ascent. At the cost of some cutting, the pair gained access to the east ridge via a subsidiary spur falling to the south. At first, the main ridge was easy but the pair soon encountered sections where Schneider had to cut and tiptoe over and around a tracery of paper-thin flakes of ice before they reached the last 300 feet of summit slope with its only barrier a single crevasse requiring a few steps. A 23,000 foot peak no doubt offered some consolation after the frustrating weeks of useless snail-like progress on Kangchenjunga. By the time the party were ready to embark upon the next objective, the Jonsong Peak, Schneider had also put in his bag the first and solo ascent of Nepal Peak, at 23,470 feet and for a few days the highest peak ascended by man.

Prior to the 1930 expedition, the highest mountain climbed was Mount Kaufmann (since renamed Pik Lenin), 23,406 feet. One of the successful summit party on that occasion had been Schneider. At 24,340 feet, the Jonsong Peak towered over these two summits by nearly a thousand feet and Schneider must have found it particularly attractive.

It is not clear when the Jonsong Peak became formally listed as amongst the expedition's objectives but it certainly was so by the time of the ascent of Ramthang Peak. Smythe had proposed it at an earlier conference when advocating, unsuccessfully, that attempts on Kangchenjunga be abandoned. When they were eventually called off, the Jonsong Peak became the chief objective and on 20 May, the upper camps were cleared and the entire party assembled at Base Camp in order to prepare for it.

The peak stands a mere six or seven miles north of the Kangchenjunga Base Camp at Pangperma. Kellas's reconnaissance had suggested that the most promising route up the mountain lay on the northern side, via the north-west ridge which he had himself attempted. It was therefore necessary for the party to establish a new Base Camp which would serve for such an attempt and it would need to be north of the Jonsong La, the route to which lay up the Jonsong Glacier and promised to be relatively uncomplicated although the height of the pass, 20,400 feet, clearly posed problems. This was the obvious route. From the main summit of Kangchenjunga, the main ridge trends in a northerly direction, first over The Twins, then down to the Nepal Gap and then, via Nepal Peak, The Pyramid and Langpo Peak, turning west to a subsidiary summit at 22,160 feet from which it falls to the Jonsong La. On the other side of that, to the north west, stands the Jonsong Peak.

The crossing of the Jonsong La was not without incident. Quite understandably, there was dissatisfaction amongst the porters, partly because of earlier logistic miscalculations and partly because they had been worked very hard, were improperly equipped, and had seen the serious injury and even death of their comrades. Immediate objections were overcome by the diplomacy of Wood Johnson, who later paid a high price for his efforts, but it proved possible to arrange for some stores to be taken over the pass immediately, with the hope that the rest would arrive later. This uneasy truce was almost shattered by Dyhrenfurth seeking, unavailingly, to insist upon what was in effect a double march, but the cracks were again papered over by Wood Johnson.

Although Kellas's report had favoured the north-west ridge (and Base Camp had therefore been sited beyond the pass and to the west so as to support an attempt in this direction) it had appeared from the south that if access could be gained to the south-east ridge from the north a route might well be made up it to the summit. A buttress, however, obscured the view of the relevant part of the north face from Base Camp and the first item on the agenda for Smythe and Wood Johnson, as they set out from base, was to turn the buttress in order to assess these possibilities. They were immediately seen to be practically negligible: an approach from the left was barred by rock precipices armed with hanging glaciers whilst further to the right, where a route might be forced up 7,000 feet of ice slopes, the obvious dangers precluded it. Yet the north-west ridge, fully in view, looked anything but straightforward. From the col, which marked the obvious point of access to the ridge from the west, and towards which there was a subsidiary ridge promising relatively easy going, the extremely long and undulating crest of the ridge swept in icy, knife-edged arcs over a series of points, each of which would have been a respectable mountain in its own right in other contexts. However, this subsidiary ridge was the best option and Camp One was accordingly pitched at its foot.

The promise of easy going was not, in the event, fulfilled. Smythe prospected it for some distance the next morning and reported favourably, but he was deceived and "hard things" were said when the party was obliged to abandon the ridge and descend to the glacier below, where the snow turned out to be in appalling condition. They eventually passed it and crested a rise above an ice-fall only to discover, contrary to expectations, that Kellas's Col still lay quite a way ahead. Camp Two was accordingly sited some distance short of it. Progress had been slow, but it was possible at least to hope for success.

Next day, the weather intervened, and a pessimist might well have abandoned the attempt by the following morning which dawned with a snowstorm. This was serious: on the first crossing of the Jonsong La it had proved possible to carry supplies sufficient only for about three days on the mountain, and time was running out. Further, the monsoon was just about due—there were traces of its advance on Kangchenjunga. It does not observe a rigid timetable and it could strike at any time. They had just about concluded that there was no option but descent when the skies miraculously cleared. Although the heavy snowfall promised to make the going hard, the slopes they had next to traverse were sufficiently easy-angled to obviate the threat of avalanche and they decided to proceed.

They soon discovered that the appearance of the ridge starting from Kellas's Col was deceptive; for some distance it was a "one-sided ridge", the edge of a snowfield which only narrowed to a true ridge some distance above and about 3,000 feet below the summit. By lunchtime they had reached a platform at the head of the snow slopes, a little below where the true ridge began. They took a rest before tackling the last few obstacles and eventually gaining the main ridge at its foot. They were disagreeably surprised. Although patently negotiable as far as the first of the several points over which the ridge made its way, thereafter it degenerated into an extremely steep-sided and serrated blade of ice and promised to become progressively only more difficult. An alternative, however, presented itself. To the west of the ridge a tributary glacier rose to the final slopes of the peak and, provided that they were able to descend to it, it looked a feasible way to the top. There were two possible routes of descent, but if porters and stores were to be taken down them, an extra day on the mountain would be needed. It made more sense to establish a camp close by and, without porters, make a bid for the summit on the morrow. Without porters, the ridge itself might still go and, if it did not, there was the glacier route.

The night was wild and bitter and although the sky dawned clear, an ice-laden wind delayed the start. It again seemed as though the attempt would have to be called off, but the wind dropped suddenly, and by 9 a.m. they were off, Schneider and Hoerlin on one rope, Smythe and Wood Johnson on the other. They soon reached the top of the first point where the difficulties commenced. By the time they had descended the far side to a small col, it had become obvious that the sharp, corniced ridge was not the way, but also that it was possible to descend to the glacier at this point and ascend it for some distance. By the time Smythe and Wood Johnson arrived at the col, Schneider and Hoerlin had already exercised this option; Wood Johnson's experience was limited (this was the first occasion on which he had worn crampons!) and whilst the others had been able to move together, Smythe and Wood Johnson had found it necessary to pitch some sections. By the time these two reached the glacier, Schneider and Hoerlin were the best part of an hour ahead. When they in turn set off up the glacier, it was immediately apparent to Smythe that inexperience was not the greatest of Wood Johnson's problems; he was soon obliged to declare himself unfit to continue. In the circumstances, altitude, and the fatigue caused by his increasing efforts to bring order out of the expedition's logistic chaos, seemed the obvious explanation, and Smythe had no compunction about yielding to Wood Johnson's exhortations to continue alone. They were later to discover that there was more to Wood Johnson's collapse than had been thought. He was ill, and it was only with great difficulty, and with Wood Johnson's own very spirited effort, that Smythe was later able to get him off the mountain without further incident.

Although by now more than an hour behind the first pair, Smythe, overestimating the potential of his fitness, set out to catch them up. His sprint carried him to within 100 yards of them but exhausted him, and they again moved ahead. Smythe made one further effort. From the glacier, it had seemed that the best way to the summit lay ahead, to the high col which separated the two summits of the peak, but it transpired that this consisted of steep ice rather than less steep snow. A better alternative was to regain the north-west ridge at a high point above the major difficulties, via a broad slabby couloir, and follow it thence to the summit. Schneider and Hoerlin had preferred rocky steps to the right of the couloir. Smythe further exhausted himself by kicking steps up the snow to the left before abandoning this way in favour of theirs. Stonefall drew his attention to the leading pair 500 feet above, nearing the crest of the ridge, whence it would be necessary to climb a further thousand feet or so to the summit. It was 3 p.m. The remaining 1,500 feet would take Smythe at least another three or four hours; he would certainly be benighted high on the mountain, and alone. The conclusion was inescapable: there was clearly no point in going on and he settled down to enjoy a pipe and savour the atmosphere and scene which surrounded him. Eventually, he descended to Wood Johnson who was now obviously far from well. While considering how best to get him off the mountain, they found time to look up and see Schneider, still leading, and Hoerlin toiling up the last slopes to the summit.

There had, thus far, been little enough to celebrate and when they first returned to Camp Two, none of the four was in any mood for it. Smythe, and especially Wood Johnson, had had a very hard time of it—the latter had managed to keep going until, and only until, porters from the camp were able to assist, and he had then collapsed. Schneider and Hoerlin returned, fatigued, well after dark. Sufficient morale, however, was soon restored and a bottle of rum circulated in celebration, though whether as a cause or consequence it is not clear.

Next day, at Camp One, they were somewhat surprised to discover Dyhrenfurth, Kurz and Wieland bent on attempting the climb. Wood Johnson clearly needed to go down to base for a rest and Schneider and Hoerlin, after their success on Jonsong Peak, had eyes on the Dodang Peak, after a rest at base. Smythe preferred to stay up and have another shot at Jonsong Peak, despite the attractions of a rest at base camp. Accordingly, the following morning, armed with the supplies that had now been brought over the pass, and at last with good going on well-crusted snow, Smythe was again on his way up to the site of the former Camp Two where he arrived, clearly still in fair condition, an hour ahead of the rest. The improved going had meant that there was still a good bit of the day left and Dyhrenfurth insisted upon a higher site for Camp Two, despite the previous experience of attempts to double march the porters. By the time the lunch-time platform below the start of the ridge had been gained, they had, understandably, had enough and camp was pitched there. It proved to be excessively vulnerable to the tempestuous winds which, together with a certain reluctance on the part of the porters, put a stop to any further attempt the next day, and the opportunity was taken to move it to a more sheltered location. Smythe and Kurz, meanwhile, had reconnoitred a route to the glacier more suitable for porters, and Wieland and Dyhrenfurth had gone out later and started to prepare it with a view to establishing a final camp on the glacier itself, and thus shortening the final day's climb to the summit.

It fell to Smythe, assisted by Kurz, to complete the route to the glacier on the following day and, apart from a hair-raising incident when Smythe, unroped and prospecting the best way for porters across the bergschrund, saved himself by a single axe placement at the cost of a sprained wrist, Camp Three was established uneventfully. The customary gale greeted the party as they set out for the summit the following morning. Its inconvenience was doubled for the going had turned to ice the snow in the couloir leading up to the north west ridge and Smythe, in the lead, had to cut steps until it was feasible to take to the rocks on the right. Here it was remarked that Nemu, Smythe's servant, was going badly. He had given himself practically no rest since first leaving Base Camp several days previously; the price was now exacted and he had to go down. After the comparative shelter of the couloir, they had expected again to confront the gale when they broke out on to the ridge, but to the pleasant surprise of Kurz, now leading, and Tsinabo, his servant, it had abated somewhat. But the ridge itself did not spare them and it was necessary to traverse out on the rotten rocks of the western face in order to ascend about 200 feet to more easily-angled slabs above. These in turn gave out to slopes of loose sharp scree overlaying a frozen base, making it impossible to sustain the rhythm desirable for relatively painless progress at 24,000 feet. The going eased with the final snow-slopes immediately before the summit, and then all that was needed was a brief struggle with an incipient cornice before it was attained.

Whether he engaged in the customary ceremony of the summit pipe Smythe does not record. Probably not; when Greene insisted upon a cigarette on the summit of Kamet a year later, Smythe rather regarded it as a step into the unknown. The overwhelming view which surrounded them may well have been a sufficient "high" in itself and enough to fill the short stay that was permitted by the half-gale which was blowing. They were able, amongst other things, to satisfy themselves that even had they succeeded in forcing a way on to the north ridge on Kangchenjunga, they would almost certainly have failed to follow it to the summit. They were also able to appreciate the true scale of Everest, still some scores of miles to the west, and Smythe could sense the first promptings of the challenge which he was to face three times in the years immediately ahead.

Dyhrenfurth and Lewa had not arrived and the summit party encountered them, still ascending and with about an hour to go, only some little time after commencing the descent. On reaching a sheltered spot, while Kurz continued the descent, Smythe stopped in order to take in the spectacle more fully and was joined by Wieland. Eventually, the two descended to camp together, resting on the point above the camp to search the ridge unavailingly for signs of Dyhrenfurth and Lewa—not that there was any undue cause for anxiety, for although Dyhrenfurth had handicapped himself by wearing the expedition boots, he was accompanied by Lewa, and the two might reasonably expect help from the moon if forced to complete the descent at night. But it was 9 p.m. before Dyhrenfurth slumped into the snow outside Smythe's tent. They had had a rough time of it: the wind had worsened, raising clouds of driven snow, and the moon had withheld the expected assistance. Smythe's comment is that "Lewa had done simply magnificently".

So also, as it turned out, had Dyhrenfurth for, not content with the main summit, the pair had, perhaps unwisely, traversed the ridge to the subsidiary summit before reversing their steps and commencing the descent proper. Or perhaps it was, at last and after a series of failures, the long-awaited triumph of the will.

The success on Jonsong Peak effectively brought the climbing to an end. The return journey to Darjeeling yielded valuable new information about the area surrounding Kangchenjunga and brought news of the success of Schneider and Hoerlin on the Dodang Peak. In the final analysis, therefore, although the expedition had clearly failed in its main objective, and had cost the tragic loss of Chettan, there were considerable compensations.

Looking back, it is easy to see several reasons why it had been destined to fail in its attempt to climb Kangchenjunga. First of all, it was badly organized and the opportunities were insufficiently well researched. The failure to solve the logistic problems, due largely to an absence of communication and consultaltion on Dyhrenfurth's part had, as one of its consequences, a deleterious effect on the morale of the porters. Another consequence was a dilution of the strength of climbing members, partly as a result of illness caused by bad diet, and partly by reason of the demands made on their time in trying to repair some of the damage caused by the defective transport arrangements.

Secondly, even had one of the chosen routes been technically feasible, neither of them was justifiable. The north ridge route was threatened continuously by ice avalanches from the cliffs above. One of them took Chettan's life and wiped out the results of many days' endeavour on the face; it was a blessing that that was all the harm it did. Another avalanche overwhelmed the site of a camp which had been occupied continuously until a couple of days before. This danger was obvious throughout to all who had eyes to see and Smythe, who spent longer on the face than anyone, repeatedly drew attention to it. The pity is that he did not do so more forcefully. The north-west ridge route would have necessitated a series of high altitude camps along the ridge; the party would have been unwarrantably extended and in the likely event of bad weather it is probable that leading groups would have been cut off and lost.

Thirdly, it seems almost certain that neither route was within the technical competence of any party, given the limitations of experience and equipment of the time. Freshfield had said merely that the mountain might have been climbed via that face. There is, I suppose, a certain compulsion for an expedition to give it a go, once months have been spent in preparation and weeks in getting there; nevertheless, when noses had actually been rubbed up against the problems, the conclusion might quite reasonably have been drawn, as subsequent events have suggested, that Kangchenjunga simply is not climbable from that side by traditional methods, without modern equipment and techniques.

Nevertheless, for particular individuals, something was gained. Schneider in particular added to the bag he had started to fill in the Pamirs just previously, and at the end of the Kangchenjunga expedition could boast, if he were so inclined, the most remarkable collection of high summits of any mountaineer of the time. For Smythe, there was similar consolation—Ramthang Peak and Jonsong Peak represented a good "catch". But the real benefits were to be found elsewhere. The entire experience, on a first visit to the Himalaya, was invaluable. The particular experience of climate and climbing conditions in that part of the Himalaya was to stand him in good stead later. And finally, although it may sound cynical to suggest it, Smythe must have learned a great deal from the mistakes of others about the problems of organizing an expedition to a major Himalayan peak. The International Expedition of 1930 left a great deal to be desired in the areas of man-management and transport logistics. When, upon his return, he set about organizing his own expedition, he knew the evils to avoid and succeeded, strikingly, in avoiding them.

CHAPTER VIII

*Kamet Conquered**

RESTRICTIONS ON ACCESS to the Himalaya, which we tend nowadays to associate with changes on the political map after the Second World War, were by no means unknown in the earlier days of exploration. At times in the pre-war era the frontiers of Tibet and Nepal were both closed to Europeans whilst, even in other areas, the obtaining of permission to enter could be something of a lottery. The opportunities for Himalayan climbing were thus severely restricted in 1931. Everest and lesser giants such as Annapurna, Dhaulagiri, Gosainthan and Cho Oyo were out of bounds whilst others such as Nanga Parbat and Kangchenjunga were, as we have seen, open to assault only by what proved to be the more dangerous and less accessible routes. Of the great triumvirate of peaks, K2 (or Mount Godwin-Austen as it was still then referred to) alone was politically eligible and its height, difficulty and remoteness made it an unsuitable objective for a relatively small, private party, as, indeed, it has consistently proved to be on a number of more recent occasions.

When Smythe first conceived the idea of a private expedition to a major Himaylan summit, his options were practically confined to the Kumaon and Garwhal and part of the Sikkim Himalaya. The most attractive choice lay between Nanda Devi in the Kumaon and Kamet which crowned the Garwhal Himalaya. There was little to choose between the two, so far as was then known, in terms of technical difficulty and altitude. Nanda Devi, however, posed an access problem from which Kamet was free, for Nanda Devi stood, at that time and for some years thereafter, inviolate in her sacred sanctuary. The mystery of approaching her feet, let alone her summit, had yet to be unravelled. Kamet, on the other hand, had not only been approached but had been attempted several times.

Some seventy of the world's summits exceed the magic figure of 25,000 feet: in 1930, none had ever been climbed. Kamet, 25,447 feet

*See p.213 for a map of the Garwhal area

(7756 m) appears to have been an object of interest to the Schlagintweit brothers as early as 1855, although it is not certain whether the peak which they actually attempted was Kamet itself or a neighbouring lower summit. The area was reconnoitred by officers of the Survey of India on a couple of occasions in the latter part of the nineteenth century and was then subjected to more serious scrutiny by a celebrated trio, Longstaff, Mumm and Bruce in 1907; Meade paid his first visit in 1910. Kamet next attracted the attention of Morris Slingsby and de Crespigny in 1911. This time, Slingsby led determined attempts on the mountain, and reached the col which bears his name, though between it and the summit of Kamet stands Eastern Ibi Gamin, a considerable mountain in its own right. Slingsby's second attempt on the latter ended in a storm at about 23,000 feet.

Meade returned in 1912 with a team of Alpine guides that included the incomparable Franz Lochmatter, the creator of a series of the most extraordinary routes in the Alps during the previous decade. Some of the party, following in Slingsby's footsteps, reached a similar height but, more important, came to understand the true stature of Eastern Ibi Gamin, concluding that a more feasible route must be found, and quite possibly would be found, via the col between Eastern Ibi Gamin and Kamet itself. Renewing the attack in 1913 with Pierre Blanc, Meade reached this now eponymous col but was stopped there by poor weather and lack of acclimatization.

The first world war put a stop to any further attempts, but in 1920 Kellas and Morshead mounted an attempt and reached a point about 100 feet above Meade's col. This time, porters put an end to any further progress; and there, in 1931, things stood. Kamet was by now well-known. An apparently feasible route had been reconnoitred and explored; but the mountain had nevertheless resisted all attempts, some near heroic, by a catalogue of names representing the best mountaineers of the day. Kamet may not now be ranked among the most difficult mountains in the Himalaya, but it is abundantly clear that measured against the technical standards and equipment of the time it was far from being a pushover.

The Kamet expedition was the first and only major expedition which Smythe organized and led. There were to be six British members, all climbers though with medical and transport specialists amongst them. Smythe considered four to be adequate for smaller peaks and, taking account of health and altitude difficulties, eight or ten to be necessary for the highest peaks. For Kamet, six would yield either three teams of two, or two of three, as needed. He favoured a mix, socially and professionally, maintaining that "wide divergencies of opinions seldom matter. It is the small divergencies of opinions that count for so much." The preferred age was 24 to 35; extreme youth lacked the relevant experience and skill and, particularly important, the right mental attitude; mere athleticism alone would not do. The youngest member chosen, Eric Shipton, whose first Himalayan adventure this was, and who had rejected the chance of making a fortune mining gold in order to embark upon it, was 23. The others were in their thirties. They were E. B. Beauman, a RAF Wing Commander of wide Alpine experience; E. St J. Birnie, on the staff of the Governor of Bengal, with some Himalayan experience, particularly in arranging transport; Raymond Greene, a doctor, son of Smythe's former headmaster (and brother of Graham and Hugh), with an extensive experience on British rock and in the Alps, some of it with Smythe; and R. L. Holdsworth, teacher, all-round athlete, Alpinist and, as a botanist, a catalyst to one of Smythe's later passions. Holdsworth also had a smattering of Hindustani.

There were to be eight Darjeeling Sherpas and some 60 porters for the carry-in, the best of whom were to carry to the lower camps. So far as the timing of the assault was concerned, Kamet offered fewer climatic problems than most other great Himalayan peaks. It is set well back from the main Himalayan range, constituting the high point of a northerly spur, the Zaskar range, and enjoys considerable protection from the onslaught of the monsoon in July and August. Whilst it was clearly desirable to be on the mountain earlier than this, failure to attain the summit before the monsoon broke would not necessarily be fatal. It was decided, therefore, to aim to establish the party on the mountain so as to be in a position to go for the top in June.

Smythe, accompanied by Shipton, arrived in Ranikhet, the starting point of the expedition and about 90 miles south of Kamet, on 22 April 1931. They were there ahead of the rest of the party in order to make final preparations, although Birnie was already busy provisioning and packing in the less salubrious atmosphere of Calcutta. He arrived with his charges on 10 May and the porters set off under the command of Lewa, the sirdar, on 13 May. The remaining three members of the party, Beauman, Greene and Holdsworth, arrived at Ranikhet on 14 May. Final preparations occupied three further days; a fourth was devoted to travel to Baijnath, the roadhead from which the walk-in began. It occupied eighteen days, including rest days and the occasional training excursion, the party arriving at Base Camp on 6 June. The gradual acclimatization which the leisurely walk-in allowed paid dividends later.

The site chosen for Base Camp was a stony pasture by the Dhaoli River which emerges from the snow of the merged Rankani and East Kamet glaciers some ten miles, as the crow flies, east of the summit of Kamet. A complex spur falling from Eastern Ibi Gamin and containing several peaks over 20,000 feet divides the two glaciers. Kamet stands at the head of the East Kamet glacier, the more southerly branch of the two. It was up this branch that the route was to go. Base Camp was at 15,500 feet, amongst complex terminal moraines and within easy reach of an adequate supply of juniper wood for fuel. Things so far had gone without a hitch. With minor exceptions, the entire expedition continued in that vein.

The plan was to establish Camps One and Two on or near the East Kamet glacier, at about 16,500 and 18,500 feet respectively. The work of stocking these camps required the selection of six local porters to assist the Darjeeling men. The first objective was the establishment of an advanced base, stocked with fuel and provisions for a month, from which the actual summit assaults would be launched, via intermediate camps. The exact location of the advanced base fell to be determined by circumstances, but, clearly, the higher the better was the governing maxim, and the effective choice seemed to be between Camps Three and Four.

June 7, set aside for preparations for the establishment of Camps One and Two, also witnessed the first success, with Holdsworth and Shipton ascending a 17,000 foot peak near the base. On 8 June these two, with Greene and Smythe, duly established Camp One as planned, moving to the projected Camp Two the next day, while Beauman and Birnie went up to One. Camp One was on the fell-side above the glacier very near Kellas's site, according to the locals. Camp Two required a five mile ascending trudge up the glacier trough, through a gorge and then, after the glacier turned to the north west, bringing Kamet into view, a hard pull up a steep slope which proved too much for at least one of the porters. Lewa, the sirdar, revealed his true mettle, not for the last time, adding the abandoned 50lb load to his own. The first site chosen for Camp Two lasted only a day: closer inspection revealed a threat from hanging glaciers on Mana Peak to the south-west of Kamet and the camp was moved up the mountainside opposite, well out of range. Birnie and Beauman duly arrived there with porters from Camp One at 2 p.m.

June 11 at Camp Two was devoted to rest, acclimatization and anticipation of the problems of establishing Camps Three, Four and Five. Previous expeditions had discovered the unlikely route to Camp Three and no serious difficulty was expected. Camp Three was scheduled for a small glacier plateau forming a shelf roughly halfway between the East Kamet Glacier and Meade's Col. The direct route from the glacier, however, lies up impassable ice-draped precipices. The actual route Smythe described as a "remarkable line of least resistance", credit for which he readily and rightly attributed to Meade. It is not easy to understand why Meade ever prospected it, for it starts up a gully apparently destined to deposit a party on the wrong side of a great rocky outlier of Eastern Ibi Gamin. But Meade had discovered that this rock peak did not thrust a continuous barrier in the direction of Eastern Ibi Gamin and was, in fact, separated from it by an easy snow plateau, enabling a simple traverse to the Camp Three site to be made. In the event, poor snow conditions turned it into a strenuous plod before Camp Three was duly established at about 20,500 feet. The ascent of the intervening 2,000 feet from Camp Two in a mere two hours spoke well of the acclimatization of the party of Greene, Holdsworth, Shipton and Smythe.

So far, so good. But Smythe, who seems to have researched his projects exhaustively beforehand, knew that, at least in technical terms, the mountain had not yet posed its significant problems. Planning and organization alone had been needed; Meade had shown the relatively safe and easy way. He had also reported on one of the two sections of the route where technical difficulties were to be anticipated. This was the passage from Camp Three to Camp Four, the projected site for which was on an ice-knoll at about 22,000 feet, well over a thousand feet above Camp Three and a similar distance below Meade's Col. Two things were known about this section of the route: it was technically hard, but it had been negotiated when parties had twice previously reached Meade's Col; the other section which might present difficulties was that above the Col leading to the summit. Here no man had previously ventured and only close inspection would reveal what the problems were and whether they would prove soluble.

The challenge betweens Camps Three and Four was presented by a precipice of rock and ice approximately 1,000 feet high. The fact that previous parties had negotiated it, meant no more than that it had proved vulnerable to the best mountaineers of the day some decades previously when conditions, as is notoriously the case with mixed walls of this kind, might well have been quite different. A ten-foot rock step can in one season be an insuperable barrier to the summit of a 25,000 foot peak, in another it might be an insignificant feature by reason of a chance three-foot ramp of snow.

The party had proceeded to Camp Three on 13 June and an ideal schedule would have provided for it to proceed straightway to Camp Four. The dawn of 14 June, however, revealed that the party as a whole was as yet not sufficiently well-acclimatized to push on immediately. Three of the porters were in poor shape and Beauman was feeling unwell. In the event, it mattered little, for a closer scrutiny soon revealed that there was no safe, easy and obvious route up the wall and that some days of prospecting and experiment would be well spent. Smythe and Shipton were still going well and embarked upon the task.

First impressions were far from encouraging. The foot of the precipice lay a third of a mile from the camp, and Smythe and Shipton were feeling the effects of altitude; they also witnessed the alarming spectacle of the precipice perversely steepening as they approached it. Due to foreshortening, the cliff had appeared moderately steep when seen from the camp. Now it became more forbidding with each step taken. Slabs became walls and what at first had seemed steep but climbable rock was now seen to overhang impossibly. In the Himalaya, furthermore, Alpine experience of snow and ice can be deceptive. In the Alps, it persists relatively rarely at an angle that is impossible for the mountaineer of average ability. No such assumption is warranted in the Himalaya (or, for that matter, the Andes) where the different conditions frequently produce ice-slopes near the vertical.

However, there appeared to be a possibility of climbing the cliff if access could be gained to its lower left-hand end, from where a rising traverse might be made along a line of weakness to the right of the steepest portion of the ice-bulge above, and thence up steep mixed ground to the top of the bulge where Camp Four was to be sited. The pair accordingly set off up preliminary thinly-crusted snow-slopes only to realize, as they struggled to the foot of the face, that the route was less practicable than had at first seemed to be the case. Access to the lower left-hand end of the ramp was barred by a smooth repellent rock wall of about 100 feet, whilst the ramp itself, if gained, offered only snow of unknown condition, at about 50 degrees, interspersed with apparently verglassed granite slabs. It may be that they were unduly discouraged; but whatever route was settled upon had not merely to be feasible for a couple of technically skilled and experienced mountaineers but had also to be made safe and accessible for laden porters. So, in deteriorating weather, the two returned to camp to find that the day had not lacked progress: Birnie, with porters, had ascended from Camp Two and consolidated the position at Camp Three which was becoming the effective advanced base.

The next day saw Smythe, Shipton, Holdsworth, Greene, Birnie and Nima Dorje investigating elsewhere. The 1,000 foot precipice blocking their way to Camp Four abutted, on the right, the glacier falling from Meade's Col, ending abruptly in ice-cliffs, up to 300 feet in height, overhanging a rock wall. Clearly, no route lay that way, but between this feature and the cliffs of Eastern Ibi Gamin, a steep couloir offered possibilities if an initial hard section could be avoided via a traverse in from the right to a point above.

As the party (less Birnie who, not yet fully acclimatized, had returned to camp) approached the foot of the couloir, they realized that they had been deceived yet again. The initial section that they had thought to be climbable but best avoided turned out to be impassable: the traverse in lay along a ramp of 60-degree snow. When Smythe entered the couloir he found hard ice beneath a layer of snow. He proceeded notwithstanding until a combination of increasing steepness and likelihood of avalanche coupled with abundant evidence of frequent rock-fall rendered a second retreat inevitable.

Strangely, this further set-back did not depress the party. Shipton's comment was, "We have had a grand day's mountaineering", and the day had proved that as a party, they were fit, able and harmonious. The easy options appeared to have been foreclosed and if this left only a direct assault on the precipice, so be it.

June 16 began in this positive mood. Shipton and Holdsworth favoured a narrow couloir just to the left of the hanging glacier which looked promising above an initial pitch of jammed boulders coated in green ice. Smythe, Birnie and Greene preferred the mixed ground to the left of this couloir starting up slabs which, if dry, would have been easy but which were in fact verglassed and complicated by powder snow. The party accordingly split in order to try both routes.

Shipton and Holdsworth encountered difficult climbing in the initial pitch but once established in the couloir found themselves on feasible although very steep snow. Smythe's party, too, found slow going initially, every hold having to be cleared of snow and ice. A steep shallow couloir of well-consolidated snow followed this initial wall until another wall of about 20 feet barred the way. Smythe had to invest 30 minutes' effort on this before hauling himself over the top, followed by his companions. Easier mixed ground led at last to a resting place which offered time to contemplate the next problem. Above them reared an unclimbable granite overhang, but a snow ramp led up and right into a corner where escape was possible via an outward-sloping slab. Thence mixed ground again led up to the final slopes beneath the bulge.

At this point the two routes almost converged and Shipton and Holdsworth joined the others for a lunchtime conference. Although the ground thus far had been successfully reconnoitred, the general opinion was that neither route was at all suitable for laden porters, even with a fair bit of fixed rope. And immediately ahead, as Shipton and Holdsworth had discovered, the snow gradually thinned into a 300-foot slope of black ice which would clearly require a great deal of hard work. There seemed to be a way of avoiding the worst, initial sections of both routes; the slanting shelf which sloped downwards from the first resting place on the Smythe route might result in a more practicable line of ascent. This shelf, a bank of exceedingly steep snow, led along the top of the cliff which had deterred Shipton and Smythe earlier and they cannot have been optimistic about the prospects until, quite suddenly, they discovered that the cliff was not, as it had seemed to be, continuous, but was pierced by an obscure narrow couloir which, although steep, consisted of well-consolidated snow in which good steps could be kicked. The day's activities ended on a note of hope.

Next day Smythe, Birnie and Shipton, the others lacking form for one reason or another, quickly reached the previous day's high point via the couloir and ramp and turned to examine the 300 foot slope of black ice. This proved to be ice of the worst kind, of a plastic quality which yields to the pick of the axe without fragmenting, and then refuses to surrender it—arduous work at an altitude of 22,000 feet. Smythe made precious little progress in fifteen minutes' cutting and was about to hand over to Shipton when it occurred to the pair that it would be sensible to exhaust one very unlikely possibility before finally sentencing the party to the hard labour of the black ice. By all the odds, the precipitous snow slope to the right was incapable of holding snow of a sufficient depth to facilitate the kicking of sizeable steps. At first, indeed, the snow did constitute merely the thinnest of cloaks for the ice but the further they went, the deeper it became until they found themselves on several feet of well-consolidated snow adhering firmly to the ice beneath and capitulating readily to Shipton's boots. Directly above, the snow clearly thinned to nothing again, but by working further to the right it was possible to kick steps for a considerable distance before, 100 feet from the top, the snow finally yielded to ice, this time white and brittle, in which good steps were easily sculpted. The route to Camp Four was open, and the path to the summit revealed for the first time.

Over sardines, peaches, tea and a pipe, the party was able to study the way ahead. They had hoped that the route to Meade's Col and Camp Four would consist of a simple snow slope; instead, their gaze fell upon a complex of crevasses and serac walls of up to 100 feet in height. These, however, threatened no more than detour and irritating delay at worst. It seemed that the way to the summit could well be open, although the 2,000 feet above Meade's Col remained to be studied at close quarters.

At Camp Three that night, the party assembled a multitude of good reasons for departing from the earlier immutable resolve not to rush the mountain prematurely. The weather might not hold; several of the party were in prime peak condition and the rest should be ready for a second assault should the first one fail; Birnie's logistics had been perfect and Camp Three was bountifully stocked. However, the ranks of the porters had been thinned by altitude sickness and it might not be easy, if they delayed, to maintain an adequate level of supply to the higher camps. They were, in the event, unanimous in deciding to press an assault with all due haste, provided, of course, that it proved possible to establish and provision Camps Four and Five.

The establishment of Camp Four fell to Smythe and Shipton (both of whom had gone continuously well), Holdsworth, now recovered from an earache which had handicapped him for several days, and, by no means least, the high-level porters. Tents were pitched and loads dumped. Holdsworth descended with most of the porters to Camp Three leaving Smythe, Shipton, Lewa and Nima Dorje on the ice-bulge.

For these four, intended as the first assault party, 19 June was a rest day, justified by seven continuous days of activity establishing Camp Four. The others, including Beauman who had been slow to acclimatize, made another carry to Camp Four where the team, plus seven additional porters, remained in order to set about establishing the next camp.

Camp Five was destined for Meade's Col, at a height of about 23,500 feet. The morning of 20 June dawned cold but brilliantly clear. An hour after sunrise, Smythe, Shipton, Holdsworth and the nine porters were en route, enjoying easy going for the first two or three hundred feet until the sun rendered the snow tedious. More serious, however, was the serac barrier which looked, from a distance, as though it spanned the whole flank beneath the Col from the precipitous east face of Kamet to the ice-slopes of Eastern Ibi Gamin. If no break could be found, it would be necessary to turn the barrier via these latter ice-slopes involving a lengthy detour and much step-cutting. Fortunately, one relative weakness appeared. To the right, a segment of the wall had slumped forward allowing a passage to be forced up the corner between it and the ice-cliff to the left. Although a mere dozen steps in good ice required to be cut, the effort involved by the altitude and blazing sun did not augur well should the summit require prolonged ice-work. An interminable and exhausting plod up poor snow followed. Halfway up, it proved too much for one of the local men who had not expected to go so high: from that point on, Lewa again carried a double load.

The conditions rendered progress slow and if the porters, who were now lagging some distance behind, were to be able to descend that day, as planned, their loads would have to be deposited. Camp Five was therefore stationed on a horizontal shelf some 300 feet below the Col proper. Tents were pitched and tea brewed and the porters, less Nima Dorje and Lewa, descended.

This might or might not be the last camp. The summit slopes

rose more than 2,000 feet above and presented several possibilities, although no certainty that the summit could be reached in a single day's climb. A moderately steep but not intimidating rib ran up from Col to summit and would have been an obvious line had not the westerly wind stripped it bare of all but gleaming black ice. The flanks of this rib seemed unpromising. What remained were the slopes rising from the camp directly to the summit with the rib on the right and the precipitous East Face of Kamet falling away on the left. These slopes were concave and the hollow centre presented bands of seracs which suggested that the best line lay to the left, or eastern side of the slope. This, however, culminated in a steep final section of several hundred feet which looked intimidating even without taking foreshortening into account. It could not be assumed that these slopes would go. It seemed likely, even if they would, that the final 400 feet would take several hours of laborious cutting and, if this were so, both rib and flank would require the extra camp originally contemplated before fitness and weather had raised hopes that it would not be needed. Whereas the rib would almost certainly require an additional camp, it was distinctly possible that the flank would not. Only when they reached the final 400 feet would they know. The flank was therefore the choice for the first attempt.

The night was bitterly cold and they slept fully clothed. Shipton, who had been feeling unwell, slept badly, Holdsworth and Smythe rather better. It seems not to have occurred to Shipton that he might not tread the summit next day. It would, indeed, have been a bitter blow had he been denied the chance, since he and Smythe had provided the spearhead throughout the entire climb.

June 21 arrived. Smythe was awake in time to see the dawn illuminating the summit but the bitter cold drove him back into his bag to spend a considerable time restoring the circulation to numbed hands. It was 8 a.m. before the party set off, fortified by sardines, fruit and tea. They climbed on two ropes, Shipton with Lewa and Smythe with Nima Dorje and Holdsworth. Nima Dorje's load included 20lbs of photographic equipment.

The route to the foot of the north flank lay initially up an easy incline on uncomfortably soft snow. Smythe, Holdsworth and Shipton took fifteen-minute turns stamping a trail up the 30–40 degree slope, which gradually steepened. After an hour, the camp was 500 feet below, the Col had been topped and only Eastern Ibi Gamin rose above the slopes on which they stood. They took a short break for second breakfast and filming and set off again. The thinness of the air was making itself felt and the snow was deteriorating, crusting just insufficiently to take the whole weight. In such conditions, large feet can be a blessing; I have in such conditions found easy going on the crust whilst my eight-stone daughter with tiny feet has had to endure a miserable time of it. The rate of progress fell to about 300 feet per hour; leads fell from 100 to 50 feet. The upper edges of crevasses needed occasional step-cutting and Eastern Ibi Gamin still loomed over them. Nevertheless, the final steep slopes gradually neared. Then ice appeared, the snow thinned and a whole hour's cutting had to be invested in gaining one hundred feet to a large red boulder selected as the next resting place.

Nima Dorje, who was lumbered with the photographic equipment, had been finding the going difficult and now, at about 25,000 feet, turned back, a mere 300 feet or so below the summit. Ahead lay the steep final ice-wall at an average angle of about 50 degrees. The climbing, furthermore, was now serious for a slip which would previously have led at little risk to easier slopes below would now carry a party over the eastern precipices to the glacier thousands of feet beneath. Fortunately, however, the snow was good in parts and the party were spared the continuous cutting which would have put an end to the attempt on grounds of time. Even so, progress was slow and it seemed an age before Smythe hauled himself on to the ill-defined ridge which capped the wall.

Here, they had hoped to find themselves on the summit, but they were to be disappointed. The ridge rose to a point 30 yards away but slopes of rock and snow behind it indicated higher ground, perhaps some distance off, ready access to which was in no way assured. The party set out along the razor-edged ridge and soon topped the nearby point. The ridge fell gently to a shallow gap and from there rose a mere few feet to a small snow cone.

At 4.30 p.m., eight and a half hours after setting out from Camp Five, first Lewa and then the others stepped up to the summit of Kamet. Lewa, who had performed miracles on the carry up, was pretty well exhausted as Smythe handed him to the lead and gave him the honour as a gesture of recognition of the indispensable role played by the porters, particularly the Darjeeling men, whose sacrifice was not yet fully appreciated.

It was bitterly cold on top and a few minutes of photography and filming left Smythe's hands numb and lifeless. In order to be certain of not failing by inches, the party followed the ridge a few yards further to another snow mound. Holdsworth smoked a determined pipe as all sat in the snow and gazed out. Far away on the north-western horizon a range of high snow peaks could be detected. It could only be the Karakoram, 250 to 300 miles distant. They stayed on the summit for half an hour and then, weary but conscious of the need to maintain all caution, set off down.

The snow of the final slope had at last yielded to the sun and the going was easier. Lewa was, nevertheless, making hard going of it and looked far from well; Smythe relieved him of his load. Bit by bit, Eastern Ibi Gamin rose before them. They unroped; the cold intensified. As they approached the tents of Camp Five Birnie came out to greet them with tea.

The fierce cold encountered on the descent took its toll. Lewa, now utterly exhausted, was found to have badly frozen feet which resisted all efforts to restore circulation. Holdsworth and Shipton were also affected. Only Smythe escaped unscathed. Holdsworth and Shipton recovered completely but it was some time before it was known that Lewa's feet had been saved, although in the event he lost the end joints of all his toes.

It is trite but true that the success of putting a man on a Himalayan summit is not his but that of the party as a whole. The ascent of Smythe, Shipton, Holdsworth and Lewa was certainly founded on team effort. All that being said, there is a special satisfaction in placing one's own two feet on the highest point of a mountain and it had been contemplated throughout that, if circumstances permitted it, everyone would have a chance. Accordingly, there was to be a second summit bid as soon as possible. The first priority for 22 June, however, was to secure Lewa's removal from the heights with all due haste and it was therefore on 23 June that the second party embarked on the attempt. It consisted of Greene, Birnie and Kesar Singh. Beauman, although he had pulled his weight in the lower camps, was still not altitude fit and regretfully therefore had to pass up the opportunity.

The inclusion of Kesar Singh requires explanation. Birnie and Greene were keen to have a porter along on their attempt but the experience of Nima Dorje and, particularly, Lewa, on the first ascent had demoralized the Darjeeling men to such an extent that none of them was willing to venture higher. Kesar Singh was a Bhotia, a local man and, according to Smythe, a plausible and likeable rascal with the lust for adventure in his veins. He could not be disabused of the erroneous notion that he would see England from the top of the mountain and entertained the no doubt accurate one that success would enormously enhance his local standing. Smythe thought highly of the mountaineering potential of the Bhotias and considered that it exceeded even that of the Sherpas.

The second party set out at 6.45 a.m. Progress was again very slow, although the route finding had been done by the first party and the second merely followed their tracks. Greene exhausted himself by leading for the whole of the first two hours, and stopped to rest whilst urging the others on. They found the going very hard and after another hour abandoned rucsacs and rope in order to travel lighter. Greene had obviously decided to continue and was following slowly about half an hour behind. A further three hours brought them to the foot of the final ice-slopes where they discovered that the steps made by the first party had been obliterated by their descent and a protracted spell of cutting was needed. Eventually, however, the ridge was topped and Birnie and Kesar Singh, with Greene behind them, followed its knife-edge to Kamet's summit. All the able members of the expedition and two of the porters, a Sherpa and a Bhotia, had stood on top.

For the second party the excitement was not yet over. The earlier abandonment of the rope might not have mattered had Kesar Singh been properly shod but he had preferred the cloth bindings customary amongst the Bhotias and now found himself unable to hold, without assistance, in the steps descending the summit ice-slopes. Using Birnie as a brake, they managed and eventually reached the camp in an exhausted state.

Kesar Singh had the last laugh. His cloth-bindings kept out the cold, whatever their inadequacies in other respects, whilst Birnie had to endure severe frostbite of a toe and Greene's finger-tips suffered.

The remainder of the party spent the day recuperating. There had been some talk of an attempt on Eastern Ibi Gamin from Meade's Col but although Beauman, who had denied himself the chance of Kamet, was keen, the others were too spent. Holdsworth summoned the energy to descend from Meade's Col on ski, but found it an unpleasant experience.

The weather determined attempts thereafter. For exactly as long as was necessary it had been clement if cold; but 24 June brought vicious clouds and fiercely-driven snow. The attempt on Eastern Ibi Gamin was finally abandoned and camp was struck. Camp Four was reached by lunch-time then it too was cleared and taken, partly by porters, partly by gravity to Camp Three, by nightfall. All descended uneventfully to Camp Two the next day where they found Lewa in a serious condition. Beauman, Shipton and four others undertook the onerous task of getting him down off the mountain forthwith. June 26 saw the completion of the clearing of Camp Three and by the next day all had returned to Base Camp, although not without incident for it was hidden in a maze of moraines and not easy to locate.

An evening of relative revelry followed. The voice of Gracie Fields and the tones of Kreisler's violin accompanied the despatch of a bottle of brandy, a deal of tobacco and a parade of young reminiscence. They had abundant cause to celebrate.

The ascent of Kamet was a seminal advance in Himalayan mountaineering. As a climb not at all unproblematical, it involved difficult technical work and route finding, and no peak which had repelled Longstaff, Bruce, Mumm, Meade, Brocherel, Pierre Blanc, Kellas, Slingsby, Franz Lochmatter and Morshead could be considered easy. The party enjoyed excellent weather but less than perfect snow conditions. It benefited from Smythe's organization, Birnie's logistics and the all-round strength of climbers and leading porters. Most of all, however, it demonstrated that Himalayan peaks of over 25,000 feet could be climbed, and it restored a morale shattered by the succession of failures on high peaks which was the legacy of the 1920s. The Everest Committee recognized this and sought to capitalize on most of the assets of the Kamet expedition. Four of the team —Smythe, Greene, Birnie and Shipton—formed the core of the 1933 Everest expedition, with Birnie expected to organize porterage as well as climb. One option, strangely, they did not take up: Smythe's organizing ability and leadership.

The conquest of Kamet, whilst the major, was not the only object of the expedition; nor was it the only success. Between them, members of the expedition in various combinations ascended a dozen peaks and explored extensive areas hitherto little known. Shipton proved to have an almost insatiable appetite for bagging and reached eleven of the summits. Smythe confined his activities rather more.

On 9 July, the party crossed the Bhyundar Pass into the Bhyundar Valley and proceeded down the valley, eventually reaching Mana after crossing the Khanta Khal Pass. From Mana they set out, after two days of recuperation, organization and planning, for a venture into the Badrinath range. The tentative objective was to cross the range via a new pass leading from the Arwa Valley to the Gangotri Glacier system, tentative at least in part because existing maps were unreliable and it was not at all certain that there was any such pass.

The party left Mana on 15 July equipped for a two week foray, and set out up the Sarsuti Valley, off which the Arwa Valley branches. They soon had cause to doubt the accuracy of the maps, for what at first appeared to be the snout of the twelve mile long glacier which was supposed to occupy the Arwa Valley turned out to belong to a side valley, the former valley presenting nothing but boulder slopes for many miles before diluting itself in a series of branches. Twelve distinct glaciers were identified, none of them in the Arwa Valley proper.

At the first fork, the party decided to follow the apparently more imposing western branch. After a short distance, this branch divided into two, and there, two days out from Mana, they camped. The following day, Smythe, Shipton, Greene and Nima Parji made an easy ascent of a nearby peak of about 19,500 feet, ostensibly for purposes of reconnaissance, and did indeed discover a mountain of 23,000 feet unmarked on the map. They spent several hours on top basking in a warm sun and, not for the first or last time, Smythe voiced a sybaritic preference for easy routes up lesser mountains. A 1,500 foot glissade brought them quickly back to camp, where the others reported the discovery of a suitable camp-site at about 19,000 feet in the vicinity of what could prove to be the watershed which the party aimed to cross. From this site, two days later, the party climbed to a 20,000 foot col and from there gazed down on yet another glacier system which, logic dictated, must merge with the Gangotri system. From the col, Smythe and Shipton followed the steep ridge to the north of the col and within half an hour stood on a virgin summit of approximately 20,800 feet, from which they again glimpsed a fang of snow and ice, first seen on the way to the 19,000 foot camp, and decided to attempt it. It rose to nearly 22,000 feet and was to earn the name of Avalanche Peak.

On 21 July, Smythe, Shipton and Nima Dorji set out with this objective in mind. The intended route involved crossing the glacier and climbing a steep 600 foot slope to a col on the steep north-east ridge, thence following a rising traverse line across the east face of the mountain to the south-east ridge which should lend access to the summit.

The glacier presented heavy going but the 50 degree slope was in good order and axes were needed only to hack down the cornice which protected the col. There hopes died. A bitter wind drove them to shelter and deteriorated during the following three quarters of an hour. An hour later they were back in camp gulping down hot tea.

The following day they returned to the attack, again in dubious weather which, however, held, and they were soon at the col and embarking on the traverse on foul snow. Mists were swirling but no technical difficulty presented itself and before long a steep 200 foot slope led them out on to the south-east ridge, where they took a second breakfast before setting out up the corniced edge. Although the snow thinned at points, and parts of the route were exceedingly steep, they were spared bare ice and duly reached the top. They did not remain long; anxiety that the waxing sun might melt the thin coat of snow on the ridge, and necessitate step-cutting, drove them down and they were soon back at the col on the north-east ridge.

From here, the temptation of a sitting glissade to the glacier floor proved irresistible. The snow appears to have been of that lightly crusted but wet and consolidated variety which, given a start, will flow under its own weight but solidify under pressure, and it is not uncommon in these circumstances to find oneself sliding at the tail of a small avalanche, as did Smythe on this occasion. But behind him Shipton and Nima Dorji were creating their own avalanches and when Smythe sought to check his rate of descent, these struck him and carried him away. He tried again and again to brake but was able to make little impression against the tons of snow carrying him down inexorably towards the bergschrund. Seconds later, he found himself buried to the chest, crushed by the solid but now stationary snow, below the bergschrund, having been carried over its upper lip which overtopped its lower lip at least fifteen feet. He released himself with a struggle and, after his companions had restored circulation to frozen hands, made his way painfully back to camp where Greene diagnosed bruising and a broken rib which restricted his activity for some days.

The party now split into three in order to maximize opportunities. Beauman, Greene and Smythe returned to Mana, Greene and Smythe later ascending the Alaknanda Valley to find the religiously significant but, in the end, banal source of the Alaknanda River in a dirty glacier snout. Birnie with porters made the projected crossing to the Gangotri side of the range returning by a different pass whilst Shipton and Holdsworth bagged a trio of 20,000 foot peaks in the vicinity of the 19,000 foot camp.

There, effectively, the expedition ended. By no means all their mountaineering objectives had been attained. The opportunity of climbing Eastern Ibi Gamin had been declined and although some possibilities had been considered no attempt had been made, as had been hoped, on Mana Peak. Nevertheless, it had been an extraordinarily fruitful trip carried through without loss of life and with no serious harm other than Lewa's frostbite injuries. On a more personal level, it had had another effect. It had introduced Smythe to the Bhyundar Valley—the Valley of Flowers—which came to represent the mountain ideal to him and to which he was to return to enjoy his most inspiring mountain experience.

For Smythe, 1931 was a year not only of professional achievement but also of significant change in personal terms for in that year he married his first wife, Kathleen. They lived at first in North London in King Henry's Road, later at Brunner Close before moving to Abinger in Surrey. Kathleen was to bear him three sons over the next few years and one of them was destined to pursue a career similar to, if less distinguished than that of his father.

CHAPTER IX

Everest★

SEVEN EXPEDITIONS BY British teams to Everest in the 1920s and 1930s yielded not a single ascent of the world's highest peak. Several times members of various expeditions, Smythe among them, climbed to within a thousand feet of the summit but the peak remained inviolate. It was the spirit of Mallory which infused the expeditions of the 1920s; and, as Walter Unsworth states in *Everest*, his now classic work on the mountain, "It is the ghost of Smythe which hovers over the 1933 and 1936 expeditions."

The pre-war attempts on Everest were the fond children of the Everest Committee which was itself the brainchild of the Alpine Club and the Royal Geographical Society and came into being once the idea of climbing the world's highest mountain had taken root in the climbing establishment. They were unique in another respect: personal relationships among members when actually on expedition were frequently happy, but the same cannot be said of the organization as a whole. The machinations of the Everest Committee turned out to be no different from those of any other committee. By contrast with many of the private expeditions of the time, which were successful, the Everest expeditions failed before that of 1953, itself a successor to the modified "Committee" expedition of 1938.

Smythe first appears upon the Everest scene as an unsuccessful candidate for the 1924 expedition. At the time of selection, he was a mere 23 years old. He had had an unusually extensive experience for his age, but he was, nevertheless, young, totally without Himalayan experience and, perhaps most important of all, insufficiently well connected. He had, as we have seen, met T. H. Somervell during his early Yorkshire Rambler days and had climbed with him at Almscliff and in the Lakes, and was, after Somervell had returned from the 1922 expedition, to climb with him in the Dolomites and, in preparation for the 1924 expedition, in the Bernese Oberland. But, while Smythe

★See p.214 for a map showing Everest

could quite properly have been declined because more able and experienced participants were available (although if this were admitted, it becomes extraordinarily hard to make out any sort of case for the inclusion of Sandy Irvine), he was condemned on Somervell's unfavourable report:

> A bad mountaineer, always slipping and knocking stones down and an intolerable companion. Nobody in our party could stick him for more than a few days, owing to his irritating self-sufficiency. However, he is a very good goer for his age (23 or 24) and carries on well without getting tired himself, though his incessant conversation makes others tired.

This is an extraordinary catalogue of charges, and it did not inhibit Somervell from using him as a workhorse in the Alps, testing equipment for the 1924 expedition, or from climbing with Smythe in the Dolomites in 1923. Perhaps Somervell's major criticism lay elsewhere. If so, he was not alone in finding Smythe lacking in the social graces. Others found him to be odd, irresponsible, categorical and dogmatic. But it seems peculiar, in the context of selection for a mountaineering expedition to remote heights, to find "self-sufficiency" listed as a vice.

The simple fact of the matter is that Smythe's face didn't fit. Somervell's did. He was a Christian gentleman with impeccable establishment credentials of whom Sir Francis Younghusband, doyen of that establishment and one of the prime movers and most active members of the Committee to which Somervell reported, was later to write, in his foreword to Somervell's *After Everest* (1936): "He is a thorough-going English Christian, with all the gay courage of the unadulterated Englishman and all his incapacity to see anything but good in the worst." *Res ipsa loquitur*; Younghusband clearly forgot that on at least one occasion Somervell had risen above his limitations and contrived to detect some evil in the young Smythe.

The selection of Irvine for the 1924 expedition provides an interesting contrast. Irvine was only twenty-one but had rowed for Oxford and created a good impression on a college expedition to Spitzbergen. He had some unspecified experience of climbing in Wales and the Oberland. He was proposed by George Abraham, endorsed by Meade, supported by Odell and selected within a fortnight. Perhaps most significant of all, he turned out to be on close terms with

Mallory who would have liked to share a cabin with him on the voyage out but who was frustrated in this respect by the prior allocation of the berth to another expedition member. Mallory's later preference of Irvine as a summit-bid companion rather than either Odell or Norton was distinctly odd. Smythe later said so unambiguously; Longstaff commented upon it; R. L. G. Irving made the point in more subdued terms. Irvine did sterling work of the donkey variety on the 1924 expedition, and it would have been an extraordinary man who, offered a place, would have declined it. Irvine seized his luck, for luck it was, with the possible consequence that Everest was not climbed. Irvine, like Gino Watkins, was one of those golden boys who made a name at school, embellished it at Oxbridge, became known, and attracted an extraordinary reverence very early in life.

The same clique, drawn from the higher echelons of the Alpine Club and the Royal Geographical Society, was still in charge when permission next came from Lhasa for an attempt on Everest to be made in 1933. By this time, Smythe was at his personal peak and there was no way he could be overlooked.

The Committee first had to choose a leader. It has been said, with considerable justification, that Smythe was the obvious man. As a climber he was universally regarded as the man most likely to succeed. As a climber *and* leader, he had succeeded, on Kamet, in the most comprehensive way imaginable. He had the Kangchenjunga experience behind him. And the Kamet team which he led was likely to, and in the event did, form the core of the 1933 party.

The Committee was denied the services of Norton and Geoffrey Bruce, both tied up on military duties. George Finch, never in any case popular with the Committee, had retired from climbing. Odell and Crawford were available and it is not obvious why they were bypassed; Crawford, particularly, considered himself to be leadership material and the discussions which preceded the 1936 Expedition showed that he did not lack support. None of the other survivors of the 1920s' expeditions was both available and young enough, but there was one man who had applied to go on the 1924 expedition at the prime of his climbing life and been rejected. This was Hugh Ruttledge. The Committee turned to him and he was appointed leader at the age of forty-four and on the explicit understanding that he was not expected to go high.

Responsibility for the failure of the 1933 expedition to reach the summit can hardly be laid at Ruttledge's door. In the Indian Civil Service, he had considerable experience of the Himalaya; the expedition was reasonably well-organized. Ruttledge seems to have had the happy knack, at least on the 1933 expedition, of giving his lead climbers their heads when appropriate, but he was not afraid of asserting his authority when it was desirable for him to do so. The fact remains that the mantle was thrust upon him, and no matter what his qualities or the opinions of others, he himself doubted the choice, was aware of his limitations, and had already been told by the Committee, in other circumstances and when in his personal prime, that he was not good enough even to go. One suspects that, had it been left to Ruttledge, a fair-minded man, he might well have selected Smythe as leader.

There is no evidence that Smythe was considered for the leadership, at all events formally, though it seems incredible that his name should never have passed across the minds of those charged with the duty of appointment. Rather, there seems to have been a tacit unanimity to leave him out of the running. In view of his record, some attempt at explanation is required.

First of all, his deferment has to be considered against the background of the times. His predecessors as leaders of Everest expeditions (Howard-Bury, Bruce, and, after Bruce's collapse on the walk-in in 1924, Norton) were all army officers with a wide experience of India, which suggests that the most important qualification was what is described as "leadership ability" rather than climbing prowess. This mysterious quality was, in those days, associated with going to the right school and the right university. It was not peculiar to officers in the armed services, but was an essential qualification for a successful career in such a capacity. In the Himalaya, mountaineering involved an expedition, the conducting of a campaign against an adversary which, if successful, would result in conquest. This chief quality, then, was man-management but of the right sort. It did not matter that Smythe had already led a successful expedition; he remained a failed product of a second-rank school who had attended no university, let alone the right one, who had never distinguished himself in any athletic sphere and whose only lasting links with the mountaineering establishment, apart from those forged by membership of the Yorkshire Ramblers, came at a later stage. His one short flirtation with a service career, in the RAF, had ended ignominiously in his being invalided out. He was not the type. It is not, of course, argued that the source to which the Committee looked was incapable of producing the right sort of leader: Bruce and Norton seem to have been exemplary in that capacity and if the proposition ever needed vindication it surely got it with John Hunt's triumph in 1953. What was wrong was the apparent belief that this was the only background from which such a man could emerge.

Smythe did not think so, and this was his second sin. During the early part of his mountaineering career, his interest in Everest amounted almost to an obsession, and he clearly thought about it a great deal. After his Kangchenjunga and Kamet experiences he had dared to present the Committee with a lengthy memorandum on how to mount a successful Everest expedition. We may safely assume that this communication would not have been well received by a Committee conscious of the fact that it had on two previous occasions failed to deliver the promised goods to a voracious British public. And if the memorandum did not get the message across, an application by Smythe for permission to lead a private expedition to Everest must certainly have done so.

There was a third and more subtle reason. In the age of the amateur there was, about Smythe, the stench of professionalism. It is not so much that Smythe made money out of his mountaineering by writing about it. Many others, including stalwarts of the climbing establishment, did that. Smythe's vice seems to have been that he actually needed his earnings from this source—he lived on them, and came to live reasonably well on them.

Finally, since the pre-war Everest expeditions were designed by Committee and, until the 1938 expedition, the Committee kept a fairly tight rein on the composition of parties, no matter who led, the team would have to include the best climbers from within the establishment; and it cannot be assumed either that they would all gladly have accepted Smythe's leadership, as would a team selected entirely by him, or that his personality was up to asserting such leadership. The members of the Kamet expedition were hand-picked by Smythe. It was his drive which initiated the adventure and his motivation which inspired it. His organization was exemplary and he assumed and discharged responsibility quietly and efficiently. An Everest Committee expedition was bound, inevitably, to be different in crucial respects.

Whilst it might be possible to overlook Smythe's claims to the leadership there was no escaping the fact that his record unambiguously established that as a climber he was the man most likely to succeed in climbing Everest and his membership of the party was a foregone conclusion. Odell and Crawford survived from the 1920s expeditions along with Shebbeare as a transport officer. The Kamet team yielded, in addition to Smythe, Shipton, Birnie and Greene. Other old acquaintances of Smythe who were included were Wood Johnson who had served so well on Dyhrenfurth's Kangchenjunga expedition in 1930, and Jack Longland with whom Smythe had climbed in Wales, particularly on the celebrated "Longland's" on Cloggy.

Smythe joined up with the others in Darjeeling at the end of February. The advance party set out on 3 March and the rest five days later. By 17 April, they were at Base Camp and on 2 May, Smythe, Shipton and porters left Camp Two and established Camp Three at what was now becoming the customary site on a side moraine beneath the east face of the north peak of Everest, or Changtse. Before nightfall, a walk on the glacier gave Smythe his first view of the North Col and after losing the next day to foul weather, Boustead, Shipton, Longland and Smythe were able to set out to reconnoitre a route up to it.

The North Col was the key to the North Ridge which was long regarded as the only feasible route to the summit, and which finally fell to a Chinese expedition in 1960, if their accounts are to be believed. The technical difficulties of the route are concentrated in two sections: first the slopes leading up to the North Col, between approximately 22,500 and 24,500 feet; the second involves negotiating the first and second steps above the north east shoulder at a height of around 28,000 feet, or turning them via the Great Couloir which breaches them to the west. These latter difficulties are obviously much complicated by altitude and cold.

The degree of difficulty presented by the North Col slopes varies from year to year. Steep and glaciated, the face is in a state of constant motion, usually imperceptible but occasionally in the form of ice avalanches which have claimed a number of lives. The problem is one of finding and, if necessary, improving a way through a maze of crevasses and ice-cliffs which will prove passable for porters carrying to Camp Four, pitched on or near the Col, and functioning as an advanced base for the servicing of higher camps. Pre-war Everest expeditions followed a pattern of establishing Camp Five at about 25,500 feet and Camp Six at 27,000 feet plus, from which summit assaults were launched.

On the first reconnaissance, Longland was obliged to retreat by reason of illness before confronting the North Col slopes but Smythe, Shipton and Boustead got straight at it. Taking it in turns, they kicked steps up the first relatively easy 400 feet, taking an hour and a half to do so, and then started cutting up a steeper section before calling it a day and returning to camp. A fierce wind the next day prevented a resumption of the work although others made the journey from Camp Two and fortified the Camp Three party for the actual assault. In spite of continuing foul weather, this began in earnest on 7 May.

It was Birnie, Boustead, Longland, Ruttledge, Shipton and Smythe who were charged with the task. Nima Tendrup and Pasang carried gear to equip the route. The start was not auspicious: Pasang had to retreat and Nima Tendrup was not going well; the initial work done two days previously had been negated by the wind and cutting would have to begin again. The ferocious wind descending from the Col prevented even that, and they all retreated to Camp Three.

In order to avoid fatigue from the long trudge back and forth between Camp Three and the foot of the North Col slopes each day, Ruttledge decided to establish a temporary camp, Camp Three A, at the foot of the slopes. The following day Greene, Longland, Shipton and Smythe set off; Wager, Wyn Harris, Birnie and Boustead were to follow up as a second shift party. After Camp Three A was set up the afternoon was spent re-establishing the route on the lower slopes and fixing rope up the first 200 feet of the steeper section above, beneath a large crevasse. That proved to be all that was possible until 12 May due to heavy snowfall, carrying with it the risk of avalanche. It was Boustead and Wager who set about clearing a way until the steeper section was reached when Shipton and Smythe took over the lead, cutting up the slope which reached 50 degrees just below the great crevasse. After a short rest there, the party proceeded, entering a snow-bowl which soon swept up to what, in 1933, was the crux of the North Col section, an ice-cliff which stretched across the full length of the accessible slopes, reaching a height of over 100 feet but, at its weakest point, 40 feet in height, the first fifteen vertical to overhanging. In all other respects vicious, it had for Smythe the virtue of being not quite so intimidating as the Kangchenjunga wall which he, Schneider and Wieland had scaled.

The lead again fell to Smythe. Tensioned on an ice-piton (an extremely rare instance of artificial climbing by Smythe!) he managed to cut holds up to the bulge which marked the top of the overhanging section. Exhausted by the effort of labouring at the rubbery, plastic ice (hand- as well as foot-holds had had to be cut and his fingers were lifeless), he descended for a rest and then went up again and, at the second effort, managed to haul himself into a large step cut into the 70 degree wall that crowned the overhanging section. There remained an even longer and still demanding stretch of cutting before first hard névé and then good snow was reached and he was able to tread a platform, belay himself and rest. He then brought up Shipton. The two of them were able to find a way through the easier slopes above and reach the shelf below the Col which had been fixed upon as a possible camp-site before descending to Camp Three A, a great day's work behind them.

Measured against the technical standards of the day, Smythe's lead of the ice-wall was climbing of the highest order. Notwithstanding that Smythe himself rated it easier than the wall on Kangchenjunga, others in the party recognized it as a remarkable piece of work and one experienced colleague, years later, reckoned it the finest piece of ice-work he had ever seen. Its immediate effect, though, was to raise and dash hopes, and lead to retreat and frustration before the party really came to grips with the mountain. Camp Five was eventually established, after the first attempt had subsided in disagreement or misunderstanding in trying weather conditions, and sterling work of the less glamorous but equally necessary type had ensured that Camp Four, below the Col, was sufficiently well-stocked for there to be no obstacle to the establishment of the high camps on that account. As events worked out, although it had been contemplated that it would be Shipton and Smythe who would be the spearhead of the attack on the summit, it was Wyn Harris, Greene, Birnie and Boustead who were in position to establish Camp Six, should the opportunity arise, and it was now intended that Wyn Harris and Greene should sleep there and mount the first attempt. But Greene, unfortunately, had spent himself, and Wager took his place. Shipton and Smythe were to follow up the next day and make the second attempt, weather permitting.

It did not permit even the establishment of Camp Six. When Smythe and Shipton arrived at Camp Five to discover that none of the sitting tenants had been able to move up, two of them volunteered to go down and thus vacate places for Shipton and Smythe, but to no avail. The weather pinned them down in Camp Five and although there was talk of a dash to the summit from there, sanity prevailed and after two days of inaction, dwindling stocks of food made it necessary for the whole party to retreat and regroup. The biting hurricane had taken its toll, particularly of porters, most of whom were suffering from frostbite in some degree, two seriously.

The weather had also had its effects on Camp Four which, situated some 200 feet below the crest of the Col, was now threatened by avalanches from the slope of freshly-accumulated snow above. It had to be struck and repitched on the Col itself. There, Wyn Harris, Wager, Longland, Birnie, Shipton and Smythe were to remain, if necessary for two or three weeks in order to be in a position to launch an attack with the minimum of delay should the opportunity arise. But time was pressing: news had arrived that the monsoon was developing and its arrival would put a stop to all further attempts.

At last there was a break in the weather. The first good day had, frustratingly, to be devoted to getting up porters and further supplies from Camp Three but, on the morning of 28 May, Wyn Harris, Wager, Longland and Birnie were able to set off for Camp Five and it was obvious to Smythe and Shipton on the next day that they, with the exception of Birnie who had had to descend because of an injured leg, would proceed to establish Camp Six. Smythe and Shipton accordingly set off for Camp Five and duly arrived pretty well exhausted in deteriorating weather eventually to greet Longland after his epic descent with the porters from Camp Six which had been successfully set up at 27,400 feet. Wyn Harris and Wager had remained there, poised for a summit attempt on the following day.

In a sense, Wager and Wyn Harris were stalking horses. Previous expeditions had not given a clear view whether the route via the ridge or that via the Great Couloir offered the better possibility. Both had been reconnoitred. Norton and Somervell had concluded in favour of a traverse, later named after Norton, across the Yellow Band to the right so as to seek access to the summit pyramid via the Great Couloir. It had remained Mallory's opinion, however, that the route via the second step and the ridge was to be preferred and it was to this that he had committed himself and Irvine in 1924, with what results, other than their disappearance, it was not known.

The primary responsibility of Wager and Wyn Harris was to explore possible routes, and this they discharged in exemplary fashion, reporting to Smythe and Shipton in favour of Norton's Traverse when they met at Camp Six on 30 May. In a long and exhausting day they had first climbed diagonally to the left in order to get a close look at the ridge but concluded that the serrated section between the first and second steps would alone prove too difficult and had failed to find any feasible way of avoiding it. They had then traversed over to the Great Couloir and arrived there too tired and late in the day to summon up the spirit to tackle the slabby buttresses, covered in powder-snow, which offered the only exit at the far side of the couloir. It was possible that a less exhausted pair concentrating on the couloir, and arriving there earlier in the day, might be able to force a way and that was the choice of Smythe and Shipton.

The following day a blizzard confined them to the small tent. In retrospect, it probably finished what chance they ever had. Neither Shipton nor Smythe was fully fit and Shipton in particular found his condition deteriorating in the course of the day. Smythe, by contrast, felt the need for a day of recuperation. The difference in condition between the two men soon revealed itself when, a day later, they left the Camp at 7 a.m. on a morning which had started inauspiciously but then, surprisingly, cleared. Neither, initially, was in good form but weeks of poor diet and hard work on the mountain had taken their toll of Shipton and, although Smythe began to feel stronger once they were on the move, Shipton deteriorated and was eventually obliged to call a halt short of the Great Couloir. This situation had been contemplated beforehand and they agreed that Smythe should proceed alone. Shipton intended to follow if he could and, indeed, later set out again but, realizing that this might prompt Smythe to wait for him, eventually went down.

As Smythe moved steadily up, he was able to confirm Wyn Harris's and Wager's opinion of the ridge route and he made his way across the top of the Yellow Band, beneath a sheer wall, partly on outward-sloping slabby rock, partly on unexpectedly consolidated snow that meant exhausting step-cutting. The slow going which the removal of powder-snow from the rocks required was less demanding and Smythe was feeling in reasonably good shape as he approached the couloir. Even before he could see his way clear to traverse round into it he had sight of its far bank, and confidence ebbed. The buttress which he had thought he could climb to avoid the continuation of the second step above, and gain access to the summit pyramid, was plastered with fresh snow; the wind had hardly touched it. A subsidiary couloir which might offer a way was likely to be full of unstable powder and not a reasonable proposition.

Smythe did not abandon hope entirely. He first tried to edge round a steep little arête of rock on a barely sufficient ledge, then funked it and descended some twenty feet to another ledge offering easier access, and so made his way into the bed of the Great Couloir. The others who had progressed this far, Norton, Wyn Harris and Wager, had found loose, uncertain snow but Smythe, possibly at a slightly lower point, found it well-hardened and had to cut steps across. It was when he reached the rocks of the buttress at the far side that his hope waned. Although steep, the buttress was sufficiently broken and well-supplied with holds to suggest that in good, dry conditions, it could safely be passed by simple balance climbing, but the holds were all outward-sloping ledges covered in dry, sugary snow, that turned any attempt into a fearful lottery, for a slip would almost certainly be halted only by the Rongbuk Glacier thousands of feet below at the foot of the couloir. With no ambition left other than to get as high as possible, Smythe climbed up gingerly from ledge to ledge, supporting himself with his axe where he could. Suddenly, a hold broke and momentarily both feet were unsupported; only the axe prevented a fatal slip. He found himself oddly unconcerned; he later described his state of mind as comparable to that of a drunken driver whose capacities are substantially impaired but who confidently believes himself to be unaffected.

About 50 feet up, he checked his watch. Those 50 feet had taken him an hour and there were still 300 feet to go before the easier ground at the lower part of the summit pyramid was reached. He could see the summit less than 1,000 feet above. With support, he might have gone on, but the danger, and mental and physical fatigue, added to the loneliness, at last proved too much.

He remained there for some little time, almost instinctively pulling out a camera and taking the world's highest photograph. No doubt like many others on Everest at that period, he had dreamed for years of seizing the chance to stand on the summit. It was now separated from him by no greater distance than is Glyder Fach from Bwlch Tryfan, or Great End above Styhead, yet it was no more readily accessible than was the moon. He wrote, afterwards:

> I cannot enlarge on the bitterness of defeat. Those who have failed on Everest are unanimous in one thing: the relief of not having to go on outweighs all other considerations. The last 1,000 feet of Everest are not for mere flesh and blood. Whoever reaches the summit, if he does it without artificial aid, will have to rise godlike above his own frailties and his tremendous environment. Only through a Power within him and without him will he overcome a deadly fatigue and win through to success.

Almost certainly, until then, Smythe had believed that he would climb Everest in pure style. Thereafter, he never rose above doubt; he changed his mind about oxygen and came to conclude that it would require an improbable coincidence of circumstances to be crowned with success.

He set about the descent, and it is here that he describes the sense of being accompanied by another presence so real as to receive an offer of a mint when Smythe stopped for a break. It lent him a feeling of security and was probably the product of a mind distressed by a frightening solitude. With his strange companion he continued the descent and eventually, not without difficulty, returned to camp where Shipton, now somewhat recovered, welcomed him with a hot drink. Each was resigned to failure; both craved rest and comfort. For Shipton, feeling better, this desire suggested descent and he set off down to the relative comfort of Camp Five. Smythe, exhausted, preferred to stay where he was and therefore planned to go down the following morning.

As Longland had previously discovered, although the best route to Camp Five lay over relatively easy ground, poor visibility could create route-finding problems; any error could be catastrophic on the north-east face, over which it would be easy to wander. Shortly after Shipton left, bad weather struck and Shipton had a hard time of it on his way down. When Smythe awoke the following morning at Camp Six, it was soon obvious that a descent would pose problems. It was bitterly cold, an unusually severe blizzard overnight had deposited large amounts of fresh snow and the sky was scored with angry grey streaks of heavy cloud. If he was to get down at all, the sooner he started, the better.

Most of the difficulties were concentrated in the first few hundred feet and arose from the heavy snow complicating the hazards of otherwise relatively easy rock. When, some 50 feet above the bottom of the Yellow Band, Smythe could see his way clear, he stopped for a rest. No sooner had he done so than he was struck with immense force and without warning by a wind of hurricane strength which had him clinging to the rocks for dear life. The next few hundred feet were acutely dangerous. Smythe was several times nearly blown off the ridge and began to lose sensation not merely in toes and finger-tips but over his whole body. Just in time, he recognized his bearings and made his way over the crest of the north ridge and into its lee where a sheltered ledge enabled him to restore circulation at least to his body. But the descent had to be resumed and the struggle recommenced, though fortunately the wind abated somewhat with the height and Smythe at last arrived, exhausted, in sight of Camp Five. Here, two figures emerged but, in spite of his pathetic attempts to raise a shout, did no more than strike the tent and head off down to Camp Four. Too tired to cope with the effect of re-erecting the tent (in which, unknown to him, there was a Thermos flask of hot tea), he struggled on down to Camp Four and was reduced to resting every few yards before, nearing the camp, Longland spotted him and went out, with a hot drink, to meet him. A few minutes later and he was in the tent, being cosseted by McLean's cooking and massaged by a porter although some frostbite in toes and fingers remained.

The first and, so far as the 1933 expedition was concerned, effectively the last attempt ended there. The entire party left the mountain and retreated to Base Camp except for a skeleton crew of porters left in charge of gear and stocks at Camp Three. On 11 June, Crawford and Brocklebank set out again, and over the next three days all who were fit to do so, including Smythe, went up to join them. As soon as the mountain came into view, the prospect was discouraging. At Camp Three, they heard that the vanguard had been stopped by dangerous snow conditions on the slopes below the North Col. A delay of at least some days would be necessary before a further attempt was justified. Birnie, Crawford, Brocklebank and Smythe put it to use and made the ascent of the 23,000 foot peak which rises to the north of the Rapiu La, but that was the last climbing they did.

Ruttledge was forced to conclude that the 1933 expedition was over and to sound the retreat.

When permission next came from Lhasa for an attempt on Everest it was in respect of 1935 and 1936. Time did not permit a full-scale expedition in 1935 but the Everest Committee determined upon an attempt in 1936 and, at the promptings of Shipton, decided to send out a post-monsoon light-weight and cheap reconnaissance in 1935 under his leadership. Smythe did not go. As a reconnaissance it appears to have been a singular failure. It yielded no useful information not gleaned by Mallory in 1921; a glimpse into the Western Cwm prompted the opinion that a way up from that side could not be altogether ruled out, but it was to be fifteen years before exploration via Nepal established that this was to be the ultimately successful route. The party engaged in peak-bagging on a scale never before achieved in the Himalaya and no doubt greatly enjoyed the experience, but the cause of climbing Everest was advanced not one whit and the problem which faced the 1936 team was exactly that which had confronted all who had gone before.

Very soon after he had returned and reported to the Committee, Ruttledge had been asked by them to lead the next venture. Although personal relations had seemed superficially happy on the 1933 expedition, it turned out that a number of its members were far from contented with Ruttledge's leadership and unwilling to accept his reappointment. Crawford, in particular, was ambitious and his interest became known to Ruttledge who, gentleman that he was, sought to resign. Thus there were two factions, and in order to bring order into the affair, the Committee sought the views of the 1933 veterans. Longland, Wager and Brocklebank favoured Crawford. Smythe, whose word mattered more than most, and who by this time was probably resigned to the fact that in the Committee's eyes he would never be regarded as leadership material, favoured the continued appointment of Ruttledge in which view he was supported by Shipton and Wyn Harris. This fell somewhat short of a vote of confidence in Ruttledge's eyes and he persisted with his resignation, forcing the Committee to look elsewhere.

No one can accuse them of not scraping the barrel. They first of all invited Norton and Geoffrey Bruce but neither was available.

R. C. Wilson, whose experience was similar to that of Ruttledge's which many considered to be inadequate, was also unavailable. Two members of the Committee turned down offers of the leadership. Longstaff was considered but the Committee did not like his response and crossed his name off. John Morris, transport officer to the 1922 expedition, was considered, but thought not suitable. It was, however, only the military barrel that was scraped. It is hard to see what, if any, substantial objections could have been raised to Smythe's appointment. The 1933 experience could only be regarded as confirming his title, but he was not considered. He would clearly go on the expedition; it was tacitly accepted by all that he would be the unofficial climbing leader on the mountain and his word was most influential in the selection of members of the expedition but there was no question of *de jure* recognition of his *de facto* position. Quite apart from anything else, Graham Brown was now on the Committee of the Alpine Club, the halls of which were still resounding with echoes from his infamous row with Smythe over the credit for the Brenva Face climbs. At the end of the day, the Committee came back to Ruttledge and, after a narrow vote, he was finally persuaded to take on the job.

Smythe, Shipton and Wyn Harris from the 1933 expedition joined the team and Smijth-Windham was again put in charge of radio communications. They were joined by Kempson, Warren and Wigram who had been on the 1935 reconnaissance and, on Smythe's recommendation (he had climbed with them in the Alps) J. M. L. Gavin and P. R. Oliver with whom Smythe was to climb from the Bhyundar Valley in the following year. There were some surprising omissions: Tilman had been on the reconnaissance expedition and, as a result of experience there, was assumed to be incapable of going high; and Odell was not invited, apparently because he had declined a place in 1933 for business reasons. These two replied in the most effective way imaginable by succeeding on Nanda Devi, then and for some years to come the highest mountain ascended by man. Also among the omissions was Colin Kirkus. Kirkus was at the time thought to be the finest rock climber in Britain and history has only confirmed that opinion. He had accompanied Pallis on an expedition to the Kumaon in 1933. However, when he had climbed in the Alps with Smythe the previous winter, Smythe had formed an unfavourable impression of his abilities. Longland, although invited, considered it inconsistent with his opposition to Ruttledge's appointment to accept. The 1936 team thus lacked the two finest British rock-climbers of the twenties and thirties. Crawford, not surprisingly, was not asked.

Those who were not selected (and it would have been possible to construct a pretty fair Everest team out of them) had the last laugh. The 1936 expedition can be considered to have been successful on only two fronts: it gave birth to the biggest and glossiest expedition book to date; and a genuinely good time seems to have been had by all, at least so far as personal relationships were concerned.

The credit for both rests largely with Ruttledge. The controversy over the leadership selection must have left him aware of his alleged shortcomings and in so far as he could not, as an essentially good and fair-minded man, deny them, he sought to provide for them. By way of justification, he confined himself to the valid point that a climbing leader might on occasion find himself out of touch with the expedition at the sharp end of the assault and there was therefore something to be said for having, as leader, one who was not expected to go very high. Otherwise, he recognized the problems and sought to overcome them by consultation and delegation. In selecting the team, he had relied heavily on Smythe and, on the walk-in, he formally appointed him second-in-command, an act which was well-received by the others. In planning the assault, he took the advice of Smythe, Shipton and Wyn Harris and involved also Morris and Karma Paul in settling the details of particular camps. There was general concurrence in his nomination of Smythe and Shipton as the first summit party; Wyn Harris and Kempson were detailed to form the second although the latter volunteered to stand down in favour of Warren if need be. Failing this, Warren would be in the third pair with Oliver whilst the fourth was to consist of Gavin and Wigram. When the time came for the assault parties to move up to the North Col, Ruttledge supplied Smythe with a written brief but also gave him wide discretion for its implementation.

There were differences, but they were almost all of a superficial character. Ruttledge was given to poking good-natured fun at Smythe—he called him a sybarite for suggesting that each climber should have a small tent to himself—and Smythe did not invariably take the fun in the way it was intended. When, after the summit parties had pushed danger to the limit and nevertheless failed, Smythe held forth upon the virtues of a bold, optimistic attitude towards the climb, Ruttledge accused him, at least semi-frivolously, of irresponsibility and sent him into a short-lived sulk. Interviewed years later, Kempson and Warren concurred in finding Smythe to have been dogmatic and given to self-justification. On the other hand, whilst the former charged him with throwing his weight about, the latter expressly exonerated him from any show of aggression.

Otherwise, and especially so far as climbing Everest was concerned, the 1936 expedition was the least successful of all and the reason was quite simply the unusually early arrival of the monsoon.

Today, with vastly increased knowledge of the mountain and better equipment, it is possible to contemplate even winter ascents of Everest. Until recently, however, and with a considerable justification grounded in such experience as there was, it was believed that the ascent of Everest was only feasible during the relatively short period between the departure of winter and the onset of the monsoon, effectively during late May and June. Prior to the 1936 expedition, and on those occasions when it had been possible to observe the phenomenon, the monsoon had never arrived before the end of May. In 1936, it put a stop to further activity on 25 May, and the best laid plans were thwarted.

The walk-in proffered conflicting clues as to what was to happen. Early on, it was disquietingly warm, and confused cloud covered Chomiono and Kangchenjunga. When Everest first came into view it appeared to be in splendid condition: the north-west wind had blown the ridge clear of snow and it was possible to make out the buttress which had stopped Smythe in 1933 and to hope that the sun, which was shining full on it, would help. Optimism reigned and the climbers, Smythe and Shipton particularly, seized every opportunity to improve fitness and acclimatization; it was Smythe's view that both were more likely to be gained by making a series of ascents rather than by a gradual increase in altitude. Ruttledge's consultative planning ensured that things went smoothly, despite the customary blight of minor ailments, in Smythe's case some stomach trouble, and Base Camp and Camp One were established ahead of schedule; so much so that Smythe, Shipton and Ruttledge were able to advance the programme by a week and aim to be on the North Col by 15 May.

With this in mind, Smythe and Shipton left Camp Two with a

strong body of porters on 7 May. Previously, Camp Three had been situated a fair distance below the foot of the North Col slopes and Camp Three A had been placed to save time and energy in opening up the route. This time, Smythe and Shipton found a site half a mile nearer and set up Camp Three there. The others arrived over the next two days and, as soon as possible, Smythe, Shipton and Warren pushed on towards Camp Four. The slopes had changed considerably since 1933. The ice-wall which had been barely climbable then was now twice the height and avalanche debris littered the ground below. The only prospect was to start to the north where relatively easy slopes led up for 500 feet, then traverse across steep ground into the centre before making directly for the top up ice and névé at an angle of 50 degrees. Whilst not free from danger it had the merit of being safer than all alternatives.

A couple of days were lost to the weather (one, in any case, a rest day for the porters) but on the morning of 13 May it was possible to make a fresh start. Smythe, instructed by Ruttledge to do as little work as possible, as was Shipton, led off with Gavin and Rinzing. Wigram, Oliver and three of the best porters followed; Kempson, Warren and Ruttledge, concerned to make a first-hand assessment of conditions, brought up the rear. Smythe selected a line which seemed most safe from any avalanches that might fall from the slopes of North Peak and Rinzing wielded the axe in, according to Oliver, a most expert manner. It took three hours to make and equip the route over the first 500 feet, then Smythe set off on a leftward traverse which needed some hard step-cutting until a shelf above the 1933 wall was reached. Here, Gavin and Oliver changed places, and Oliver and Smythe took turns cutting steps up the steep ice leading to the crest of the Col 300 feet above. At 3.30 p.m., five and a half hours after he started, Smythe hauled himself over the top. Oliver followed a minute later. Wigram and Gavin were near to exhaustion; Smythe considered it the hardest day's work he had ever done but the route had been opened and equipped in a single day, the North Col gained and the party put in a position where, weather permitting, the chances were the best ever.

May 14 dawned fine and clear and Wyn Harris and Kempson were able to lead 46 porters up to the Col to establish Camp Four. Next day, Smythe and Shipton went up with 50 porters, including the 36 who were to remain on the Col to help establish the higher camps with Smythe and Shipton. That evening, Smythe reported that whilst it might be possible to establish the higher camps, there was too much snow for Norton's traverse to be a practicable proposition. It was best to wait. By the 17 May, conditions had deteriorated; by 18 May, there was up to two feet of fresh snow on the Col and both Shipton and Smythe counselled a tactical retreat until the weather improved. Smythe led the hazardous descent. It was effectively the final retreat of the 1936 expedition, although no one realized it at the time. Most of the climbers, other than Smythe, were suffering from minor ailments; it would be at least a week before the mountain came into condition; the physical and mental health of the party would be best served by a "holiday" and Ruttledge ordered a withdrawal to Camp One.

The next approach was determined not so much by any signs of improvement on the mountain—there were none—as by news that the monsoon had reached Darjeeling. If there was to be any chance at all of tackling the summit, it was now or never, and most probably never. Shipton and Smythe strove to scrape together the makings of optimism and on 23 May these two, with Gavin and Ruttledge went up to Camp Two, continuing to Camp Three on 24 May. Halfway there, the bad weather set in. When they looked out on the morning of 25 May, it was obvious that there could be no further advance for some time. In desperation, Shipton, Oliver and Gavin went off to the Rapiu La and went some way up the north-east ridge, which remains unclimbed to this day and which claimed the lives of Boardman and Tasker on the 1982 attempt. By 28 May, there was nothing for it but to order another withdrawal, again in storm, to Camp One.

The mountain, however, had not yet finished toying with them. The clear dawn and propitious north-west wind which ushered in 29 May were fortified by news of a "window" in the monsoon, and a new advance was fixed for 30 May. Blizzard conditions kept them in Camp Two for some days, but they then pressed on to Camp Three by 3 June where, after a close examination of the North Col slopes, Smythe, Shipton and Kempson reported that, given great caution, a further venture up them was justified. Early the following morning, Wyn Harris and Kempson set out to restore the route up the first 500 feet, followed closely by Smythe. They soon discovered that an avalanche had fallen directly across their route and debated whether or not it was right to continue. Smythe took the lead but soon concluded that the previous route along the traverse was now suicidal and set about cutting straight up extremely steep ice, just the start of about 500 feet of very difficult climbing. It was a last, desperate attempt. There was never any prospect of carving out a route suitable for porters. Shipton realized this and ordered down the porters who were following. Smythe soon concluded that the game was up and concentrated his efforts instead upon getting the whole party down safely.

It seems likely that, allowing the attempt to be thus pressed, desire and frustration had overcome their judgment. If proof were required, it was provided the next day when Shipton and Wyn Harris persuaded Ruttledge to grant one final look at the slopes and, for their trouble, were caught in an avalanche, fortunately suffering nothing more serious than fright and bruises. Even then, hope was not utterly abandoned: Smythe persuaded Ruttledge that even if the eastern approach to the North Col was now closed, some benefit at least for future expeditions might be gained by exploring the possibilities of a western approach up the Rongbuk Glacier, never before thoroughly examined; secretly, Smythe hoped that a summit attempt might still be possible and, had Ruttledge not restrained him, he might well have pressed things further. As it was, they contented themselves with the revised judgment that the western approach might well prove preferable and feasible in post-monsoon conditions and, with that small gain, left the mountain.

In spite of its inauspicious start, the failure of the 1936 expedition was nobody's fault. Certainly, the Committee made a shocking mess of the leadership selection—Ruttledge was perhaps not the very best man for the job—but the net result of the errors in selection was that the team which went out, although strong, was not the strongest that could have been formed. These errors and omissions, however, cost nothing at the end of the day: until the establishment of Camp Four on 15 May, every phase of the expedition had been carried through in exemplary manner. Thereafter, the weather would have put a stop to an attempt by any party. The most meticulous search for errors, however minor, which might have affected the eventual outcome yields nothing.

In the same way that success would have had the effect of justifying plainly wrong and perverse decisions, so also failure was taken to indicate that some features of the 1936 expedition, although in fact causally unconnected with failure, nevertheless required reconsideration. The result was that when the next expedition came into prospect a year later, changes were made.

For some time the vogue away from vast expeditions of battalion proportions and towards the smaller expedition had been growing. Its advocates were, up to a point, harking back to the early days of Himalayan exploration and ventures such as Longstaff's ascent of Trisul. Smythe was an early proponent, although his variant of the argument involved some concessions to size and difficulty and he recognized that Everest required a bigger team than Trisul: his "horses for courses" approach had been adopted on Kamet and he remained sympathetic. But by the mid-1930s the chief protagonists of the "small" expedition were Tilman and Shipton. Tilman, indeed, was solitary almost to the point of solipsism and, polemically no doubt, considered two to be large. He had, however, followed Smythe in putting his principles into practice and, having been rejected for the Everest expedition of 1936, joined in the organization of an expedition which, refused permission for its first choice, Kangchenjunga, succeeded in climbing Nanda Devi.

The failure of the 1936 expedition could in no way be attributed to its size, but it showed that a large expedition was by no means assured of success and it did nothing to falsify the argument that a smaller expedition might do just as well. In any case, money was by now in short supply and economics pointed in the direction of a small expedition even if the logic was not compelling.

Similarly, it was in no way due to a failure of leadership on the part of Ruttledge that the 1936 expedition did not gain its objective. Success might have vindicated a leader of organizational ability, but failure offered no reply to those who had argued that Everest was now a mountaineering problem and the leader should therefore be, first and foremost, an outstanding climber.

The Everest Committee had learned another lesson from the embarrassing quarrel over the leadership of the 1936 expedition and this time did not proceed to a choice without consultation. Instead, they discussed the matter with Shipton, Smythe and Warren, and with Tilman whose only flirtation with Everest had been on the 1935 expedition when he had been unable to go high. It was, nevertheless, Tilman who, a month later, emerged as leader, although no announcement was to be made for the time being. A rather strange development, later in the year, possibly sheds some light. Longstaff was almost the patron saint of the small expedition lobby and had allied himself with their aims. He had become friendly with Tilman, and when the Committee found itself short of finance for the expedition, he stepped forward with an offer which the Committee seems to have been unable to resist. Longstaff was prepared to put up £3000, more than enough to finance the sort of "small" expedition Tilman had in mind, provided that either Tilman or Shipton was confirmed as leader.

Writing in 1950, Longstaff hints, *en passant*, that the justification for Tilman's appointment lay in "a record in Africa and the Himalaya second to none" but this opinion is somewhat hyperbolic. Tilman had a good record: its high points were the traverse of Mount Kenya with Shipton in 1930, the discovery of a feasible route into the Nanda Devi sanctuary with the same partner in 1934 and the ascent of that mountain in 1936. But though a good record, it hardly stood comparison with that of Shipton or Smythe or even, for that matter, Odell, who had done practically all that Tilman had done and performed quite remarkably on Everest. Odell later let it be known that he thought that there had been serious errors in the mounting of the 1938 expedition. However, it is doubtful whether it could have succeeded as conditions were never ideal.

With the example of 1936 before them, the party had reached Rongbuk by 6 April. In addition to Smythe and Shipton it included Odell and Peter Lloyd, both of whom had been on the Nanda Devi expedition with Tilman, and Warren whom Tilman had first been reluctant to invite. The seventh member was Oliver, a veteran of the 1936 expedition. Tilman had wanted Longland but he was not available.

On 9 April, they set about establishing Base Camp. Camp One was set up on 13 April and almost immediately Tilman and Oliver set off with the first relay of stores for Camp Two which was occupied on 18 April. By 26 April, the entire party was assembled at Camp Three which was fully stocked. This was by far the longest time taken by any expedition although it was also the earliest date on which Camp Three had been completed. There were a number of reasons: the expedition started very early and was in no rush; Shipton and Smythe were both of the view that no serious attempt could be mounted until the end of May and it was clearly too bitterly cold to proceed when the party first arrived in the area. They had tackled the establishment of the first three camps in a leisurely manner partly because they had been plagued by minor illnesses—Tilman had gone sick and retreated to Rongbuk—and partly because each of the reduced number of porters had to make more carries, four relays being required for the establishment of each camp.

It was part of Tilman's plan that Shipton and Smythe, upon whom primary hopes for the summit were again fixed, should not exhaust themselves on work lower down, but should be wrapped in cotton wool and brought out only when needed. They were scheduled to go down to the Kharta Valley to graze, and, with Oliver, duly set off on 27 April. Cold and inactivity drove the rest to join them two days later and there they all stayed until the middle of May, Tilman with "a bad cough, a worse cold, stiff legs, and a temperature." Although porters had been left behind to move Camp Three nearer to the North Col slopes after a rest in Rongbuk, the cold had been inauspicious and, in his report on the expedition, Tilman refers to the period after the retreat as consisting of six days of unabated cold and wind followed by seven days of heavy snow, at Camp Three. The purported source for this information was the porters left behind. The only facts of which there was direct evidence were that, whilst the mountain had been unusually clear of snow when they left Camp Three (when it was too cold to go any further), it was covered and clearly unclimbable when next seen by the main party, returning via Rongbuk, on their way up the East Rongbuk Glacier to Camp Three which they occupied on 18 May.

They began work on the North Col slopes the following morning; although intermittent snow showers fell, they prompted only temporary discouragement, not despair. A line nearer to the centre of the slopes was chosen not because it was the easiest option but in order to avoid the traverse on which Shipton and Wyn Harris had been caught by an avalanche in 1936. Nevertheless, a short traverse to the left, about 300 feet from the top, was necessary and, with the porters who were making the passage crowding together, an avalanche, fortunately without serious consequences, was provoked. Odell and Tilman completed the traverse and by the time the route thus far had been improved and equipped they called it a day.

Smythe and Shipton, meanwhile, had returned via the Lhakpa La;

and further snow that night, which reminded them of the avalanche-potential of the North Col slopes, led to the adoption of a contingency plan. One of the few fruits of the 1936 expedition had been to suggest that the western approach to the North Col might be useful when snow conditions rendered the eastern approach unjustifiable. In spite of the resolve to save Shipton and Smythe for better things, they were given this task, to be carried out concurrently with a continuation of efforts on the eastern side. The reasoning, that this would double the chances of reaching the North Col, might well have a place if applied to a large expedition. In relation to a small one, it is arguable that, far from doubling the chances, it would spread scarce resources to such an extent as to render them negligible.

The contingency did not arise for some days. A brief improvement in the weather again prompted interest in the eastern slopes and on 23 May Shipton, Tilman, Oliver and Smythe examined the slopes, found conditions reasonably good, and a fresh start on 24 May was decided upon. Smythe and Shipton set out at 6 a.m. and by 9.30 a.m. stood on the Col. Others followed, equipping the route and leading porters. Smythe and Tilman took another fifteen porters up the next day and hopefully inspected the route above, but it remained draped in a mantle of impassable snow and there was no point in occupying a camp on the Col. There was, indeed, no point in Shipton and Smythe hanging about at Camp Three and they were to be sent down to Rongbuk to await events. Before they set off, another snow-fall revived thoughts about the western approach and the object of their retreat became not recuperation in Rongbuk but the reconnoitring and, if possible, opening up of the route on the far side of the Col. The rest, meantime, continued with the establishment of Camp Four via the eastern approach and eventually occupied it. They went further and made an effort to set up Camp Five with the young Tensing doing most of the work, but it was obviously pointless. The attempt was abandoned; and Camp Four was vacated.

Shipton and Smythe, together with Lloyd who had been convalescing at Rongbuk, were now establishing camps on the Rongbuk Glacier and Tilman ordered a conference at Lake Camp, the first of these. The chief result of the conference was a decision to abandon attempts from the eastern side, this was taken mainly in response to Smythe's urgings: he knew the ground better than anyone and regarded it as being wholly unsafe when, as had now come to be recognized, the monsoon had started. From then on, such hopes as remained were pinned on an ascent from the western side.

Oliver, who had accompanied Tilman, went down to arrange the support. Shipton, Smythe, Lloyd and Tilman headed up the Rongbuk Glacier. Over the next two days, they set up the North Face Camp, negotiated the easy ice-fall below the western slopes of the Col and established Camp Three (West) at about 21,500 feet in the middle of a broad snow terrace above the ice-fall and a mere few hundred yards from the foot of the slopes. The following morning, bitterly cold, saw Smythe and Lloyd breaking the trail, the rest following. The next 500 feet was up steep ice laid bare by an enormous avalanche over the cone of which they had made their way. They again reached more manageable snow, and 800 feet of hard-going led to the Col where Camp Four was again occupied.

It was 10 a.m. on the following morning, 6 June, before they were able to start for Camp Five; they were short of porters, and loads had to be rearranged. Smythe and Lloyd, who led off, found excellent going on well-consolidated snow up to 25,000 feet; then it abruptly ended and reverted to the heavy powder which seemed always to occupy the upper slopes. The porters, particularly Tensing, had gone well up to this point. Heavy going over the last 800 feet, however, soon took its toll and two of them collapsed with 700 feet still to go. A sudden snow-storm 300 feet below the camp-site almost brought things to a halt but finally, at 4 o'clock, the caravan arrived. Lloyd and Tilman went down almost immediately leaving Smythe, Shipton and seven porters in the camp. Looking back, Tilman noticed two of the Sherpas following; they were Tensing and Pasang. Not content with the carry to Camp Five, they had descended, picked up two abandoned loads, and re-ascended.

Any tendency towards hesitant optimism rapidly dissipated once Smythe, Shipton and the porters set off for Camp Six. A heavy wind had delayed them for a day but gave reason to hope that the ridge would have been cleared. It was not so; nor was there any recurrence of the consolidation which had made the going easier lower down. It was 4.15 before they reached a suitable site at 27,200 feet on a scree slope below the Yellow Band. The porters were utterly exhausted; it had been a truly magnificent piece of work on their part and if the Almighty were awarding points for effort this is when Tensing earned his right to be the first man to stand on the summit of Everest.

The work done, they descended leaving Shipton and Smythe in possession of Camp Six. Before 4 o'clock the following morning, these two started preparations for the attempt and were off before the sun reached the ridge, but the bitter cold drove them back, numbed, and they had to wait for the sun's rays to illuminate the slopes before they set off for a second time. Norton's traverse was out of the question, buried beneath banks of loose snow, and it was obvious also that the Great Couloir would be impassable. The only hope was that, in some strange way, a build-up of consolidated snow might have improved the ridge route and they headed in that direction. The next 40 yards took them an hour, struggling through the hip-deep snow. They pressed on but, reaching steeper ground, realized that they were in imminent danger from avalanche and had no effective choice but to give up.

Both men were in prime condition; that part of the planning at least had gone well. On the way down, they passed Lloyd (trying oxygen) and Tilman at Camp Five. This pair then went up to Camp Six and on 11 June made another attempt. They too, despite repeated efforts, were unable to reach the summit ridge and it was quite clear that if there had ever been a chance it had gone.

Almost certainly there never was a chance. There were two occasions on which the upper slopes appeared encouragingly clear of snow. On the second of these, new falls had obliterated them too soon. On the first, at the start of the assault, it was bitterly cold and Tilman settled upon retreat to the Kharta Valley to await events. He was not alone in his view that any attempt at that time would have invited serious frostbite—Shipton and Smythe concurred—but it was Tilman's decision to retreat to the Kharta, rather than to the more depressing Base Camp at Rongbuk, and it seems likely that he thus prevented the expedition from seizing any brief opportunities that might occur. Even then, several days would be needed from Camp Three, and the evidence is that no break in the weather was long enough.

The 1938 expedition left the case for the small expedition unproven. It did not stifle Tilman's advocacy of it—that was based in romance rather than reason. He defended his position by pointing out, as was the case, that the failure was not attributable to the size of the expedition. A large expedition would have found the going on the upper slopes equally impossible. Tilman considered that to place two teams of fit men above 27,000 feet, ready to seize an opportunity should it present itself, abundantly vindicated his philosophy. He has a point, but he does not consider whether he was justified. There is no doubt, of course, that all more than willingly exposed themselves to the risk; Smythe and Shipton in particular were desperate to climb the mountain. Nevertheless, the size of the expedition meant that it was stretched in order to stock the high camps at a fairly minimal level. The monsoon had started and it was quite on the cards that one or both of the assault teams might have found themselves marooned at a high camp for several days. Success would have vindicated the small expedition; tragedy would have condemned the philosophy. Neither transpired.

The 1938 expedition marked the end of Smythe's love affair with Everest. The war intervened and although he planned, afterwards, to return to the Himalaya he was dead by the time the next and ultimately successful British expedition was mounted in 1953. As a goal, it occupied his sights for the greater part of his mountaineering career; and he was not alone in this. Everest was the "third pole"—the remaining ultimate in adventure—and many were consumed with a burning ambition to be the first man to tread its summit. Although he remained obsessed, Smythe's attitude changed. Perhaps naively romantic at first, he came, eventually, almost to detest the mountain. Everest is essentially for masochists and he was no masochist. Much the greater part of any expedition was concerned with ancillary matters—walking in, establishing camps, waiting around. Even much of the climbing was not particularly interesting or challenging as such, merely painful. He further disliked the nationalistic air which came to surround the expeditions. He was not alone in regarding one of the most important products of success as being a return to more enjoyable, less trumpeted mountaineering on more interesting lower peaks; and if by any chance he was observing from another plane when Hillary and Tensing finally triumphed he would almost certainly have echoed the former's famous, "We knocked the bastard off".

The "Everest" years coincide with Smythe's first marriage. Both resulted in ultimate failure. The expeditions of 1933, 1936 and 1938 all involved prolonged absences such as to impose a strain on the soundest of relationships and even when Smythe's services were not in demand for "public" expeditions of this sort, he exercised his private choice in favour of visits to the Alps and on ventures such as the Bhyundar Valley sojourn. His books tell a tale he did not intend. His first, *Climbs and Ski Runs*, in 1929, had been inscribed "To My Mother". *Over Tyrolese Hills*, published in 1936 and his Everest book, *Camp Six*, which appeared in 1937, bear, perhaps significantly, no dedication at all. His next book was *The Valley of Flowers*, written rather innocently and somewhat uninformatively for "all who enjoy hills and the flowers that grow on hills", whilst *Mountaineering Holiday*, published in 1940, appears to be "for Jim Gavin", his companion in the adventures there described.

Then, in 1941, comes *The Mountain Vision*, dedicated, mysteriously, "To 'N'". Not long after this, his first marriage having been dissolved, he married Nona, a New Zealander and herself previously married. For the rest of his short life, she was a constant companion, sharing his love of the wild places and accompanying him on almost all his expeditions. *The Spirit of the Hills*, written in 1946, he was able to inscribe frankly "To my Wife". It is an apt testimony to their devotion and to her companionship that his last dedication, in *Mountains in Colour*, should have been to her also. By every account, they were an extraordinarily happy couple.

CHAPTER X

The Valley of Flowers

IT IS TRUE of a great deal of what Smythe did, that merely to record the ground he covered and the heights he reached is to convey only a small part of the experience which attracted him to the hills and which, as described by him, appealed to his wide audience. The indispensable dimensions of experience on his sojourn in the Bhyundar Valley in the Garwhal in 1937 were the peace, joy, fulfilment, tranquillity and beauty which he found there and which he described uniquely well in *The Valley of Flowers*, where he makes it clear that mountaineering achievement ranked lower in importance on this expedition than on any other that he undertook. But the Bhyundar Valley is a mountain valley and in that lay much of its appeal for Smythe. More to the point, whether or not climbing was an original objective of the Bhyundar venture, it certainly came to play a part and, indeed, yielded Smythe some uniquely satisfying ascents.

Parallel to Smythe's experiences in the Alps, it was amongst the less elevated Himalayan summits of the Garwhal that Smythe discovered not only his most lovely and peaceful mountain environment but also the mountaineering that most appealed to him. His love affair with the Bhyundar Valley starts with the Kamet expedition of 1931. After climbing Kamet, the party first descended to Gamsali in the Dhauli Valley and then crossed the Zaskar Range by the Bhyundar Pass, nearly 17,000 feet, descending, through mist and drizzle which cleared as the valley floor was reached, into the Bhyundar Valley. Smythe was overwhelmed by the beauty, delicacy and variety of the flora; it led to a life-long interest in Alpines, the establishment of an Alpine garden at his newly acquired country home in Sussex and, in 1937, the collection of some 250 specimens for study back in Britain.

The first real opportunity to return came in 1937; during the intervening years he had been preoccupied with the Everest expeditions. The 1937 plan was for Smythe to go out alone, later to be joined by Peter Oliver, who held an army appointment in India, for a couple of months' climbing, before collecting specimens. 1 June saw Smythe at Ranikhet where he engaged Wangdi Nurbu whom he had first met on the Kangchenjunga expedition of 1930, three hours of which Wangdi had spent in a crevasse. The acquaintance had been renewed on the Everest expeditions of 1933, where pneumonia had failed to break Wangdi's spirit, and in 1936, when he had led the North Col porters. In addition to Wangdi, Smythe recruited Pasang, whose chief virtue was his infinite trustworthiness rather than any particular mountaineering competence; Tewang, whose Everest experience covered 1924, when he reached Camp Five, and 1933; and Nurbu who was one of the 1936 Everest team. With eleven Dhotial porters in addition, Smythe set off from Ranikhet on 5 June.

The first stage, to Joshimath, involved a lorry drive to Garur, 55 miles, where the walk-in began. The first stage took them to Gwaldam, whence they descended to the Pindar Valley, camping at Tharali and transferring first to Subtal and then Ghat, deep in the Mandakini Valley. From there, they travelled via Ramni, Semkharok and the Birchi Valley to Kaliaghat; then they took the Kuari Pass (where they camped) to the Dhauli Valley and Joshimath. Here, after eight days on the move, they took a break and stocked up with the rest of the supplies needed for their stay.

Finally, leaving the remaining shreds of civilization behind them, they set off at six one morning, descended to Vishnu Prayaj where the Dhauli River joins the Alaknanda River and set off up the gorge of the latter until, after a couple of miles, they reached the junction with the Bhyundar Valley entering from the true left, or east, of the Alaknanda. Up this they went until they found the perfect site for the first base camp, at the uppermost end of a shelf of green turf, 500 feet above the valley floor and with birch forests above and below. Here the Dhotial porters were paid off.

It was obviously desirable to spend some time acclimatizing. A day was spent exploring the immediate neighbourhood and examining the first plant specimens. The second day saw a training and reconnaissance climb on the 17,000 foot peak which rose at the back of the camp; before breaking for lunch they were able to observe Nilkanta, and conclude that the south-east ridge alone seemed to offer any possibility from that side. After lunch, a ridge with 500 feet of difficult climbing tested them before a long intermittent glissade brought them back from the summit to the camp. They then spent a further two days in the cause of botany before finally setting out farther afield.

Their immediate objective was the head of the valley. The main feature here is the Bhyundar Pass which Smythe had crossed six years before, but their aim on this occasion was a snow col to the south-east separated from the Bhyundar Pass by an unnamed peak of about 19,000 feet and framed on the other side by Rataban, a fine summit of more than 20,000 feet which was their primary objective. The snow col was defended by an ice-fall which, however, could easily be avoided by making for the Bhyundar Pass, to which they carried bundles of timber and beneath which they camped. Next day they traversed snow slopes in a south easterly direction towards the snow col to camp there. Previous observations of Rataban had led them to conclude that a direct assault on the north ridge, which fell to the snow col, would prove the ridge to be inaccessible, but they thought that they might reach it via the west face. That afternoon, Smythe climbed the unnamed peak of 19,000 feet from the col, solo, in one hour, ostensibly to make observations but, one suspects, simply in order to have a summit underfoot. It was as well: an overnight storm turned to a blizzard and at 5 a.m. they decided to retreat while they still could. However, this first venture had given them the opportunity to observe a snow peak to the south of the Bhyundar Valley and they settled upon that as their next objective. Without any delay at all, they set off towards it and camped the first night on a rocky rib between two gullies low on its south-east face.

At 6 a.m. next day they set out on what promised to be a long haul to the top if, indeed, it proved possible at all. They were able to kick steps up an initial gully leading through a rock band to a snow ramp which rose to the right and which they followed until it steepened and dissolved into a rock wall. Another gully offered a route through the wall and led to the crest of a ridge which took them up on to the steep snow face of the mountain. After a second breakfast, they tackled first a 50 foot ice-wall, then made their way up steep snow slopes to the névé which supported the summit ridge. They reached it in swirling mist but then had to endure the disappointment of a false summit followed by a gap in the ridge, with an ice step to climb on the far side, before finally gaining access to the summit in a fierce cold wind. The 5,000 feet of quite complicated ascent from the camp had taken less than five hours. A further two saw them down again, uneventfully except for Norbu almost pulling Smythe off the mountain by an enthusiastic and unnotified leap down the last few feet of the ice-wall while Smythe was gently lowering him. It was as well to have a significant success under their belts, for their next venture was frustrated: bad weather put a stop to an attempt on a 20,000 foot peak to the north of the Khanta Khal Pass and confined them to a scramble on a minor rock peak before giving up.

A feature of the valley which had interested them was its entire north wall consisting of a series of summits of about 20,000 feet with few breaches. Bent first of all on reconnaissance, they established a camp some 2,500 feet above the valley floor on a rock rib and Smythe went to survey prospects for the following day, a line of some promise being found after initial problems. Smythe and Wangdi set off up it at 5 a.m. the following morning. A slabby ridge gave access to a glaciated area across which a sloping shelf led to a snowfield and then about 3,000 feet of mixed ground, predominantly rock. The pair came to a halt in a steep gully at about 18,500 feet, where wet snow threatened to avalanche and from which it was obviously right to descend. Again, there was consolation in defeat. A satellite of Nilgiri Parbat, at about 19,000 feet, yielded an excellent climb and also gave Wangdi the chance to demonstrate his excellent mountaineering quality on the descent.

Nilgiri Parbat itself figured in their next plan. On 16 July, they set off to explore the glacier-filled valley via the snow col below the peak, in order to reconnoitre a route from the north or north-west. Crossing the snow pass, the party descended a glacier ice-fall on the far side, then easier snow slopes to the main glacier below. From here, the north face of Nilgiri Parbat was in profile. It disclosed an average slope of about 40 degrees and might well be climbable. Camp was pitched on the main glacier below the ice-fall; Smythe would have preferred to be higher but the porters, their nervous energy spent on fretting about abominable snowmen earlier, were having a bad day and dragging their feet. At least it gave Smythe time to consider the possibilities. A push to the summit would involve 6,500 feet of climbing; and any time spent avoiding danger or overcoming difficulty would reduce the chance of success.

They set off at 6 a.m., negotiating an ice-fall to a small glacier plateau. They then followed a snow slope, and then a subsidiary snow ridge where the more serious difficulties had to be turned. They were thus able to gain access to a buttress ridge, some step cutting being involved, which they hoped would carry them well up the north face. Mist hindered progress, but eventually they reached the top of the buttress ridge that led to a shelf down which they were able to traverse to the foot of a 400 foot snow couloir. Cutting steps all the way up the very steep snow, they came out on a blade-like ice-ridge leading to a little plateau above which the last 2,500 feet of the face remained to be climbed. It was 10 a.m. They continued on up, at times kicking steps but at times having to cut. The mist was stifling and oppressive and Wangdi took a turn at leading. The crux came with a vertical ice-wall which they were able to surmount by using the steep corner provided by faulting in the ice. Then a long snow slope followed, until finally steep névé up which they had to cut led them out to the north-east ridge. Their troubles were not quite over. Wearily, they had to cross one point before following the ridge, in a fierce cold wind, to the narrow point that formed a summit which would accommodate only one at a time. The freezing wind permitted only a short stay, then they were off down, arriving back at camp, after a wearying and exhausting descent, at 7 p.m. For Smythe, however, the day was one of his most rewarding in the mountains. He came to regard Nilgiri Parbat as the most beautiful summit on which he ever set eyes and he described it as "the finest snow and ice-peak I have ever climbed."

He and Wangdi no doubt considered that they had earned a break. Oliver was due to join them in a couple of days and the 20th and 21st of July were spent pottering in and about the base camp. On the 22nd, Oliver arrived and before very long, having settled upon Mana Peak as their main objective, they were planning the stages of an attempt via the Banke Glacier area, which would be reached over the head of the Bhyundar Valley by the Bhyundar Pass. En route, they settled upon an attempt on Rataban from the col as being a good preliminary, but Oliver had subjected himself to a very speedy walk-in and was not yet acclimatized sufficiently for a mountain in excess of 20,000 feet. He found the going very hard indeed and at about 19,000 feet they decided to retreat.

The porters were going through a lethargic phase and the first camp in the Banke Valley area was short of the objective they had in mind. The high ground which separates the Banke Glacier valley from the East Kamet Glacier to the north consists not, as was at one time thought, of a simple ridge alone. The ridge, containing several high points and dominating the south west flank of the East Kamet Glacier, is bolstered on the Banke Glacier side by a high glacier plateau above the Banke Glacier and buttressed by the ramparts which immediately overlook the glacier. Smythe and Oliver had hoped to camp on this plateau. Instead they had to camp short of it at about 15,500 feet, and it was not until the following day that they were able to establish a higher camp at which they remained while the porters descended. The immediate objective was a point on the ridge, at 21,140 feet, ostensibly for purposes of establishing if Mana Peak could be approached along the glacier plateau, turning higher points on the ridge which otherwise would pose insuperable obstacles to an approach from this direction. Leaving camp at 5.15 a.m., they made their way up to a col in the ridge, overlooking the East Kamet Glacier up which Smythe had passed six years previously on the way to Kamet, and from there made their way easily up the 1,200 foot slope which led to the summit. This, alas, failed to yield the information required.

They decided to press camps further up the plateau hoping to see more from one of the points further west along the ridge towards Mana Peak. The logistics of doing this delayed them necessarily and it was 4 August before they were able to set out again. They were soon at a height suitable for a further camp and, it being still early in the day, Smythe and Oliver decided to make for point 22,481 on the ridge. They needed to know whether the plateau continued to the eastern foot of Mana Peak rendering access from this side possible, or whether in effect it ended with the spur which point 22,481 threw down to the south into the plateau.

Smythe and Oliver set out via this spur but thick mists prevented observation lower down and they decided to press on up the spur. They were brought to a halt by an unclimbable rock step, which they avoided by prolonged step-cutting up very steep ice of the worst kind—as strenuous a piece of work as Smythe ever undertook. When it came to an end they found themselves on the ridge again, now mixed and broken initially, later pinnacled and leading to the final summit pyramid, and then the summit itself. The mists still prevented any final answer to their question; they descended without incident, and a re-ascent of the first part of the route next day yielded the information they sought. The plateau did indeed end at the spur they had climbed; there was no way beyond. Mana Peak was, in effect, unattainable from the east and there was nothing left for it but to retreat and think again.

It was clear that the best approach to the mountain was from the west or south-west, via the Banke Glacier with camps en route. Further supplies would be needed and it was 8 August before they set off up the Banke Valley. The initial view of the Mana Peak, from the Banke Glacier to the south, was discouraging, and their hopes narrowed to an ascent from the area of the Zaskar Pass, at the head of the glacier, where they arrived on the third day out. It might be possible, by traversing point 21,500 feet to the north of the pass, to reach the plateau south-west of Mana Peak and above the 3,000 foot ice-fall which fell to the Banke Glacier to the east of the Zaskar Pass and point 21,500 feet. And from the plateau, it might be possible to gain the Kamet–Mana Peak ridge and follow it to the latter summit. It was therefore decided to press on immediately and establish a camp as high on the ridge leading up to point 21,500 feet as was possible that night, with a view to pushing straight for the summit of Mana Peak the following day. In any case, they lacked supplies for a longer stay.

Setting out at 5 a.m., Smythe and Oliver made their way up the ridge to broken rocks, then a chimney, more broken rocks, and some slabs to a wall now verglassed after the recent weather. The ice was cleared by axe, and the ridge then followed to the summit of the point, from which it was an easy matter to descend some 300 feet to the snow plateau above the ice-fall. The tentative plan now was to cross the glacier to the foot of the north-west, or Kamet, ridge, climb up to it and follow it to the summit. However, the slope up to the ridge was extremely steep, extending above a bergschrund for over 1,000 feet of ice below the crest. They had previously dismissed the south ridge of Mana Peak as being too difficult and dangerous, especially a rock step about 1,000 feet below the summit; now, faced with even greater difficulties, they considered those dangers perhaps overstated and decided, *faut de mieux*, to have a look at the south ridge.

The obvious line of approach meant a descent of another three or four hundred feet to gain access to a subsidiary ridge which took them to the foot of a 400 foot wall defending the south ridge proper. This wall proved extremely strenuous and it was 10 a.m. before they were able to rest and eat on the crest of the south ridge. They then set out along the ridge, uneventfully for the first hour. It steepened when three towers obstructed the way, although they could be turned on the left; but, while climbing a wall by a granite step, Oliver decided he had better quit. He had not had Smythe's acclimatization and had done at least his fair share of the work. After some discussion, and without any great enthusiasm on Oliver's part, Smythe decided to continue alone.

Conditions were now perfect. Smythe followed a broad ledge to the foot of a 150 foot wall. A very steep couloir led for 100 feet through this, then a traverse along ledges led first to relatively easy going, then to a 35 foot slab, and the steep section was finally conquered. As far as could be recalled, that was the end of the difficulties; the rest was a trudge. It must have come as an unpleasant surprise to find the way along the ridge blocked by an immense boulder which could only be passed by crawling *underneath*, regaining the crest at the far side via a ledge and a pull-up. A final step of 50 feet was overcome by a gully to the left and at 1.30 p.m. Smythe stepped on to the summit at the end of the hardest of the very many solitary climbs of his career.

Almost immediately he set off down to rejoin Oliver who by this time had recovered sufficiently to wander about and take photographs. Except for having to recut some of the steps, they were able to return to camp uneventfully and, after much tea, press on down to the Zaskar Pass camp from which they retreated the following day. "So," later wrote Smythe, "ended the longest, grandest and hardest mountain climb of our lives." It had involved them in a total of five or six thousand feet of ascent over several miles, a great deal of it spent in exhausting technical climbing. It was the excess of hard work at altitude which had done for Oliver. Smythe, fortunately, was supremely fit; and in bringing his tally of 7,000 metre peaks to five (no 8,000 metre peak was climbed until 1952), Smythe could at that time claim more than any man, alive or dead, except, possibly, Erwin Schneider.

They descended to Badrinath on about 13 August and spent several days in recovering and reprovisioning. They did not know it at the

The Ramthang Peak — Smythe's first 7,000m summit

Nilgiri Parbat — "the longest and finest snow and ice expedition of my mountaineering experience"

Kamet

The Bhyundar Valley

Unnamed snow peak of about 6,000m above the Bhyundar Valley

The Windachtal from near Fiegl's Gasthaus. The Pfaffenschneid/
Zuckerhütl appears in the top left-hand corner

Mount Robson, north face

Members of the 1936 Everest expedition:
Smijth-Windham, Oliver, Humphreys, Warren
Shipton, Smythe, Ruttledge, Morris, Wyn Harris
Gavin, Wigram, Kempton

View from 26,000 feet on Everest

time, but their tour was effectively over, so far as mountaineering success was concerned. They now had in mind attempts on Nilkanta and Dunagiri, but they were perhaps biting off too much. On Nilkanta, they spent a day in reconnaissance up to about 19,000 feet on its south-east ridge, then rain imprisoned them in a lower camp for several days. On 22 August, they pushed a camp up the ridge willy-nilly and, next day, set off for the summit, but hailstorms and blizzard put a stop to the attempt at 19,500 feet, about 2,000 feet from the summit. A foot of new snow forced a final retreat. It would have been astonishing if they had succeeded. It was to be many decades before a team finally climbed Nilkanta—the first authenticated ascent was as late as 1974.

Dunagiri, by contrast, fell to a team led by André Roch two years later, but is still not an easy mountain. It was September by the time Smythe and Oliver were en route. They established a camp at about 21,000 feet on the south-west ridge, with over 2,000 feet to go to the summit. There, they endured five days of fierce storms and blizzards before setting out, somewhat optimistically, at 6 a.m. on 13 September. The ridge was by now treacherously corniced. It eventually collapsed under Oliver but miraculously he landed on the ridge itself, and still they pressed on. Only when they found themselves out on the south-east face in deep, steep, unconsolidated snow on top of ice, did they decided to go down. They had, said Smythe, pushed their attempt to the limit of what was justified; some would say they had pressed it some way beyond and were quite lucky to get off the mountain at all.

It was now time for Oliver to rejoin his regiment. The climbing was over. Smythe returned to the Bhyundar Valley to wind up the botanical work and collect further specimens and then return home. They had visited none of the great mountains which had grabbed the headlines in the 1930s. They had climbed in teams of one, two or three, depending on the circumstances, but ranking as small even by Tilman's definition—there is no evidence that their plans ever occupied even the back of an envelope. At the same time, the tour was not without quantitative achievement: some dozen new peaks, most of them over 20,000 feet, including Nilgiri Parbat and Mana Peak. Best of all, Smythe tells us, it was "the happiest mountaineering partnership of my experience".

CHAPTER XI

Alpine Ways

SOME MOUNTAINEERS PREFER climbing from a centre, while others prefer traversing from A to B. Nothing illustrates the "mountain wanderer" in Smythe better than the journey which he undertook in the early spring of 1934. He travelled alone, climbed few peaks hardly any of which were generally known, and yet he made a journey at least as rewarding in its way as had been the Everest expedition of the previous year.

Towards the end of March, he travelled out by train to Bludenz and from there proceeded by train and bus via Schruns to Partenen where the wandering proper began. Its first section was a traverse of the Silvretta where he had been so happy on previous visits. Setting off for the Madlener Haus, for the first night, he headed up the Gross Vermunt Valley. He was unfit, overloaded, had sent his sealskins on in error to Klosters and arrived at the hut to find it crowded with skiers. Fortunately, he intended only an overnight break there and at 5 a.m. next day was off to the Wiesbadner Hut where, by 9 a.m., he was enjoying a second breakfast. The only "rule" he had for the journey was not to climb out and back from the same centre, though he broke it straight away for, from the Wiesbadner Hut, he left for the Dreiländerspitze, about 10,500 feet, intending to return to the hut before crossing into Switzerland over the Silvretta Pass. From the hut he took the left-hand branch of the Vermunt Glacier to the Jam Joch from which, in some mysterious way, he purports to have reached a point on the north-west ridge, which he then followed over a minor summit to the top. There he sat and brewed up lemonade before running back to the hut on ski.

His plan was to enter Switzerland the following day although the weather had looked doubtful for a while. Leaving the hut, he crossed to the southern branch of the Vermunt Glacier which leads up to the Fuorcla del Confin and the border. Just before the Fuorcla, he diverted from this route and, finding his way amongst crowds of skiers, ascended the Piz Buin from the Fuorcla Buin before crossing over into Switzerland, traversing to the Silvretta Pass and, by this time more than satiated with the company of skiers, running down the glacier, past the hut, past Sardasca Alp straight to Klosters where he spent the next night.

Smythe had little time for "expensive and fashionable" Alpine resorts such as Klosters. He became paranoiac about exploitation as a tourist. Even so, it was as nothing by comparison with Davos, to which he made the short journey by train, continuing on the Parsenn Railway, then just two years old, to the Weissfluhjoch. Today that journey reminds the traveller of nothing so much as a Rhondda coal-tip. *C'est magnifique, mais ce n'est pas une montagne.* The entire route up has been remoulded, restructured and decorated, presumably in the interests of the winter hordes whose only interest is in riding up and skiing down as unproblematically as possible. It requires a courageous flight of the imagination to envisage what the Parsenn must originally have looked like.

On arrival, Smythe was not disposed to hang around at the joch. He had intended to take in the summit of the Weissfluh, but even in those days the surroundings of the Weissfluhjoch station were unattractive, so instead he clipped on his ski and pointed down the Fondei Valley for Langwies. The following day he went on by train to Arosa. He had planned to traverse the Arosa Weisshorn from Langwies to the Arosa Hörnli Hut, but, preferring the intelligence of the stationmaster to that of his ski-touring map, he ascended to the Carmenna Pass, and then, making a detour in order to avoid a couple overwhelmed, on the path, by an all-consuming passion, followed the south-south-west ridge of the Weisshorn to the summit —not all that easy to find amongst the debris left by Easter trippers. He descended almost immediately and then, following the ridge south and traversing the eastern slopes of the Plattenhorn, reached the Hörnli Hut where he spent an uncomfortable night. He awoke with a chill and, to the amazement of the keeper, who could not believe that anyone would voluntarily go to Chur, set off down. Preferring the descent in the direction of Parpan, he circled round the cwm at the head of the Urdenbach valley and made for the Urdenfürggli from where, it being still early in the day, he climbed the Parpaner Schwarzhorn, the south ridge of which proved not lacking in interest. A biting wind and absence of shelter sent him down almost immediately via the Spinazmanntobel Valley which gave him a fine run all the way to Tschiertschen. From there, by contrast, he had to endure a painful and dusty trudge six miles down the road to Chur.

Although a dozen attractive summits are within a stone's throw of its massive church tower, Chur is emphatically a town of the plain, not of the mountains. It is heavily industrialized and does not pander to the self-indulgent leisure of the tourist. Viewed in itself and apart from its environment it remains no more or less attractive now than it was when Smythe passed the night there before moving on to the next stage of his tour.

He had intended to enter the Glarus mountains via Flims and the Segnes Pass but, doubtful about the wisdom of descending the pass on ski, decided instead to travel by train to Wallenstadt for a day around the lake and then, next day, doubled back to Flums with a view to crossing the Spitzmeilen into the Glarus. He was clearly now stronger and fitter and managed the 5,500 foot walk up to the Spitzmeilen Hut with a heavily-laden sac without undue suffering. The following morning ambiguous weather signs made it necessary to set about the traverse of the pass with some urgency if he was not to be storm-bound. The pass, however, is no great distance above the hut and, once there and with no perceptible deterioration in the weather, the proud little summit of the Spitzmeilen and then the Weissmeilen proved irresistible before he descended via the Mühlebachthal to Engi in the Sernftal in now more threatening weather. From Engi, he set off to walk up the valley to Elm but, once half-way, and having stopped for refreshment, he succumbed again to the temptation of the railway and rode the last three miles to find lodging in Elm for the night.

The next day, 9 April, was lost to the weather. However, the 10th was more encouraging and Smythe set out to cross the Richetli Pass to Linthal. There was no time to lounge on the Pass as the snow slopes on the far side were steep and better crossed sooner rather than later, especially in view of the continuing uncertain weather. He was, therefore, soon down to the Durnachtal and installed for the night in Linthal, well-remembered from the time of his apprenticeship. The next few days were to see him treading old familiar ground on more than one occasion.

The following section of his route lay up the valley as far as

Stolden, then bore right through the forest, over the Altenoren Alp, and rose to the Clariden Hut. He had intended to revisit the Claridenstock, but the dubious state of the weather next day delayed his start and, by the time he was tentatively on his way, there was insufficient time for the climb. He crossed the Clariden Pass and ran down to the Hüfi Hut for an overnight stop before continuing down the Maderanertal, where there was some risk of avalanche, to Amsteg.

There is a very obvious and direct route from Amsteg to Andermatt, his next port-of-call. Both road and rail have used it, and Smythe had thought that this section of the tour would be best quickly bridged by train, but in Amsteg he heard of an alternative which he resolved to follow. A couple of miles up the valley from Amsteg, a branch valley enters from the east. This is the Fellital. It leads up to the Fellilücke with a lift of nearly 6,000 feet over five or six miles. Three miles up the valley Smythe spent the night at the Tresch Hut. Realizing that there was some avalanche risk at the approach to the pass, he had intended an early start, but overslept, and it was 8.30 a.m. before he left the hut. Higher up, he stopped to weigh the pros and cons of continuing and, deciding that he just about had time to reach the pass before the morning sun made the danger substantial, set off for it. About 200 feet from the top, and just clear of danger, the avalanche struck; a start twenty minutes later would have put a stop to this and any future touring. As it was he reached the pass and idled in the sun for three hours before beginning the run down to Oberalp and then Andermatt.

He was stuck in Andermatt for four days, and there are vastly better places to be marooned. The surrounding terrain is more like Rannoch Moor than the Alps and, with all due respect to the manifold delights of Kinloch Rannoch, there are better places to spend four days in the rain. It was 20 April before he was able to get going again and it now began to appear as if it might not be possible to weave the whole of his original grand design. This had included yet another attempt to traverse the Oberland glaciers from the Grimsel Pass to the Lötschental, a venture on which he had been frustrated on more than one occasion; but he could keep his options open for a while. He took a bus to Realp where he left the Urseren Valley, making his way via the Wyttenwasser Alp to the Rotondo Hut and again reviving memories of earlier times when, twelve years previously, he had endured a frightening descent from the Rotondo Hut in a blizzard.

After a night at the hut, he was soon at the Lecki Pass from which he scrambled to the summit of the Stellibodenhorn before descending to the Mutten Glacier, Mutten Alp and, after a long pull over the Thierberg, the Furka Pass. He followed the road down to Gletsch; he still had a theoretical choice of routes the next day.

In the morning it was immediately obvious that the preferred option of the high Oberland glaciers was not open to him, so he went down to Oberwald through storm and blizzard and, after drying out overnight, by train to Brig, Goppenstein and, via the Lötschberg Tunnel, to Kandersteg where he spent a couple of days visiting the Lake of Thun and Bern before setting out on the last leg of the tour.

Here again there were options, but the preferred route was to ascend to the Gemmi Pass, then traverse the Wildstrubel and Wildhorn. As Smythe set off for the Gemmi the weather was doubtful and by the time he reached the plain of the Spittalmatte it seemed obvious that the long, high-level traverse of the Wildstrubel and Glacier de la Plaine Morte would not be a sensible undertaking for a lone mountaineer. He therefore settled down, lit a pipe, took out his map and travelled in the imagination the ground denied him in reality. He had not, previously, climbed the Wildstrubel, but he had read accounts of it, and it is therefore perhaps not surprising that his imaginary account of the traverse should be so accurate, for it captures what is the peculiar essence of this particular tour. There is nothing difficult or dangerous about the traverse from the Gemmi to the Wildstrubel Hut (unless it be locating the latter at the end of the long trudge across the Glacier de la Plaine Morte). Its peculiar characteristic is the quite unwarranted air of mystery and remoteness which it exudes, even though the route is rarely more than an hour or two away from fondue and a bottle of Dôle. The atmosphere is partly a matter of history: Sir Leslie Stephen and Thomas Hinchliff were both here in the early days and Conway passed this way on the original end-to-end traverse of the Alps. Partly, too, it is due to the peculiar topography: at no point on the ten-mile traverse, not even on the summit of the mountain, is it possible to appreciate just how close, in reality, civilization is. The ascent via the Lämmern Glacier yields only a backward view of the retreating Gemmi; the rest is enclosed by the Wildstrubel horseshoe. The descent via the Glacier de la Plaine Morte is notorious. Although the glacier is no more than two miles wide at its widest point, it appears to go on for ever, so flat and featureless is it.

Smythe was eventually able to traverse the mountain in reality. For the present he had to be content with a lower-level traverse—of the valleys and sub-ranges of the lower northern slopes of the western Oberland.

From Kandersteg he made his way to Adelboden not via the more commonly travelled and slightly lower Bunderchrinde but by the pass, to the north, that separates the Bunderspitz from the Chlyne [Klein] Lohner. In Adelboden, he put up at the Gasthaus Kreuz which, whilst it may, like pretty well everything else hereabouts, have gone somewhat upmarket, remains run by the same family offering the same high standard of hospitality. From Adelboden, he traversed the Hahnenmoos to Lenk and, next day, walked up the Ronewald Valley and followed the flanks of the Haslerberg to the Trüttlisberg Pass, from which he diverted for the few minutes required in order to bag the Tube before descending to Lauenen. Here, a break for refreshment gave birth to the idea of devoting his last night to a bivouac on the Höhi Wispile. The coldness of the night, possibly coupled with a heightened sobriety, made this idea much less attractive in reality than it had been in imagination and, fortunately, a cosy and unmarked hut on the ridge spared him the experience.

And so he arrived at the final day of the tour. Walking along the ridge of the Wispile, he descended to Gstaad and boarded the train for Montreux. There was a moment when, passing through Château d'Oex, he was briefly tempted to revive the experience of that first daring adventure on Mont Cray, but it was resisted.

Thus ended what in almost all respects was a wholly unremarkable tour. Perhaps an unusual feature is that it started at one end of the Swiss Alps and finished at the other; it also serves as a reminder that the delights of the Alps can be savoured other than between 1 July and 15 September in each year. Otherwise its only unusual feature is the obscurity, by reference to contemporary British notions, of the ground covered. How many have heard of the Spitzmeilen or the Parpaner Schwarzhorn? Yet if they doubt whether such enterprises could possibly be rewarding by comparison with, say, the South Face of the Fou or whatever it is that is currently fashionable, the only way to find out is to sample it. It is, no doubt, a matter partly of motivation and partly of temperament but, for some (and Smythe was clearly one), obscure peaks in obscure places have just as much to offer as any of the more heavily trafficked highways of Alpine endeavour.

The next year, in the summer of 1935, he again arrived in Bludenz, this time with Campbell Secord. They intended to traverse the main groups of the Tyrol in an easterly direction.

The point of embarkation was again the Madlener Hut but when they set out, in glorious weather, at 5.45 a.m., they were bound for the Jamtal Hut, intending to reach the Jamtal Glacier by traversing the Bieltalspitze. Taking in the humble Bieltalerkopf on the way, they reached a notch in the ridge to the north of the Bieltalspitze from which they made the ascent, then descended the same way and continued down to the Jamtal Glacier and the hut. At five next morning, they set off for the Flutchthorn which they intended to traverse on the way to the Heidelberger Hut in the Fimber Tal. Taking a second breakfast at the Schneejoch, they then climbed the south-east ridge of the Flutchthorn which rises from it, not without complications and difficulty, to stand on the summit. The continuation along the summit ridge now seemed less attractive than a doze, and when they eventually moved, it was down the ordinary route to the Krönen Glacier from which, after recrossing the Schneejoch, they made their way down the Fimber Tal to the Heidelberger Hut. From here, next day, they completed the traverse of the Silvretta by crossing the Zeblasjoch to the Samnaun Tal and descending to Pfunds.

Pfunds is one of a number of gateways into the Ötztal Alps. It is today at one and the same time one of the most attractive, most unusual, and least frequently used. Its attractions must speak for themselves; but it will readily be admitted that a 10,000 foot pass leading nowhere in particular is an unusual feature, and it ought not to be a surprise that the pass is infrequently used since practically all the terrain to which it grants access is today more readily reached by road. Smythe and Secord, less than enamoured by the comforts of such accommodation as they found in Pfunds, decided against spending a day on the valley floor and to make instead for the Hohenzollern Hut, two hours short of the pass, the Riffljoch. They took a day off there instead.

Next day, they were soon in the area of the Riffljoch and lunched on the summit of the Rifflkarspitze which stands to the north east of the pass and 500 feet above it. After lunch, the Glockturm itself beckoned and, not satisfied even with that, Smythe and Secord set off up what they thought to be the inescapable rock face of the Riffljochturm, Secord leading a severe section before, from the summit, they discovered a much easier line of ascent. A good day's scrambling behind them, they then descended to a crowded Gepatsch Hut where they were accommodated, there being nowhere else, along with the bread and sugar.

The classic way to traverse the Ötztal Alps is east to west, or vice versa, rather than north to south; and from the west there are three possible starts. Of these, the Radurschel Tal route, which Smythe and Secord followed, can be the best or worst according as to whether the descent to the Gepatsch Hut is avoided or not. The Gepatsch Hut is not without virtue—it would be a good place for a picnic. But it is an incongruous port of call on a high-level traverse designed to avoid the delights of civilization for a few days. It is, in fact, quite possible to avoid the descent to the Gepatsch Hut and hold on to some of the character of the undertaking by descending the cwm of the Riffl from the pass as far as the ski road and then turning south and camping or bivouacking before traversing the Weisseespitze via the west ridge and east flank next day. It appears to be possible today to take mechanical assistance to reach the Ober Falginjoch for the west ridge; and on a clear day, the plod down from the summit and across the Gepatsch Glacier to the Brandenburger Hut is a splendidly idle walk of a couple of hours.

Smythe and Secord followed the altogether less enterprising and more boring trudge from the Gepatsch Hut to the Brandenburger Hut in deteriorating weather. Bad weather persisted the following morning and prudence dictated that they abandon a projected attempt on the Weisskugel. They decided, instead, to traverse the Fluchtkogel to the Gepatsch Joch and from there descend the Gross Vernagt Glacier to the Vernagt Hut. There is nothing at all difficult about this undertaking except that, much like crossing Trafalgar Square, it can be tricky in thick mist. Their notion, of following the south-west ridge to the summit, instead of the normal approach up the glacier, was, no doubt, good in principle but rendered somewhat less so in practice by their mistaking an earlier point on the ridge for the summit itself. As a result, they never reached the Gepatsch Joch but instead, returned somewhat humiliated to the Brandenburger Hut at the end of a long and not particularly fruitful day.

The next stage in their expedition was the traverse of the Guslar Joch, from which they made the easy ascent of the Kesselwandspitze before proceeding to the Vernagt Hut and then the Breslauer Hut from which they intended to climb the Wildspitze. This they determined to do via the south buttress by which the mountain is rarely climbed and which proved to be less intimidating than had appeared from below. Arriving at the south summit ahead of parties using the ordinary route from the Breslauer Hut, they sat for an hour, then traversed the icy crest to the north summit and descended by the steeper and rather more difficult north-east ridge back to the Breslauer Hut where, after a shave and a gargantuan meal, they yielded to the temptation of the fleshpots of Sölden and completed their traverse of the Ötztal mountains that evening. They were in position to embark upon the next leg of the journey the following day.

The Stubai Alps occupy an area of about 600 square miles south-west of Innsbruck. They are bounded on the east by the Brenner Pass, traversed now by the slowest motorway in Europe, and on the west by the Ötztal, which separates them from the group of that name. Small and compact, they are gentle mountains by Alpine standards. Although hard rock is to be found, long, classic rock routes do not abound. The climbing on the higher peaks is mixed, mostly on relatively easy ice and snow; the lower slopes understandably attract mountain walkers in considerable numbers. They are, then, relatively humble mountains, a quality which does not seem to have abated Smythe's enthusiasm one whit.

The backbone of the Stubai Alps consists of a complex ridge running in an east-west direction culminating in the Zuckerhütl, the highest summit of the range, reaching 3,505 metres. The second highest summit is the Pfaffenschneid, immediately west of and barely lower than the Zuckerhütl and, some (including Smythe) would consider, really no more than a twin summit of the Zuckerhütl. The *voie normale* of the Zuckerhütl ascends and descends its east ridge, a snow arête which steepens near the summit for a few metres to up to 55 degrees. Heavily trafficked, it normally contains a series of bucket steps negotiable even by the most incompetent lounge lizard. It can, however, offer the worst sort of ice and impart a sense of seriousness often lacking on routes of much greater difficulty. This east ridge descends to the Pfaffensattel from which easy snow slopes rise for a few hundred feet to the summit of the Wilder Pfaff. The east ridge of this mountain descends, via a subsidiary snow spur, to the Müller Hut, from whence there is a choice of ways to the summit of the next peak to the east, the Wilder Freiger. From the Wilder Freiger, a long and somewhat tortuous descent leads to the Nürnberger Hut and, thence, back to the floor of the Stubaital. It was this traverse, Pfaffenschneid–Zuckerhütl–Wilder Pfaff–Wilder Freiger, on which Smythe and Secord were bent.

Nowadays it is customary to embark upon this traverse from the Hildesheimer Hut which sits on a rocky promontory looking eastwards over the Pfaffen Glacier on to the north-western flank and fine-pointed summit of the Pfaffenschneid. The Hildesheimer Hut can be reached easily from the Stubaital by taking the Mutterbergalm cable cars to the Eisgrat. Those who have mastered the art of travelling by ski-tow in climbing boots can, indeed, employ artificial means the whole way to what is now known as the Eisjoch; the rest must plod 800 feet or so up the piste. From the Eisjoch, there is some compensation to be derived by bagging the Schaufelspitze and the Stubaier Wildspitze before descending easily to the Hildesheimer Hut. Once the trappings of the ski industry are left behind, this way in has the merit of going through high mountain country and, if done alone, conveys a wholly deceptive air of remoteness. However, it involves abjuring what is undoubtedly the more classic traditional and gentle walk-in via the beautiful Windachtal from Sölden, which Smythe and Secord took.

The Windachtal forms a swathe running in an easterly direction from Sölden, in the Ötztal, into the heart of the Stubai. For the first couple of miles, which Secord likened to the Rockies but with a path, there is an old rough road leading to the collection of chalets amongst which Fiegl's Gasthaus still nestles. The length of the walk-in from Sölden to the hut must rank amongst Fiegl's most precious assets—about eight miles over which 5,000 feet of altitude are involved. On a warm summer's day it is impossible to resist the temptation of at least a couple of beers at Fiegl's before approaching the foot of the last long haul up to the hut. Smythe and Secord sensibly decided to spend the night there and go straight on to the traverse the next day.

From Fiegl's, a level couple of miles along the valley floor leads to a choice of paths mounting the balance of 3,000 feet or so of heather and boulder slopes to the hut and the start of the traverse. From the hut, all routes circle the rocky cwm to its north-east and join the Pfaffen Glacier at about 10,000 feet. For about a hundred yards the track follows the true right-hand side of the glacier to the top of a rise and here the first route branches off.

It is a delightful, easy route, and the classic way up the Pfaffenschneid. It crosses the glacier, lightly crevassed at this point, negotiates a small bergschrund which can be pleasingly problematical, then snow slopes, then another bergschrund before taking the rocky crest of the west ridge—a scramble with the odd bit of II—1,500 feet to the summit. Smythe and Secord, however, disdained it. From just below the summit of the Pfaffenschneid, a snowy spur projects into the Pfaffen Glacier in a northerly direction and Smythe's preference for an ascent via this relatively undistinguished path is yet another indication of his predelection for snow and ice rather than rock, given the choice. The spur is certainly no easier than the ridge and in some conditions could be markedly more difficult.

The summit of the Pfaffenschneid offers a short rocky scramble, then an easy and classic piece of mountaineering in miniature leads along the summit ridge and up to the Zuckerhütl just a few minutes away. Descending the snowy arête of the ordinary route, to the Pfaffensattel, they set off up the snow slopes to the top of the Wilder Pfaff, Secord finding the most difficult line possible, then descended easily for a break at the Müller Hut. From there, they followed the south-west ridge of the Wilder Freiger, a pleasant scramble, to its summit and, a little more than two hours of racing and glissading later, sat outside a hostelry in Ranalt confronting tankards of foaming beer. From there, they travelled by bus to Innsbruck to the accompaniment of Smythe bemoaning the spoliation wrought in the Stubaital by the demands of tourism since his days of innocence there some twelve years previously.

Three days in Innsbruck sufficed to recharge batteries and late in the day on 15 July Smythe and Secord arrived at the Geraer Hut for the ascent of the Olperer. On the way in, they had remarked upon the fine-looking south-west ridge of the Fussstein, twin summit of the Olperer, which rises directly above the hut and resolved to climb it, and traverse the Fussstein–Olperer summit ridge before descending to the hut. They embarked on this enterprise the following morning

—Smythe in particular was slow to get going and the ridge was not without incident but five hours later they were relaxing in the sun on top of the Fussstein. The traverse to the Olperer provided its share of excitement. Taken in the direction Fussstein–Olperer, it is still considered to be quite hard, even today, but Smythe and Secord contrived to avoid the main difficulty by a tortuous descent, traverse and re-ascent of the face beneath the col and so reached the summit of the Olperer. They found the north ridge, by which they descended, already polluted by iron stanchions, then glissaded, then walked back to the Geraer Hut.

The following day, after a late start, they transferred to the Dominikus Hut, en route conceiving the plan of climbing the Hochferner Spitze via the spur which falls down the centre of the north-west face between the Hochferner and Griesferner, the steep and broken glaciers which adorn this face. Even getting to the foot of this face from the Dominikus Hut is a bit of an expedition and there is, today, a bivouac hut there. The climbs on the face are reputed to be the longest and hardest in the Zillertal, and Smythe and Secord were unable to gain access to the central rib which had attracted them. With some difficulty, they made their way, via the most easterly spur, on to the Griesferner but by this time they were assailed by doubts not merely about the climbing but also about the weather and accordingly decided to cross as speedily as possible to the Hochferner Spitze—Hochfeiler Col. Although they had it in mind to ascend both summits from here, prudence in the event confined them to the Hochfeiler. Adventure did not end here: descending via a somewhat convoluted route, they experienced a skirmish with Italian frontier troops before making their return, wet and exhausted, to the Dominikus Hut.

Next day, they were away early, ascending the Schlegeisental to the Furtschagl hut for breakfast, then climbing to the Schönbichler Scharte from which they climbed the Furtschagl Spitze, a rocky peak of about 10,500 feet, before descending to the positively palatial Berliner Hut in the Schwarzenstein Tal. Doubtful weather emphasized the attractions of a day at the Berliner Hut and it was 4 a.m. on the morning of 22 July before they set off for the Mösele which, whilst not quite the highest mountain in the Zillertal, bids fair to be the grandest. They did not get far: the weather closed in and sent them scurrying back to the Berliner Hut. Now, for the first time, they began to be conscious of pressure of time and, rather than sit it out at the hut resolved instead to go down in order to be further along the trail for the eventual return of good weather. They accordingly proceeded by foot, bus and train, after an overnight stop in Zell am Ziller, to Gerlos from where they went up, via the Wildgerlos Tal, to the Zittauer Hut examining on the way the summits of the peaks of the Reichen range which were their next objective.

The following day was one of determined bagging. Setting out from the hut, they traversed the Gabelkopf and then climbed the Reichenspitze by its short but difficult north-east ridge. Descending from here to the gap, they then set about the south-east ridge of the Wildgerlos Spitze which they negotiated only with considerable difficulty part of the way before being driven out on to the face to traverse to the west ridge from which they reached the south summit. The traverse from here to the north summit again extended them and even then the demands were not at an end. They descended from the Wildgerlos Spitze by its north-east ridge to the Gerlos Glacier and from here traversed the slopes of the Gabelkopf before embarking on the last ascent of the day, to the Rosskar Scharte, from which they made their different ways down to the Krimmler Tauern Hut in the Krimmler Tal.

The Krimmler Tal is the gateway to the Hohe Tauern, the last of the ranges into which their wandering was intended to take them. Their plans involved climbing from the Warnsdorfer Hut, a short afternoon's walk from the Krimmler Tauern Hut, and they were able to study the ground that they hoped to cover next day as they walked up. As one ascends the valley, the Hohe Tauern presents its north wall to view with, from left to right, the summits of the Maurer Kopfe, Simony Spitze and Dreiherren Spitze. Near the centre of the wall, a buttress rises to the summit of the Simony Spitze. Smythe and Secord planned to climb the buttress to the summit of the Simony Spitze and from it follow the crest to the west, traversing the Dreiherren Spitze by ascending its north-east ridge and descending by the north-west ridge to the Birnlücke. A reconnaissance on the evening of their arrival at the hut confirmed the possibilities and shortly after 4 a.m. next day they set out.

The glacier leading to the foot of the buttress was complex and heavily crevassed but the previous evening's research paid dividends and they were able to negotiate the difficulties without incident. The buttress presented serac walls on its lower slopes, which discouraged a direct assault, but ice-slopes to the right enabled them to gain height and traverse on to the buttress about 400 feet above its base and well clear of the dangers.

Once on the buttress, a ridge of snow in good condition led to a section of slab which was passed by means of a flared crack. Above that, ice-slopes led to the top of the buttress and, for a hundred feet or more, constant step-cutting was required. The quality of the snow then improved and they were able to kick steps to the top of the buttress where they stopped for a second breakfast before continuing up steep snow-slopes again for half an hour to the summit ridge west of the Simony Spitze. A few minutes later, after five hours' climbing, they stood on the summit, where they were greeted by the Gross Venediger and Gross Glockner to the east.

From the Simony Spitze, the ridge which they must follow rose and fell for about a mile in the direction of the Dreiherren Spitze before running up against a final pyramid of 500 feet. The climbing was not without interest, nor was the weather wholly faithful, and they had little time to spend on the summit of the Dreiherren Spitze before commencing the descent to the Birnlücke. It was slow going. It took an hour and a half to cut down a slope of 250 feet; then, in deteriorating weather, they came to an interminable pinnacled section, nowhere particularly hard but constantly demanding and inescapable until, in its lower reaches, it was possible to traverse on to the face and avoid some of the difficulties. Eventually they reached the path to the col, then descended to the glacier and finally trudged 1,500 feet uphill back to the hut after seventeen hours on the move.

One of Smythe's first Alpine ascents had been that of the Gross Venediger by the north-west ridge with J. H. B. Bell in appalling weather in 1922; now Secord and he transferred to the Kürsinger Hut with a repetition of this route in mind. They were blessed by better weather and traversed the undulating mixed ridge to the summit in four hours. Although they did not know it at the time, this was to be their last day in the hills and they were lucky to savour the best of Alpine weather as they lounged about the summit for a couple of hours before descending to the col between the Gross and Klein Venediger and taking the ordinary way down.

The tour was designed to end at Zell am See which they reached, in deteriorating weather, using public transport for the last few miles.

They had hoped to conclude their wandering with an ascent of the Gross Glockner but it was not to be.

Smythe made only one visit to the Dauphiné and even then spent little time there. It would be an exaggeration to say that he disliked it, but its rocky wildness and relative lack of contrasting form and colour made it less attractive to him than other areas. It was at the start of his last pre-war season that he set out from La Bérarde with J. M. L. Gavin. They disdained the doubtful pleasures of a crowded Pilatte Hut, bivouacked some way below it and, at dawn, made for Les Bans. Smythe justifies such a trivial exercise on the grounds of advancing years, lack of fitness and the need for training. Many would regard it as a major undertaking in its own right. Les Bans is one of those mountains where the *voie normale* really is the *voie classique*. There are other, harder, routes to be had—the north-east pillar is highly thought of by those who have ventured on it, the first of whom were Graham Brown and his guides Graven and Rodier, although they took what is described as a more obscure, less interesting and less elegant line than that now customarily followed. However, the south-south-east ridge involves route-finding on a glacier, a choice of steep snow/ice slopes to a col, and a rocky ridge with some route-finding puzzles, if the best way is to be followed, before a scramble on easy rock leads to the summit of over 12,000 feet.

For Smythe, out of condition and lacking his customary aggressiveness, the alternative, harder, start direct to the Col. W. des Bans, involving some fifteen feet of vertical ice on the upper lip of the bergschrund, lacked appeal and Gavin acquiesced in taking the easier East Col route, following the ridge westwards to the foot of the arête. Smythe, suffering from a bad attack of early season blues, followed Gavin up the ridge, nursing a splitting headache, and reached the summit with a resolve never again to climb to 12,000 feet on the first day of a tour. It is plain from his account that the appeal of the view from the summit was limited by the circumstances—objectively, it is nothing less than magnificent. But they were blessed by a warm sun and dozed reasonably contentedly for an hour before descending without incident, via a break for beer at the Carrelet Hut, to La Bérarde.

Smythe and Gavin had as their ultimate objective what is no doubt the Dauphiné's most prized gem, the traverse of La Meije. The immediate preparation for this was to be the traverse of the Barre des Écrins, ascending via the south face and then descending via the north to the Col des Écrins and returning thence via the Glacier de la Bonne Pierre to La Bérarde, thus following the itinerary of Coolidge's first classic traverse. Today, both the south and north faces are presented by the La Bérarde and Ailefroide guides respectively as *voies normales* but the former remains much less frequented than the latter.

The traverse is normally attempted from the Temple-Écrins Hut but by 1939 the old hut had been destroyed by avalanches and its replacement was still in course of construction. It was thus with a view to another bivouac that Smythe and Gavin set out from La Bérarde after lunch on the day after the Les Bans climb, pausing en route in order to savour yet again the hospitality of the Carrelet Hut. Although they had taken a low tent, they soon abandoned it in favour of a short night around the fire—it was, as Gavin remarked, "an ill avalanche that blows nobody any wood", and the remains of the old hut were put to good, if dubiously legal, purpose. By 3.30 the following morning, they were on their way to the Col des Avalanches, passing under the north-west face of the Pic Coolidge, zig-zagging up to the Glacier du Vallon de la Pilatte which they ascended until they could bear east towards the Col des Avalanches separating Le Fifre from the south face of the Barre des Écrins. Here, they were subjected to a lengthy delay in a chilling wind in order to avoid bombardment by rocks sent down by parties above, and when they eventually started up, further time was lost by assuming, unwarrantedly as it turned out, that the parties above knew where they were going. Some hours were wasted on trial and error interspersed by a good lead, by Gavin, of a difficult chimney before they concluded that a gully which they had originally rejected as impossible must offer the way. Examination soon revealed that it did so, that it was far from impossible and that it led to the fixed ropes which reassured them that they were at last on the route—and offered an efficient if athletic and unaesthetic way up to easier rocks above. These passed, they lost the route again and, Smythe's form having improved somewhat, he managed a difficult lead up thin holds at the cost only of considerable anxiety. They contrived to reach the upper snowfield, seamed with rock ribs, up which they forged a route, at times being forced to cut steps into the ice beneath now softening snow, until they came to the cliffs leading to the summit ridge. Here, steeper, firmer rock gave better climbing and they finally reached the summit ridge twelve hours after starting and nearly nine hours from the Col des Avalanches: they had wasted some four hours in route-finding errors, most uncharacteristic of Smythe.

Signs of deteriorating weather, a certain lack of enthusiasm and the lateness of the hour persuaded them to forgo the last few feet to the summit. Instead, they set off along the ridge and down over the Pic Lory towards the Dôme de Neige des Écrins, turning north from the Brèche and rapidly descending the snow-slopes of the north face to the Col des Écrins. From there, they scrambled and slid down fixed ropes, negotiated the bergschrund without serious difficulty and so made their way back to La Bérarde at the end of a sixteen-hour day.

It also proved to be the end of their sojourn in the Dauphiné. Deteriorating weather persuaded them to try their luck in the Mont Blanc range and they headed, by bus and train, for Chamonix, stopping en route to enjoy the culinary delights of Annécy. Their unspecified objective on Mont Blanc was one of the great routes on the south side of the mountain, but it transpired that conditions ruled this out for the time being and they accordingly settled on a visit to the less frequented western part of the range around the Glacier de la Trélatête. Thus it was that, after a somewhat half-hearted attempt to savour Chamonix night-life, they embarked on the bus to Les Contamines and strolled up, first through the forest, then over the rocky alp above, to the Trélatête Hotel. Five days had been lost to the weather and the transfer and, when the next day dawned reasonably fine, they decided to make for Mont Tondu, the extreme south-western peak of the Mont Blanc range and, at about 10,500 feet, somewhat of a pigmy amongst giants.

Mont Tondu is sometimes described as "little", "a good training peak" and "a good introduction to the Mont Blanc range". Smythe and Gavin ascended via the Col du Mont Tondu—not at all a glamorous way and certainly less classic than the traverse via the Col des Chasseurs and north-west ridge. However, it enabled them to survey the territory on which they next had designs. A trek up to the Col Infranchissable at the head of the Glacier de la Trélatête the following day, with, incidentally, an ascent of the Tête Carrée to the south via its north ridge, supplemented their observations.

A couple of days of sun had sufficed to consolidate the snow, freshly fallen during the poor weather, and next day they set out on the first leg of the classic traverse from Trélatête to the Col du Géant via the Aiguille de Bionnassay, the summit of Mont Blanc and the Brenva Spur. It is an exceptional traverse not so much by reason of great or sustained difficulty, most of which is concentrated on the Aiguille de Bionnassay and the descent by the Brenva Spur, the rest of the route lying over relatively easy ground, but on account of its length, beauty and classic nature. It extends over some ten miles of high mountain terrain that never falls below about 11,000 feet, rarely wavering from the most direct natural line between the two opposite points.

The first section of this traverse involves ascending the Aiguille de la Bérangère from the Trélatête Hotel and thence crossing the Dômes de Miage to the Durier Hut to the north of the Col de Miage. The Aiguille de la Bérangère is often described as a "walk" from the Trélatête Hotel and for a pair as fit as Smythe and Gavin that was, no doubt, an accurate enough description. The Hotel has the disadvantage of being little more than 6,000 feet above sea-level and the ascent to the summit of the Aiguille de la Bérangère could well be described as easy a 5,000 foot plod to the top of an 11,000 foot peak as one is likely to find anywhere in the Alps. A lazy start spared Smythe and Gavin the experience of sharing the summit with the earlier "tourists" and after a rest on top, they were soon on their way down to the Col de la Bérangère and then up and over the Dômes de Miage, not so much a peak or even a series of peaks, as a ridge, a mile and a half long, containing several points and collets with, however, less than 400 feet separating the highest and lowest points. This ridge, which is usually climbed in the opposite direction, mainly in order to avoid the long and unpleasant trudge through soft snow back down the Trélatête Glacier, rises to its last point north of the Col Infranchissable and then falls to the Col de Miage and the Durier Hut. Smythe and Gavin arrived at the hut in the afternoon to find it tiny, damp, filthy, unequipped and untenanted until the later arrival of a French party of four.

At six o'clock the following morning, they set off up the south ridge of the Aiguille de Bionnassay, certainly one of the most beautiful peaks in the Alps. The main difficulty on the south ridge is a rocky step at about half height, normally turned on the left or western side. But the early morning sun tempted them on to the mixed slopes to the right and it was only with some difficulty that they regained the corniced ridge which they then followed to the summit, reaching it at about 9 a.m. Although a leisurely stay would have been welcome, a glance at the north-east ridge which they must now descend revealed cornices which would involve traversing out on to the steep and now sun-warmed eastern slopes, and an early continuation was obviously desirable. Thin soft snow over ice necessitated the cutting of steps for much of the way but eventually they reached the Col de Bionnassay, easier ground and a break for food and rest in the now hot sun. From here, no difficulty barred the way to the slopes of the Dôme du Goûter and, a couple of hundred feet higher, the Vallot Hut where they spent the next night.

A pre-dawn start next day saw them on the summit of Mont Blanc for sunrise, then setting off down towards the Col de la Brenva in order to descend by the Brenva Spur. The tracks of parties seizing the good weather of the previous two days in order to make the ascent led them down without difficulty to the famous ice-ridge where they rested before following tracks again, away from the buttress by which the climb is usually ascended, and instead down its snowy flank to the south. Such difficulties as were presented surrendered to Gavin's axe while Smythe lazed in the sun, and soon they were at the Col Moore. Poor snow and steep slopes again brought Gavin's axe into play descending from the Col de la Fourche and before long they were ensconced in the Torino Hut where, after food and a pleasant bottle of Chianti, they endured a less pleasant night in a crowded dortoir.

They planned to continue in the line they had already followed for many miles, and to trace the frontier along the Rochefort Arête, north-west from the Col du Géant. After that, weather still permitting, they would turn their attention to one of the great southern ridges. The first part of their plan was carried through without a hitch; they found it necessary at times to move on to the flank of the arête, so narrow and corniced was the crest, but they arrived at the summit of the Aiguille without incident and made their way back by the same route to the Col du Géant. By contrast, a descent to Courmayeur, from where they intended to ascend to the old Gamba Hut, did them no good at all: Smythe slipped and injured an ankle (which still bothered him two months later), and then, in the fleshpots, he contracted a fever accompanied by a fearsome headache. Although they had intended to go straight up to the Gamba Hut, Smythe required a day's rest at the Purtud Hotel from which, after another liberal administration of Chianti, they set out in earnest.

From the Gamba Hut, they spent the first day in a reconnaissance as far as the Col du Frêney and concluded that their route of first choice, the Innominata Ridge, was feasible. It was, in a sense, an unhappy return for Smythe, for his last visit to the Col du Frêney had been in order to organize the search for a couple of young Oxford climbers who had disappeared a month previously. Their bodies were found and recovered, largely due to the skill of Adolphe Rey and the Courmayeur guides; Smythe subsequently referred to it as the only occasion on which he climbed with a guide but one suspects that had the mission not been one of such gravity he would have muddled through on his own.

The Innominata Ridge today constitutes a somewhat less demanding and serious proposition than it did in 1939. It was usual, pre-war, to do it with a bivouac; today, a bivouac hut has been placed on the Col Eccles. Smythe and Gavin, however, had been sufficiently encouraged by their reconnaissance to attempt the route in one day from the Gamba Hut, 8,000 feet below the summit, which they left at about 1.15 a.m. They made excellent progress as far as the Col du Frêney which they reached in three hours. A mis-reading of their route description caused them some delay on the way to the summit of the Pic Eccles, which they seem to have reached by a novel variation. There, they had the satisfaction of seeing German parties, who had preferred to bivouac, only a little way ahead of them and they were able to take time for a rest and second breakfast before embarking on the final sweep of the route from the Col Eccles to the summit of Mont Blanc de Courmayeur.

Most of the technical difficulty of the Innominata Ridge occurs in the negotiation of its lower section, immediately above the Col Eccles, where it rises in two steps for a few hundred feet until it is necessary to move left or right when confronted by the unclimbable granite face of Mont Blanc de Courmayeur. Gavin led the first step which Smythe, suffering it seems not only from a sprained ankle but also from general ineptitude, needed a tug to get up. Soon the second step was below them and they were moving left to tackle the great couloir, moving whenever the threat or appearance of debris, despatched by a German party above them, permitted. Although technical rock difficulties were now below them, danger was not, and to avoid it required some speedy and efficient ice-work. However, several hours after leaving the col they were restoring themselves with a snack a short walk from the summit. The last few hours had involved step-cutting almost continuously up the long slopes which link the upper crest of the Innominata Ridge with that of the Brouillard which they now followed to the top of Mont Blanc de Courmayeur. Thus far, they had climbed in effect in the lee of the mountain but they were now greeted with cold west winds, and had soon traversed the main summit and descended to the Vallot Hut where a night in this new, metal box failed to impress Smythe as memorably warm and comfortable.

The Innominata Ridge is a very high standard of mountain "wandering", if it is wandering at all, but it marked a suitable point for calling an end to the season and Smythe and Gavin descended to Chamonix and returned to England. Within a month, war had broken out and for six years Smythe's link with the mountains was of a different sort. Until he was transferred to the general staff in the Italian campaign, he was in charge of Commando Training Schools, and the ranks of post-war mountaineers contained many whose introduction to the hills was at his hands in North Wales, the Cairngorms or the Canadian Rockies to which he was to return on a number of occasions.

When Smythe returned to the Alps after the Second World War it was to Adelboden that he went first, in February 1946. His plans included the elusive traverse of the Oberland glaciers, this time from west to east. He had no particular liking for Adelboden, considering it somewhat spoilt by the demands of the skiing industry. From that point of view it is probably worse today than it was, for there are now lifts, and a mechanical device carries one up to the restaurant-crowned Hahnenmoos where Smythe skiied in 1946; but the higher mountain terrain around the town has escaped their attention and the ridge which undulates north from the Hahnenmoos to the summit of the Albristhorn at over 9,000 feet suffers a trespass only at a solitary low point. For the remaining 2,000 feet, the ridge remains much as Smythe found it when he chose it for his first post-war solitary Alpine outing.

The Albristhorn is a friendly peak and its south ridge, which Smythe followed in winter conditions, offers a friendly walk along a rolling crest. At one point, three Crib Goch-like pinnacles seem to threaten difficulties but they are neatly turned on the left. At times, broken, rocky sections suggest a scramble but nowhere is the use of the hands necessary.

Some 3,000 feet above the Hahnenmoos, the summit offers a better prospect than that enjoyed by many a grander peak. Modest though it be, the Albristhorn is the highest point for some ten miles in any direction. The southern horizon is largely occupied by the triplets of the western Oberland, Wildstrübel, Wildhorn and Diablerets, though the Glacier de la Plaine Morte attracts the eye and the humble Röhrbachstein makes a determined attempt to steal part of the scene. The Pennine Alps, including the Matterhorn and Grand Combin, occupy such gaps as the triplets leave, and Mont Blanc itself crowns the Wildhorn. To the east, the eye falls first on the Balmhorn and Altels, then, nearer, the Lohners and the Tschingelochtighorn. Behind these start the Blümlisalp peaks, eventually ceding the sky-line to Jungfrau, Mönch and Eiger. Such a prospect would certainly have reminded Smythe that he was amongst old friends: very few of these summits had escaped an earlier acquaintance.

Smythe did not bother with the last easy slopes leading to the summit of the Albristhorn. Instead, he ran quickly down to Adelboden and on the following day took the train from Frutigen to Goppenstein to prepare for the traverse of the Oberland glaciers.

Many consider, and Smythe was amongst them, that the Lötschental, to which the station at Goppenstein is the most popular gateway, is the most beautiful of the Alpine valleys. It certainly remains today one of the least spoilt, give or take a car-park covering several acres at Fafleralp. The view over the valley from the Hockenalp, which Smythe now visited, towards the Bietschhorn, Lötschentaler Breithorn and Lötschenlücke is grand—Smythe, of course, had good reason to remember the Bietschhorn. The view from the Hockenhorn, dominating the ridge a few hundred metres above Hockenalp, is not merely grand; it is breath-taking and arguably the most glorious in all the Alps. It is, furthermore, a delightful short expedition either direct from Hockenalp or from the Lötschenpass Chalet/Hotel, well within the capacities of almost anyone and practically free from all difficulty and danger.

Not all that much has changed in the Lötschental since Smythe's 1946 visit. The Pension Bietschhorn in Kippel has been spared the bland facelift visited on so many inns of character; the tree-shaded terrace still tempts one to sip and gaze all day. It is now run by the great-niece of the Belwalds who greeted Smythe; their hospitality can hardly have bettered hers. His guide on the tour that followed, Willi Lehner, still lives a mile up the road in Wiler, although he has now given up his guiding.

This was one of the few occasions in his career on which Smythe climbed with a guide, though on only one occasion was he "guided" in the normal sense of that term and that was when, as a small boy, he made his first climb. He had climbed with Adolphe Rey, but this was in the course of a search for a pair who had gone missing. His need, on the glacier traverse, was not so much of a guide as of a partner and companion for the glaciers. The length and lift of the trek from Fafleralp to the Hollandia Hut on the Lötschenlücke is quite intimidating, and it is a measure of change that when Smythe, Lehner and a porter set out in winter with heavily-laden sacs they did so not from Fafleralp but from Kippel, a further seven miles down the valley and 1,500 feet lower. Nevertheless, eight hours later they were at the Hollandia Hut, boosted by a draught of cognac on the Langgletscher, with Smythe wallowing in the rare experience of leaving to Lehner, as guide, the entire responsibility for fires, food, etc.

Smythe had a poor night. It preceded a worse day; it was soon clear that they were in for a spell of really bad weather and the wise thing was to descend without more ado. Although conditions were far from perfect, they were soon running down again to Kippel but glühwein and Frau Belwald's cooking, although considerable compensation, could not be expected to make up for yet another frustrated attempt on the traverse. It was some weeks later that Smythe took up the challenge yet again, this time of necessity without benefit of guide or porter, for the post-war foreign exchange controls had left him with insufficient means to hire them. It was to be a solitary venture, this time from east to west, with Münster as the point of departure.

Arriving at Münster fresh from the Pennine Alps, he went straight up to the Galmihorn Hut and, the following morning, made his way north–west from the hut (leaving the Kastelhorn and Hohe Gwächte to the west), on to the Münstiger Glacier, following it westwards to the Galmilücke where he lunched. He had had it in mind to climb the Galmihorn but, overwhelmed by laziness, ran instead down the Galmi Glacier to its junction with the Fiescher Glacier which he then laboriously ascended to the Finsteraarhorn Hut. Next day, he made the ascent of the Finsteraarhorn via the ordinary route, breakfasting perversely at the Hugisattel rather than the Frühstückplatz. The day after that, and a long day it was, he finally completed the elusive traverse, crossing the Grünhornlücke to the Aletschfirn, then ascending to the Lötschenlücke before running down the Langgletscher to the Lötschental. Stopping for tea at the Pension Bietschhorn in Kippel, he finally descended to Goppenstein for the train and the journey back to the fleshpots.

Between his two attempts at the Oberland traverse in 1946, Smythe fitted what has now come to be accepted as the classic ski traverse of the Alps, the Haute Route. After a couple of days skiing solo from Verbiers, he joined forces with Jimmy Belaieff and Dr Broccard. The party, or such members of it as were from time to time fit, warmed up on a tour to the Cabane de Mont Fort from which they made ski ascents of the Rosa Blanche and Mont Fort before returning to Verbier and moving to Zermatt. From the Bétemps Hut, they made the ascent of the Cima di Jazzi and the traverse of the Breithorn via the Schwarztor. Then they set out on the Haute Route.

The version of the Haute Route which seems today to be accepted as classic is that which involves traversing the Pennine Alps from Saas Fee to Chamonix. The Smythe version involved linking Zermatt and Verbiers.

The first day was devoted to leading Belaieff, snow-blinded by the descent from the Breithorn, to the Schönbiel Hut. Next day, they crossed the Col de Valpelline, traversed the Haut Glacier de Tsa de Tsan and the Col du Mont Brulé, running thence down to Arolla where they had arranged for hotel and reprovisioning. On the third day, 22 March, they continued from Arolla, via the Pas de Chèvres to the Cabane des Dix from which, feeling energetic, they made an afternoon ascent of La Luette. Finally, a long day was spent descending the Glacier du Seilon to what is now the Barrage des Dix, crossing the Rosa Blanche range and descending to Verbier.

Expeditions of the type described in this chapter are the bread and butter of the average alpinist but they were not, for that reason, any the less delectable to Smythe. Whilst the "great routes" may have yielded achievement, these more modest ventures gave fulfilment. In what was to prove to be the last chapter in his story, the North American expeditions, Smythe aptly realized both.

CHAPTER XII

Rocky Mountains

DURING THE LAST years of his life, Smythe spent as much time in the mountains of North America as anywhere. He visited them first as a servant of the King, but later visits were private, although, like Whymper before him, he was welcomed as a guest of the great railway companies.

His manner of visiting some at least of the ranges of North America was idiosyncratic. Military activities during the war gave him both pretext and opportunity for aerial reconnaissance and, among others, he overflew Mount Alberta and Mount Robson and even made a flight to Alaska where Mount McKinley impressed him as "the wildest, loneliest and most inhospitable panorama on which I have ever gazed"—impressive indeed, bearing in mind his experience of Kangchenjunga, Kamet and Everest. Military duties also took him to the Coast Range in Washington state—he was to return here again in 1947 and cross the range twice, by road. A break from duties was responsible for his first visit to the mountains of New England in 1944; he was again to return, this time in 1946, with his second wife Nona but, so far as is known, the only ascents made were those of Mount Monadnock, by car, and Mount Washington, by cog railway.

However, North America yielded a host of more orthodox mountaineering experiences. These were at first incidental to military duties and some time was spent scrambling with troops in the Colin Range to which Smythe later returned. Winter training took them to the Columbia Icefield. Soon after arriving, Smythe had teamed up with Rex Gibson for the ascent of Mount Athabasca and, later, winter conditions on Snow Dome offered a stern test to the troops. More than anything else, the war-time experience added up to an extensive and prolonged reconnaissance. At the end of it all, Smythe knew that there was a great deal to be done in the Rocky Mountains.

The first return visit came in June 1946 when Smythe, accompanied by Nona, found himself in Jasper. Using Bruno Engler as a guide/companion, and with Jack Hargreaves in charge of pack-horses, they headed into the Victoria Cross Range of mountains to the north-west of Jasper, making first for Elysium Pass, then for Barrett Pass. Although this is not particularly highly thought of as a climbing area nowadays, they nevertheless contrived to keep themselves perfectly happy first of all with the ascent of a minor peak which they named Mount Ruin, then with a traverse of Monarch Mountain which certainly seems to have been a worthwhile expedition. Later, with Engler as his partner, Smythe made the first ascent of a minor unclimbed peak and also climbed the two unclimbed summits of a three-headed peak which they named The Trident.

This was merely the overture to an extended and varied season. After the Victoria Cross Range foray, Smythe, Nona and Engler met a Mr and Mrs Gardiner at the ACC Cabin at Lake O'Hara, and Smythe, Gardiner and Engler set out for Mount Victoria. Spending the night at the hut higher up, they reached the south and highest summit of the mountain via the south-east ridge and then traversed the interesting summit ridge to the north summit some 200 feet lower, from here making their way back to the hut and then down to Lake O'Hara.

At the cabin at Lake O'Hara, a young American had arrived. This was David Wessel, at that stage almost totally inexperienced but anxious to progress in a mountaineering career. He joined the party and figured in almost all of Smythe's North American ventures thereafter. The next of these was an attempt on Mount Hungabee which the four proposed to climb via the west arête from the Opabin Pass.

All went well as far as the pass, and for some way up the ridge above it which they climbed on two ropes of two. Then, however, Gardiner and Engler, on one rope, were assailed by doubts about the weather and decided to discontinue the climb. Smythe, perhaps more optimistic but certainly never disposed to seek a corporate view of prospects, saw no reason not to go on, and he and Wessel duly reached the summit and, eventually, descended, all in glorious weather. After that, however, the going got tougher.

First, Smythe and Nona, with Mr and Mrs Gardiner, set out for the Lodge at Lake Magog with an attempt on the classic north ridge route of Mount Assiniboine in mind if not definitely decided upon.

It may safely be speculated that, once in the area, Smythe would find such a striking line on such a grand mountain utterly irresistible. In the event, others had less enthusiasm for the enterprise than he and, it having proved impossible to agree upon a party, Smythe set out alone.

He first followed the obvious broad couloir that cleaves the rock wall which defends the base of the summit pyramid of the mountain proper. It turned out to be hard work—a vast number of steps had to be cut—and had he known of the existence of the easier path which zig-zags up to the right, he would almost certainly have taken it. He reached the plinth of the mountain in due course, and thence followed the usual approach to the north ridge via the north face and made satisfactory progress until brought up against the rock step which forms the crux of this route. Recent bad weather had left it icy and dangerous, particularly for the solitary climber, and Smythe may well have pressed his attempts a bit beyond the justifiable before abandoning it and embarking upon the initially worrying descent.

Driving south from Jasper, Smythe had noticed an unusual, dolomite-like peak to the west. It was Mount Brussels and, although not one of the mightier mountains of the Rockies, it is unusual enough to have attracted a number of attempts and difficult enough to have repulsed them all. One who had been thus attracted and repulsed was Douglas Crosby, a climber from Banff, and it was in his company that Smythe and Wessel set out for their attempt.

No way up Mount Brussels is easy. The line which at that time appeared least invulnerable was the east ridge and it was this that they determined to follow. After bivouacking below, therefore, they set out to gain access to the col between Mount Brussels and Mount Christie from which the east ridge rises, at first at a relatively moderate angle but then rearing up until at one point it overhangs. The party negotiated the lower and very loose section without difficulty. The problems began immediately the ridge steepened, just beyond a gap, and they were eventually forced to the conclusion that, short of resorting to pitons, which they were not prepared to do, further progress was unjustifiable.

Mount Brussels was, in fact, climbed the following year, with the aid of pitons. It was a controversial ascent, and Smythe was among those who disapproved and let it be known that he regarded the mountain as being no more climbed by such methods than it would be if a helicopter had lowered a team on to the summit. There was nothing novel in this attitude towards artificial aids, so far as Smythe was concerned, and he was consistent in his attitude towards the use of pitons, to the point of feeling defeated on a climb where success was due to it. At the same time, it deserves to be noted in passing that, after their first defeat on the east ridge of Mount Brussels, Smythe's team conceived the idea of overcoming the pitch which had defeated them by lassooing rocks above it and climbing the rope, in its way just as "unnatural" and "artificial" as hammering in a peg.

Defeated on Mount Brussels, they plucked the consolation prize with the short climb from the col to the summit of Mount Christie via its south-west ridge. Smythe and Wessel then moved on to attempt Mount Alberta which has the reputation of being one of the most difficult peaks, some would say *the* most difficult peak, in the Rockies. Before Smythe and Wessel approached it in September 1946, it had been climbed only once and that was by a large Japanese party which had used siege tactics and spent several days on it. Following their route, but with variations, Smythe and Wessel forced a way to within 200 feet of the summit ridge before retreating. Though creditable to have gone so far, the difficulties are by no means over once the summit ridge is attained.

The consolation for defeat on Mount Alberta was the first ascent of Mount Bridgland. Smythe had remarked upon this mountain earlier when, climbing in the Victoria Cross Range, he had observed it on the far side of the Yellowhead Pass. In height, it is a modest mountain by Rockies standards, reaching less than 10,000 feet, but it is more of a climber's mountain than most. Smythe suggested it to Wessel as compensation for Alberta, and Rex Gibson's sudden appearance on the scene boosted the party to three. After a memorable camp on the lower slopes, they explored the mountain from the south west, initially via a subsidiary ridge which, they hoped, would establish them well on the main peak.

Only when they reached the crest of this ridge, after a couple of hours up grass, scree and broken rock, were they able to confirm that it offered a way, albeit a roundabout way, to the top. Bearing round in a great arc, it passed over three subsidiary summits before buttressing the final tower. The first two points on the ridge were easily gained. The third was as easily avoided by traversing its slopes to the gap beyond, and immediately before, the final peak. This latter rose gently at first but then reared up, intimidatingly steep before the summit several hundred feet above.

Gibson led off and, after three ropelengths, the party reached the ledge at which it had been agreed that Smythe would assume the lead. Declining the phenomenal chimney which cleaves the mountain on the right, Smythe managed to overcome an initial overhang by means of a corner and then followed easier slabs and short walls until the party was beneath the final overhang just short of the summit. This it proved possible to avoid by traversing along ledges on the west face until it was feasible to follow a break up easier ground to the summit, a happy hour on which was followed by a speedy descent and lunch on the col before returning to Jasper.

With confidence thus boosted, the three set off, on 9 September, for their final climb of the year. Mount Robson, highest point in the Canadian Rockies, is rarely in good condition. This 1946 attempt, on which they intended to follow the Hall-Führer variant on the south face south-south-west ridge route, was frustrated by bad weather; and Smythe fared no better when, returning in 1947 and intending to climb the mountain by the Kain, east face, route, poor conditions again ruled out an ascent although on this occasion a trudge up easy slopes yielded the summit of Rearguard Mountain—hardly an adequate substitute.

The 1947 season had begun in June, in Jasper. Smythe had, in 1946, discussed with Rex Gibson the idea of mounting a small exploratory expedition to an almost unknown part of the Rockies to the north of Jasper. In June, 1947, the party consisted of Smythe and Nona and Gibson (the seminal influences in its planning), together with Wessel and Ross and Henry Hall (an American), as climbers, and Noel Odell as climber and geologist. The expedition had formal and laudable objectives. Less formally it was for Smythe an opportunity to have "a first-rate mountaineering holiday far from an unsatisfactory civilization."

They warmed up with an attempt on Mount Colin which Smythe had noticed during the training days and which remained, in 1947, unclimbed. Gibson and Ross would take the south ridge while Smythe and Wessel would go for the north. In the event, both parties were defeated by a combination of difficulties consisting of a steep wall, and the inexperience of the juniors on the ropes, Ross and Wessel, whom Smythe and Gibson were reluctant to expose to the hazards involved. Smythe was not sure the north ridge would go, but Gibson thought that the south ridge would. When, in August, Smythe, Ross and Odell returned to the mountain, they reached the summit via the south ridge for the first ascent. Smythe had, however, used a piton for protection on the crux section and considered that it deprived the ascent of legitimacy. This may perhaps be a pedantic point, but it was a real one for Smythe who was never able to speak of the ascent with any of the satisfaction which would normally attach to such an adventure. Nor did it help that they were able to complete the traverse by descending the north ridge and establishing its viability as a route. A later ascent of Mount Louis via the south-east face (Kain) route with Odell no doubt offered some consolation and also some excitement, for Odell was struck by lightning on the descent.

They were now ready for what was undoubtedly the greatest achievement of the 1947 season and probably also its most memorable feature: the exploration of the Lloyd George Mountains.

There are still unclimbed peaks in the Rockies: at least, there is no record of climbs on many of the vast number of subsidiary peaks which lie within the immense area between the more popular and better-known regions of Alaska to the north and Banff-Jasper to the south. Within this huge area, there are hundreds of peaks of 6,000 to 9,000 feet and a few that are higher. At the end of the Second World War, this area was even less well-explored, and the part of it which particularly interested Smythe had hardly been penetrated at all.

In north-east British Columbia today, about 200 miles north-west of Fort St John and about a hundred miles south-west of Fort Nelson, lies the Kwadacha Wilderness Park; within 40 years of the peaks of the Lloyd George Range first being visited by Smythe's expedition, the area has been thus packaged and labelled for future consumption. Prior to 1947 these summits were virgin. Haworth and Chesterfield had penetrated as far as the lakes which now bear their names and crossed the range between them but no one had succeeded in gaining access to the high mountain country to the north-east which they drained. As Smythe readily admitted, the problems of approaching the range had been vastly more severe when the only transport available was canoe and foot. By 1947 air transport had begun to open up the hitherto secret mountain fastnesses of the Rockies. Certainly, the 1947 party did not intend to do it the hard way.

Odell, Hall, Smythe and his wife went by train from Jasper to Vanderhoof from where they took a taxi to Fort St James. Things almost went to plan; the plane they had arranged duly took off as arranged and deposited the four of them at Lake Haworth. The following morning Gibson, Wessel and Ross were to be flown in from Fort Nelson, on the Alaska Highway, the itinerary which they had chosen to follow.

The base camp which they established on the shores of Lake Haworth, under Nona's supervision, served them very well indeed for the whole of the expedition. The lake, six miles long and one mile wide, lies along a south-west/north-east axis, and camp was pitched near the north-west shore. Behind, largely afforested slopes led only to minor summits; across the lake to the south-east, three more significant peaks arose, later to be named Cloudmaker, Little Cloudmaker and Mount Chesterfield. The head of the lake steals the scene: here a mighty cirque of rock and ice vulnerable, in the event (although not immediately obviously so), at two points leads to the terrain above and beyond, which comprises the great Lloyd George icefield and the three summits which crown it, Mount Lloyd George, Mount Glendower and Mount Criccieth. The two points of access proved to be, on the left, a narrow valley which curved round towards a high bowl occupied by a stagnant glacier from which they found routes to Mount Glendower; and, on the right, the Llanberis Glacier, consisting mainly of a difficult-looking ice-fall some 3,000 feet in height, via which the massive ice-field above contrives to find its way to Lake Haworth. To the right of the Llanberis Glacier, walls and slopes protect the peaks which buttress the ice-field to the east.

The routes of egress from the valley to the mountains above did not immediately reveal themselves. Reconnaissance parties went out on 4 July and one, consisting of Gibson, Wessel and Ross, reported that the possibilities of the Llanberis Glacier were worth further examination. These three accordingly went up the glacier on 5 July and succeeded in reaching the ice-field above, thus establishing that there was a feasible route via the true left side of the glacier even if it was neither easy nor wholly safe. Hall, Odell and Smythe, meanwhile, had a less demanding day in view. The plane was due to fly back in with the rest of their stores and it had been arranged to use it for a couple of hours in order to have a look at the surrounding area as well as the Lloyd George Range itself. In addition to all its other benefits, this air reconnaissance disclosed the approach to the Lloyd George summits from the west, via the stagnant glacier valley. There was no reason now why an attempt should not be made on the summits once weather permitted.

On 6 July, after a morning of bad weather, Smythe and Odell took advantage of an afternoon break to ascend a minor peak of about 6,800 feet behind the camp. They were able to gain new perspectives before bad weather drove them down again. For a week thereafter the weather prevented all but short trips and minor climbs. However, by 14 July it had improved enough for a trip from the Lake to the stagnant glacier confirming that an attempt might be made from there on Mount Glendower; and on the afternoon of 15 July they left in two parties.

They climbed as two parties because two distinct routes were in prospect. One of these was to follow a long couloir which emerged at a point high on the west-south-west ridge of Mount Glendower; Gibson, Hall and Ross were to go for this. The second route followed broken slopes leading to a point lower down on the same ridge which would then have to be followed to the summit. This, Smythe, Odell and Wessel were to climb. They found no significant difficulties in gaining access to the ridge and, once on the ridge, easily traversed a point on it to a gap beyond. Here, the trouble began. The ridge ahead was dangerously corniced and it was necessary to take to the face in order to avoid the dangers. This posed no great technical difficulties, for the face was not unduly steep and could easily have been negotiated; but the snow was deep and yielding, Smythe was overcome by a sudden conviction that they were on very dangerous ground and no one questioned his suggestion to retreat. The disappointment was partial, for the others succeeded in the couloir and were able to reach the summit without encountering deterrent dangers. At least one of the mountaineering objectives of the expedition had been attained.

A second followed. At dawn the next day, the entire party, except for Nona who remained in charge of camp, set out for Mount Lloyd George. Taking the Llanberis Glacier route reconnoitred some two weeks earlier they went up past the ice-fall and cliffs to the left until the angle eased and they emerged on to the ice-field. From here, the poor quality of the snow tired them, but no difficulties at all were encountered until, just for the hell of it, they chose a pitch of steep but easily avoidable snow below the summit. The descent by the same route was notable only for even more appalling snow on the ice-field and even greater danger of serac-fall descending the glacier back to the camp.

As soon as the weather eased again, Smythe and Wessel set out to seek yet another success. From the camp, they had looked across the lake to the peaks which crowned the terrain of the south eastern shore. Because these peaks seemed to attract bad weather they had earned the name Cloudmaker. They stood a little more than 8,000 feet in height and a way not merely to their summits, but to their feet, would have to be found. It appeared that a valley which debouched into the lake at the far side might offer a route, although so thick and impenetrable were the banks of the lake that Smythe and Wessel accomplished the first part of the journey on a crude raft, repelling an attack by a bear en route.

As they had thought, the valley led round to slopes which tumbled down from the summit ridge of the Little Cloudmaker and they were able to reach the summit without difficulty. Resting there perhaps longer than, with benefit of hindsight, was desirable, they were suddenly reminded by signs of deteriorating weather that if they wished to take in the main Cloudmaker summit, they had best be off. Descending to the col between the two peaks, they then ascended via a subsidiary ridge to the main west ridge and followed this, accompanied by the rumble of distant thunder, to the point at which it abuts against a 200 foot wall which guards the summit. Then the storm broke. Finding such little shelter as they could, each in turn felt the secondary effects of nearby flashes of lightning and both were soaked through by the time the freezing storm had passed. The summit lacked all attraction; they descended to their gear and set off down the mountainside until, 1,500 feet down, and now warmer and drier, they stopped, exchanged glances and set off back up as one man. Conditions were far from good, and rain and drizzle accompanied them, but eventually they arrived. The mission accomplished and a small cairn built, they dashed off down in the last of the light, collected timber for a fire and settled in for the night, glowing with contentment.

The sole remaining objective was one they had fixed upon when they first saw the ice-field and summits above—the traverse of the Mount Lloyd George–Mount Glendower ridge, a passage which appears to have something in common with the Dom–Taschhorn or Midi–Plan traverses in pre-commercialized condition. On 26 July, they left camp with this traverse in mind and, although delayed by doubts about the weather, reached the summit of Mount Lloyd George by the same route as previously and in the same time, ten hours. Not without some hesitation, in view of the weather, they then took the narrow and, at points corniced ridge leading as they thought to Mount Glendower. They soon discovered that the ridge was not continuous, but broken by a steep rift, and they had to make a devious descent and re-ascent by the north-east slopes of Mount Glendower, over appalling and deteriorating snow in order to reach its summit. Descending by the couloir route established on the first ascent of Mount Glendower, they returned to camp without incident, and to a delicious meal prepared by Nona, 21 hours after departing. It proved to be the last venture of the expedition and on 30 July they flew away from the Lloyd George wilderness and back to the joys of civilization.

Although he was not to know it, the return from the Lloyd George expedition was the last significant act of Smythe's mountaineering career. During the few remaining years of his life he of course returned to the Alps and savoured again the delights of Britain's hills. For much of the time, however, he was preoccupied with writing, for this was the most prolific phase of his literary career; and the evidence suggests also that domestic life was rewarding and his Sussex garden distracting.

He never became totally proof to the charm of the remote places. He planned a solitary return to his beloved Bhyundar Valley but it was not to be. At the very point of embarking upon it, death intervened.

CHAPTER XIII

A Mountain Visionary

WHAT THEN, AT the end of it all, does one conclude about Smythe? Although the concern of this account has been to review the career of the mountaineer, in the final analysis he cannot be separated entirely from the man and better to appreciate the former one must at least speculate about the latter.

As was suggested at the start, the seeds of Smythe's mountaineering career were sown in early childhood when the death of his father deprived him of an important influence and when ill-health caused his mother to insulate him from the experiences and influences which might have taken a father's place. As a result, Smythe undertook social burdens which no young person should be asked to bear and which it took him many years to learn to carry. It is merely ironic that, as Raymond Greene later diagnosed, much of this was unnecessary.

Nevertheless, it left its mark upon the man who emerged, perhaps not physically but certainly psychologically. Smythe's physique was undoubtedly consistent with protracted ill-health in childhood—small and slight in stature, he appeared "incongruously frail", "incongruously" so because of the extraordinary strength and stamina which he seemed effortlessly to summon when the occasion arose. Psychologically, however, the causal connection with his childhood is easier to assume. He emerged from his schooldays without ever having learned by experience how to cope comfortably with social relationships; he emerged burdened with the doubts of others and himself as to his ability to excel at anything at all. Most of all, and very likely for these reasons, he emerged with what is only inadequately described as an unusual capacity for fulfilment through the mountain experience in all its aspects.

The first of these matters resulted in a misinterpretation of his character which plagued him all his life and which led to intense animosities. Some thought him stand-offish and "insufferably self-sufficient", others thought him to be egotistic and self-opinionated. There were those who found his conversation (when they were fortunate enough to experience it) "banal" or "dogmatic". Graham Brown came to hate him with an incomprehensible passionate intensity. In private notes written for his own eyes only he insulted and derided Smythe. Those who knew him better appreciated not merely that he was shy and reserved but also, beneath it, highly-strung. This emotional energy gave him an "immense enthusiasm" which inspired others and a determination which, once a plan was embarked upon, allowed nothing to stand in the way. The Kangchenjunga and Everest experiences were severe tests of character. Observers found Smythe to be "imperturbable, reliable and good-tempered" throughout subject only to some hesitancy in coping with jokes against himself.

Smythe was himself aware of those facets of his personality which gave rise to comment. Indeed, he positively cultivated some of them. He had, he says, a knack of detaching himself from his surroundings and becoming wholly introspective; this he regarded as being worth much more on a mountain than mere brute strength or stamina.

Once he had decided to make a career out of mountaineering, self-doubt about his ability to excel caused him to go at it in an almost ruthless manner—his living was, after all, to depend upon it. The will to succeed sometimes caused him to appear unreliable as, for example, in the publication of accounts of the Brenva Face climbs. He led Graham Brown to understand that he, Smythe, would not rush into print and then, to his later regret, reneged on the understanding for selfish motives.

It was this aspect of his personality which many, including some stalwarts of the pre-war climbing establishment, found insufferably "pushy". For these stalwarts, modesty, the amateur tradition and subtle self-deprecation were among the virtues. It would be presumptuous to be critical of them, for although some did singularly little, others were mountaineers of rare distinction and significant attainment; and in any case, criticism would stem from a standpoint merely of alternative and in no way necessarily superior values. The contrast with Smythe's career and attitudes is, nevertheless, marked. He failed at a second-rank school, attended Faraday College without conspicuous success and taught himself by soloing in the Tyrol. Socially awkward and unsure, slight in stature almost to the point of frailty, it took him time to master the art of understatement. Like

Whymper and Mummery before him, he had no birthright to succeed and was by some resented for excelling nevertheless. Worse still, his semi-professionalism was heavily dependent upon self-publicity. He succeeded in establishing himself in the popular imagination as the leading exponent of mountaineering of the day—a reputation due not simply to his deserving it but also to his personally making his merits obvious. Some were revolted by this—Lord Schuster, President of the Alpine Club, for example, could hardly contain himself and reminded an audience, sarcastically, that there had actually been "great men before Mr Smythe appeared on the scene."

There was, in all this, a combination of understanding and misunderstanding, and the final judgment is not necessarily euphemistic or over-gentle to his memory. He was, according to T. S. Blakeney of the Alpine Club, "The most unassuming of men and would probably never have credited that his death could evoke the flood of private tributes that has poured in from all parts of the world."

As he matured, so life sanded down the rough edges of his personality but not before it had given him a view of the world the main tenets of which were ineradicable by time. His early difficulties in getting on with people in a civilized, urbane social environment caused him initially simply to prefer a solitary mountain life but then to endow that experience with mystical qualities. The need he felt to disabuse himself and others of the notion that he was an awkward weakling caused him, first to strive for, and then to develop a philosophy concerning challenge and adventure. These in turn he translated into a reasoned objection to what he referred to as "civilization" particularly as manifested in technological advance but also, to some extent, in social organization. In many ways, he had a low opinion of man as a species. He was repelled by man's cruelty to man and by his infatuation with material goods and his blindness to nature. His experience in the Bhyundar Valley gave him the view that "it is the ugliness man creates that leads to discontentment and war; the ugliness of greed and the ugliness that greed begets; a vast ocean of ugliness in which he perishes miserably."

In the light of these values, it is possible the better to understand some of the idiosyncratic ideas with which Smythe was associated. His preference for solitary climbing might have been explained on grounds of necessity, but it continued even when he had the choice of companionship, and was always tempered by a sense of obligation to warn others about the hazards of the enterprise.

His suspicion of large expeditions did not prevent him enjoying the company of a few chosen and proven companions. With them he could avoid the contentiousness and quarrelling which he disliked; once a person revealed such a tendency, he said, it was best to leave him severely alone. He speaks of the importance of having, as companions, men who are "temperamentally in phase", in another place emphasizing that it is the small, not the large differences in personality and experience which matter. Which of us can put his hand on his heart and say that there is no ring of truth in Smythe's statement that:

> Your friend in civilisation may become your enemy on a mountain; his very snore assumes a new and repellent note; his tricks at the mess table, the sound of his mastication, the scarcely concealed triumph with which he appropriates the choicest titbits, the absurd manner in which he walks, even the cut of his clothes and the colour of the patch on the seat of his trousers, may induce an irritation and loathing almost beyond endurance.

Tilman and Shipton are usually thought of as being the staunchest advocates of the small expedition. This was, however, the normal type until it was displaced, for the highest and most demanding peaks, by the large, siege-type expedition. Longstaff climbed Trisul with a couple of porters in 1907 shortly before the Duke of Abruzzi mustered a battalion for K2. Smythe's successful Kamet expedition in 1931, like that to Nanda Devi, which Tilman accompanied, five years later, was a reversion to a smaller type.

This was undoubtedly Smythe's preference. But Tilman and Shipton were probably more emotionally committed to the idea while Smythe remained more rational and discriminating. He considered, for example, that "for peaks within easy reach, the ultra-small party loses its point and inadequate porterage merely complicates an expedition", and at one time he considered that siege by a large expedition was the only avenue to success on the highest mountains. Later, he revised this opinion and took a more favourable view of the prospects of a small expedition, even on Everest, at least until the 1938 expedition. Of that venture, there were those who did not hesitate to express the view that its small size was one of the factors which caused it to perform less ably than it otherwise might. Smythe was not among those who published such views, but he privately voiced reservations.

The philosophy of adventure also explains Smythe's attitude towards guided climbing. To abandon responsibility for a climb to a guide was to destroy much of the purpose of climbing and he never, as an adult mountaineer, did so. No one, as Blakeney pointed out, owed less to professionals, a fact for which Smythe incurred opprobrium in some quarters. He was wrongly thought to dislike guides—nothing could be further from the truth: they ranked high in both affection and admiration. It was the phenomenon of being guided that he disliked and it caused him to overstate the case somewhat. His admitted caricature of the early Alpinists as gentlemen dragged up by local peasants and sustained by brandy carried by armies of porters contains, like all caricature, a grain of truth, but could have been put more felicitously. In *Edward Whymper*, his words are:

> . . . no one with an ounce of adventurous pioneering instinct in him can tolerate for long being bear-led up and down mountains by professionals so superior in skill to himself that climbs are little more than a matter of routine. It is better fun to tackle less difficult ascents without guides.

It is hardly surprising that such sentiments should have excited the wrath of such as Schuster who had followed the traditional pattern and been "bear-led", like Whymper, whom Schuster adored, up most of his major peaks. It remains the case, notwithstanding, that for mountaineers of Smythe's motivation, where a guide acts as guide, it is he who takes the lion's share of striving to meet the challenge. There can be satisfaction in guided climbing but it is impossible ever wholly to escape from its vicariousness. The client may believe that he could have met the challenge on his own; he may be right. But the fact remains that he didn't.

Finally, the dislike of "civilization" and mechanical things explains Smythe's preference for a pure style of climbing. He disliked not only motor roads and téléfériques but objected, famously, to the use of pitons. Since he objected neither to axe nor crampons, we can only speculate what his view would have been on such things as Friends and Pterodactyls. It is impossible, here, to escape a charge of irrationality. If pegs are unethical, what about ropes, or Vibram soles or even training for fitness? Smythe's less than wholly satisfactory answer to this was to appeal to reasonableness in all things, but appeals to "reasonableness" are, at best, appeals to current convention or, at worst, unargued reassertions of a person's prejudices. If so, it was a prejudice which Smythe sustained throughout his life. In the Rockies, in 1947, a first ascent rendered possible only by the use of a piton gave him no satisfaction, and on another climb he retreated rather than resort to such aid. When the mountain was, shortly thereafter, "climbed" by a party which "nailed" its way up, Smythe refused to recognize the ascent. These are the particular implications of Smythe's philosophy of adventure.

In attempting to assess Smythe's mountaineering achievement, chiefly as a climber, but also as author and photographer, there is no shortage of opinions. On his standing as a climber, they range from the extremes of Graham Brown to that of Sir Francis Younghusband, that he was "the ideal mountaineer", though he was, perhaps, partial: he relied upon Smythe for a supply of strawberries in old age. Graham Brown's charge of cowardice is specific and serious: he claimed personally to have experienced it on the Route Major and to have heard, at three removes, "that Smythe had a reputation for funking it on Kangchenjunga."

We shall never know for sure whether the Route Major incident sprang from fear or whether it was the product of a rational consideration of risks. On Kangchenjunga, we have rather better evidence. It is true that Smythe formed the opinion that the chosen face was unjustifiable as too risky. He admitted to fear; but his fear and judgment did not keep him off the mountain. On the contrary, he played the major role at the sharp end of the assault where he remained longer than anyone. Was he, then, guilty, if not of cowardice, of over-caution, itself no mean vice in the context of Himalayan mountaineering where boldness may be at a premium? Events proved conclusively otherwise: the apprehended avalanche did occur, the wall collapsed and Chettan was killed.

On the Route Major it is perfectly possible that Smythe actually lost his nerve. They had been on the move for ten or eleven hours after a bivouac on an unknown face. It was late in the day and they did not know what difficulties might lie ahead—it was, in fact, dark before they reached the Vallot Hut. It must have looked like at least even money on a second bivouac if they continued, with what consequences one can only guess. It is at least arguable that retreat, although difficult, was the proper course. They could not know that they would encounter no further difficulties and yet run out of daylight.

It is impossible to say whether Smythe's suggestion sprang from cowardice or from a strong mountaineering sense. This was an era when a high proportion of the pioneers succeeded in killing themselves. Roch points out that of the first thirty to climb the South Ridge of the Aiguille Noire de Peuterey, one of the "hard" routes of the day, more than a half later died young in the mountains. Smythe, by contrast, was a notoriously safe mountaineer. He makes his attitude clear in *Edward Whymper*: one should be willing to accept "defeat" (not, note, "retreat" or any other voluntary response) on account of risk just as much as on account of technical difficulty or impossible conditions. Neither Smythe nor any member of a party of which he had charge ever suffered death or serious injury on a mountain while at the same time an unexcelled record of achievement was compiled. Had he been less "cowardly", he might have added to the record the summit of Everest in 1933. It was early in the day; he was fit and going well; he had less than 1,000 feet to go, but the risk was too great and he acknowledged defeat. To some, this may have been "funking it"; others went on record as recognizing it as "the final triumph of judgment".

Of one slightly different crime Smythe was guilty. On both Kangchenjunga and the Route Major, he failed to press his view. On Kangchenjunga, this would have meant rebelling—perhaps a lot to ask of a young man on his first Himalayan expedition under the leadership of the overbearing Dyhrenfurth. He was, in any case, always a loyal and faithful expedition member, even under clearly inferior leaders and despite an alleged arrogance. On the Route Major, he seems to have allowed the obsession of Graham Brown, admittedly an older and stubborn man, to win the day too easily.

As to his technical competence, some had reservations. Lunn thought him "not in the first flight as a rock climber" but "one of the greatest mountaineers of the day". Shipton observed Smythe as closely as anyone, and it was his assessment that Smythe was "sound rather than brilliant". Another Everest companion, Jack Longland, in summarizing progress generally in the inter-war years, regarded Smythe's contribution as most significant. Other leading mountaineers of the day, such as Greene, Beauman, Blakeney and MacPhee held him in very high regard, but were ranked amongst relatively few friends and may therefore have been partial in their judgment.

"Sound rather than brilliant" seems to me to be a fair assessment of the man as a rock-climber, although it can also be said of all the best-known British inter-war Himalayan mountaineers, with the exception of Jack Longland. Smythe belonged to the group that would second the harder routes of the day, such as Longland's on Cloggy, or with Bell on the Plan, rather than to the small and select group of pioneers who led them. On ice, by contrast, word was that he was brilliant, if any British climber was. His leading on Kangchenjunga seems to have been in the highest technical class, which is where Bell placed his contribution on the Plan route, whilst his leading on Everest yielded what was described by a colleague of wide experience as the finest example of technical ice-climbing ever seen. It is easy to forget that crampons were an innovation and that the modern axe was four decades away.

What all this overlooks is that Smythe purported to be not a rock-climber as such, but a mountaineer and if what is being assessed is the ability to travel with maximum safety over difficult high-mountain terrain in the worst conditions, then Smythe *was*, in the view of many who travelled with him, brilliant. MacPhee was not alone in regarding the first successful descent of the Rochers Gruber after their traverse of the Aiguille Blanche as a remarkable *tour de force*. Others, such as Bell, spoke of his extraordinary stamina and remarkable route-finding ability. On Everest, he went, alone, as high as very few ever had, and endured a desperate solo descent. On none of his Himalayan expeditions did anyone stay high longer than he. His record of achievements speaks for itself.

As a leader and expedition organizer his contribution is easier to assess, although events conspired to limit the experience. Raymond Greene said of Smythe's role in the Kamet venture that he was "the best kind of leader for such an enterprise, the leader who makes all the plans with meticulous care and having, as it were, created the world leaves it to run itself, giving it only a gentle push if it slows down or begins to wobble on its axis, but remaining personally inconspicuous." Part of the secret was the effort he made to get together the right team for the task in hand. The three true expeditions of which he had charge were all highly successful. All were "small". It is entirely speculative what sort of job he would have made of handling a large expedition, though, of all leaders of British expeditions to the Himalayas in the inter-war years, none exceeded Smythe's level of success and few approached it.

As an author, Smythe is again the subject of conflicting judgments. There were those leading members of the climbing establishment of the day, such as Schuster (reviewing in the *Alpine Journal*), to whom he was "a copious (perhaps a too copious) writer of Alpine books" and Lunn (in the *Dictionary of National Biography*, 1941–50), who thought his "literary reputation suffered from the fact that he rather overwrote himself." Others, such as Raymond Greene (in his obituary in the *Alpine Journal*), pointed to the rather obvious proposition that "he is not to be blamed because the public liked his work—such a judgment smacks of snobbery and puts him in the condemned cell with many a better writer. Rather should we be grateful to him for bringing a love of mountain adventure into the lives of thousands who would never otherwise have known it."

It is at least paradoxical that his two most vociferous critics should have formed an unfavourable view of his work. The mountaineering career of neither came anywhere near the distinction of Smythe's yet out of it each carved remarkable literary achievements. Lunn overwrote to an extent never dreamed of by Smythe and, incidentally, made a handsome living out of it, presumably evading the charge of professionalism by reason only of not needing the money. Schuster gave to the world surely the two most turgid mountaineering books ever written.

Some disliked the views expressed in his books and let this colour their criticism of their literary merits. Schuster, in particular, revered Whymper and could not forgive what he conceived to be Smythe's criticism of him. Of Smythe, he said that "his lack of sympathy with Whymper as a man amounted to a positive dislike and he was overfond of the clichés and half-truths with which a certain school likes to belabour the Victorian age and those who lived in it." He paraphrases Smythe's view of Whymper's *Travels Amongst the Great Andes of the Equator* as being that "things happened and they were chronicled—that was all", but surely this is a fair view. Is there, anywhere in the annals of mountaineering, a flatter, duller, more frankly factual account of any major expedition? Is there perhaps a hint of paranoia in some of the charges levelled against Smythe as author by some of his contemporaries? Or was there, more likely, envy in some quarters, at his popularity in others, engendered largely by his own books? Those who could not, or would not, write accounts of their exploits or who, more likely, had no significant exploits to write about, would not take kindly to the fame which attached to Smythe, very largely as a result of self-publicity which, if not a crime, at least fell short of the ideal of gentlemanly behaviour.

Indeed, the more serious charge levelled against him was that he was a professional who climbed to write and wrote for money. It is a curious parallel that, as Smythe points out in his biography of Whymper, the success of the latter's *Scrambles* . . . caused him to be accused of profiting out of the Matterhorn tragedy which, of course, he undoubtedly did. Raymond Greene gave the lie in Smythe's case in his obituary:

> The view that he climbed mountains not for love of mountains but for love of the gain they brought him is as absurd as to suggest that Shelley pursued Harriet in order afterwards to write love poems. His was too simple a soul for such twisted insincerity. Mountains were the symbols of his religion and his books his testimony.

This is not to say that the possibility of writing, profitably, about his exploits never entered his head. It most certainly did; he would, for example, negotiate a publishing contract before even setting a foot abroad on a projected expedition. But, apart from one questionable assertion by Graham Brown, there is no evidence that Smythe's primary motivation was ever other than climbing mountains for the love of it.

Whatever the summary of judgment at his death, the facts remain, first, that his books were well-received by the cognoscenti of the day and, second, that they were extraordinarily popular. With one exception, all were well-reviewed in the leading contemporary journals. The one exception was his photographic album on the Rocky Mountains, reviewed by a Canadian in the *Canadian Alpine*

Journal, who obviously resented the phenomenon of a foreigner daring to comment on the Rockies at all. And they all sold well. Smythe was, no doubt, grateful but was nevertheless undoubtedly sincere when he said that "the most satisfactory and satisfying success was that success which achieves not material gain but spiritual contentment and happiness."

Criticism of Smythe as author is today more muted but it is still there. His books "had a great vogue at the time" but "his somewhat romantic philosophy of climbing is little echoed today." This is a view held only in some quarters; it still resounds repeatedly in others. His books, for example, enjoyed and still do enjoy a reverence in France not generally accorded to them in Britain. The British today are not awfully keen on philosophy at all, regarding it rather as a harmless hobby for eccentrics. The French are much more comfortable in the presence of mysticism and romance. Herzog voices the Gallic view both of Smythe's books, and of the film which he made of the Kamet climb, in the most complimentary terms.

It would be easy to pitch the debate on too elevated a plane. What it boils down to is this: there are many who value the mountains because they offer peace, beauty, solitude, grandeur and an unsurpassable feeling of well-being and mark a contrast with the harsh, overmechanized, brutal and often vicious realities of life in human society. Equally, there are some who do not. In his own day, Smythe suffered from unpopularity in certain circles at the same time as enjoying enormous popularity with the public at large. Today the philosophy for which he stood flourishes among thousands of ordinary and humble adherents of the pastime; but it is those whose voices tend to be heard who find their satisfaction otherwise, and, in their contributions to the debate, in the climbing journals, rarely bother to say whether or not they had a good day out. For such, Smythe's approach to the hills would indeed appear romantic; this is not disputed. What is most vigorously contested is the notion that there is only one way to enjoy the mountain experience.

It is, perhaps, Smythe's unique achievement as a writer that he belonged to both worlds and addressed both contemporary audiences. He was, not of course alone, at one and the same time in the van of achievement and, in that sense, one of the "hard" men of the day, and at the same time highly critical of those, such as the Munich School, for whom the "*Blitz am Berg*" was everything. There is no shortage of deeds of "derring do" in books such as *The Kangchenjunga Adventure* which provoke a sympathetic hearing without ever prompting a desire to leave one's armchair. At the other extreme, most reading, say, *Over Tyrolese Hills*, would be able not merely to sympathize with the author but to wish to emulate, for he here describes the sort of exploits which the humblest and most modest of mountaineers might reasonably undertake, and he does so in terms of, if anything, even greater affection. Even today, some readers will be provoked to leave their armchairs, others to recall what it was like last time they did. Vast numbers in both categories will have no difficulty in understanding the call which drew Smythe to the hills. Anyone who looks outside the ranks of the élite will readily find that the same attitudes prevail today. Smythe's greatest literary endeavour was to try to express his delight in mountains in a way, sometimes mysterious, sometimes reverential and sometimes irreverent, which most ordinary mountaineers, not preoccupied with ever more remarkable attainments, understood. The many thousands who, over the years, have savoured his books, gave the lie, in the most unambiguous way, to his critics.

As a photographer, Smythe almost succeeded in avoiding criticism entirely. There was an occasion when, pulling out his tiny *Etui* and quickly taking a picture, he was brusquely dismissed, by an old gentleman manfully struggling with thirty pounds of hand-and-stand camera, as a "snapshotter" but apart from this he was allowed to go his way without comment.

He was, reputedly, blessed with a sound technical knowledge—a spell working with Kodak Ltd in the 1920s was, no doubt, a great help. He was certainly prolific; and he was popular. In all, he produced ten albums, the least attractive of which is the Rocky Mountains volume, many of the plates in which lack definition and suffer from poor colour which was at that time, admittedly, still in its infancy. Apart from his albums, his photographs still appear frequently in other sources, from newspapers to glossy expedition books.

He was, however, rather more than merely popular and prolific. He is acknowledged to have been one of the best, if not the best, exponent of the "art" of the camera of his day. It is not overstating his standing to regard him, amongst British mountain photographers, as inheriting the mantle of the Abrahams brothers, passing it on, eventually, to the likes of Douglas Milner and W. A. Poucher. It is probably fair to say that, had he never set foot on the Brenva Face or the summit of Kamet, his place in mountaineering history would be assured simply as, at the very least, one of the most outstanding mountain photographers not merely of his day, but ever. It was, for all that, merely one of the minor strings on his bow.

None of this reaches the heart of the man. Grading his achievement, assessing his books, evaluating his photography all fall short of describing the compulsion of the hills for Smythe. Escape and challenge there certainly were. But he could have found solitude and adventure equally on the ocean or in the desert. He speaks, more than once, of the "pure air" of the mountains and it is plain that, in doing so, he is speaking figuratively as well as literally. He toys with psychological explanations—man is not quite as totally emancipated from primitive superstition about high places as he likes to think: a residuum of dread to some extent accounts for the obsession. But there is more to it than that. In the final analysis, it is hard to better his own attempt to explain:

> Deeply engrained in the mountaineer is a desire for adventure far and high and to attain to some indefinable spiritual degree of attunement with the beauties of the universe. The zest for physical exercise and good health, the application of technique and skill to a difficult problem, are powerful material motives, yet they cannot be the only motives in mountaineering. Failing to observe beauty, we are as men dead. Fully to enjoy the hills it is necessary to heed beauty and to discern through beauty a peace that knows no mental or physical limitations and is concerned with no material formulae.

It was this sort of declaration of faith which led to the accusation in some quarters that Smythe was attempting to carve a religion out of his mountaineering. His experience in India, indeed, caused him to think. He began to understand that the secret of earthly happiness lay in simplicity of living, and he developed an interest in meditation, as a Westerner somewhat before his time, recognizing the limitations of the intellect and the importance of feeling uncluttered by thought. "He is indeed great," he said, "who can conquer his own cleverness."

Lunn thought him to be at his worst in this respect, but Lunn himself might easily be described as being a religious freak of a different sort and might well feel discomfited by Smythe's gropings towards pantheism. On a less theological level, thousands will be able to bear witness to feelings engendered by the mountain experience which certainly have a "spiritual" content and which it would not be out of place to describe, in a broad sense, as religious, although some might prefer to restrict that term to a narrower meaning. But to those unreceptive to such sentiments, such claims will be as incomprehensible as is the notion of vision to one who has never known sight, and may therefore seem false.

Speculation about motives seems to be one of those journeys that it is more entertaining to make than to complete. Smythe, whatever the reason, made a great impression and has probably influenced attitudes towards mountaineering more than any figure this century. If there is any doubt about the genuineness of the man, the experience of his last days in Darjeeling in 1949 may resolve it. Tensing observed his grasp of reality slipping. Smythe first could not remember his own name and, when he did, could not remember the month of the year. He tried October, then settled for December. It was in fact May. Later, walking, he demanded his ice-axe, though the nearest snow was miles distant. And so he lapsed into delirium. In hospital, now separated from the real world, he talked on about great climbs and great mountains. They were his life.

I believe Smythe's influence to have been greatly beneficial. I remember well the occasion when this first became clear to me. It was on an early visit to the Alps; I was unfit and had just trudged despairingly up from Les Contamines to the Trélatête Hotel. I slumped down at the dining table, with a beer, opposite the only other occupant of the room, a grizzled and weather-beaten old French guide reduced to escorting wealthy schoolboys over passes, and utterly content to do it. I ventured a "Bonjour" in my best French. "Ah," he said, "you are Eengleesh. Ah! Frong Smeet; 'e have the vision of the mountains."

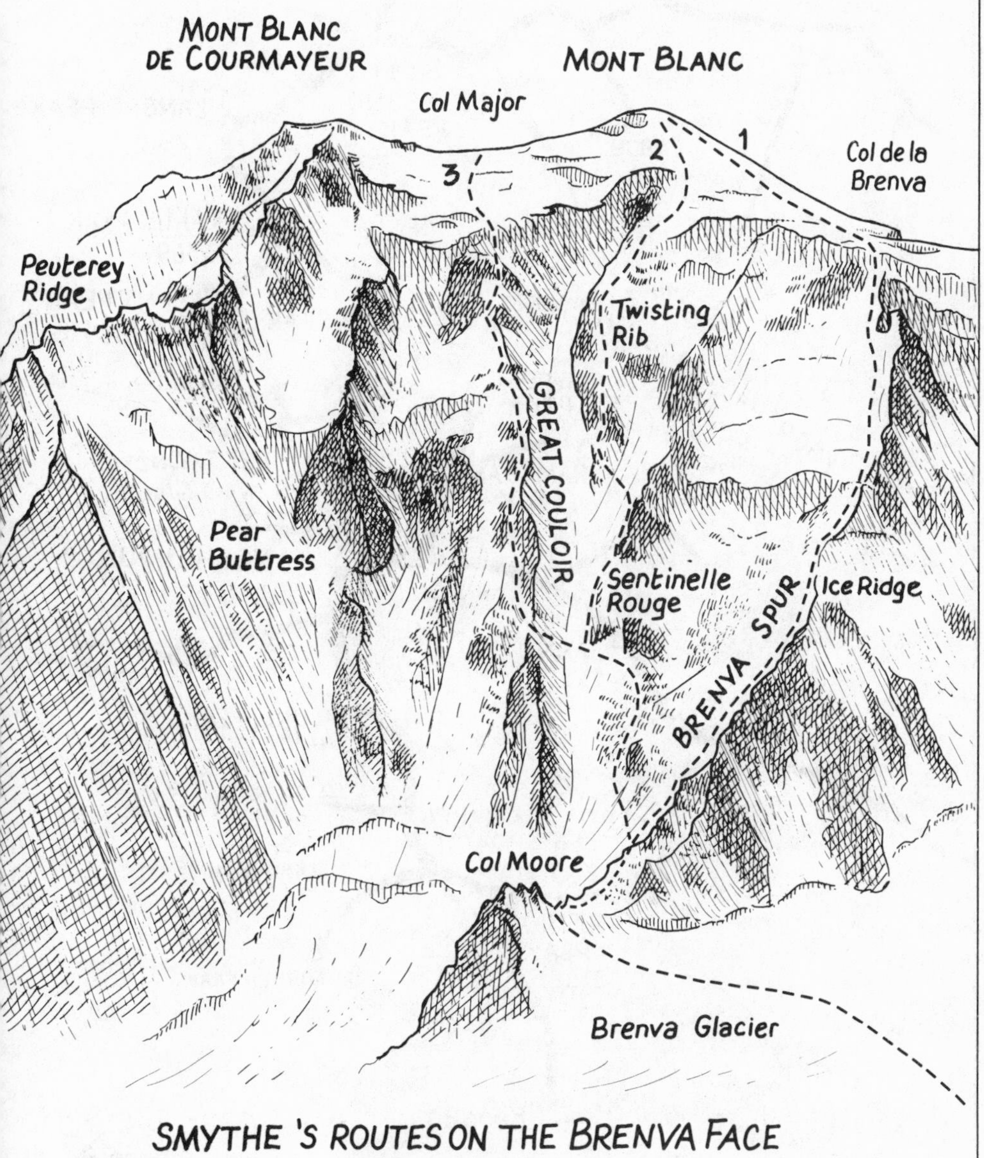

SMYTHE 'S ROUTES ON THE BRENVA FACE

1. Old Brenva
2. Red Sentinel
3. Route Major

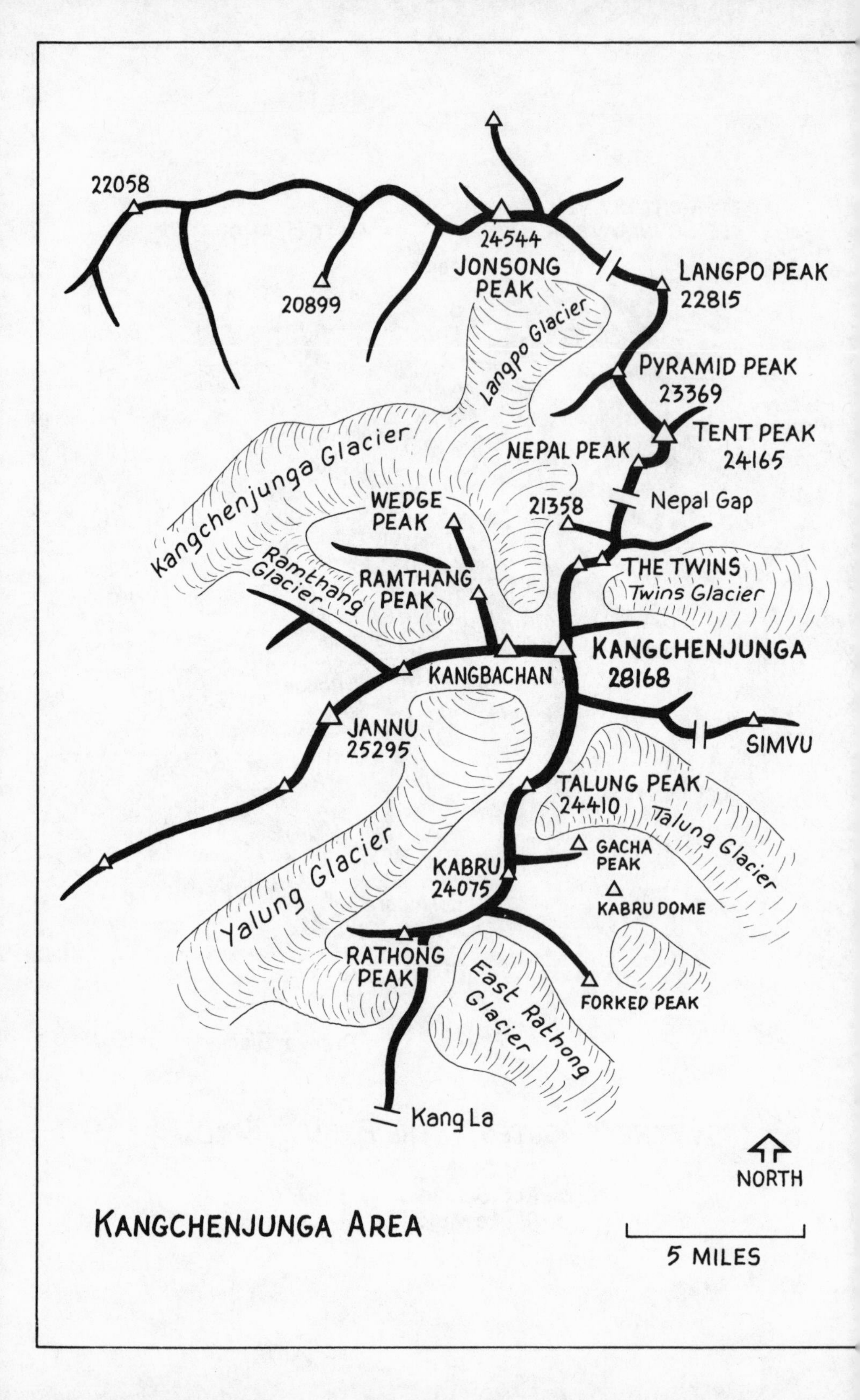

KANGCHENJUNGA AREA

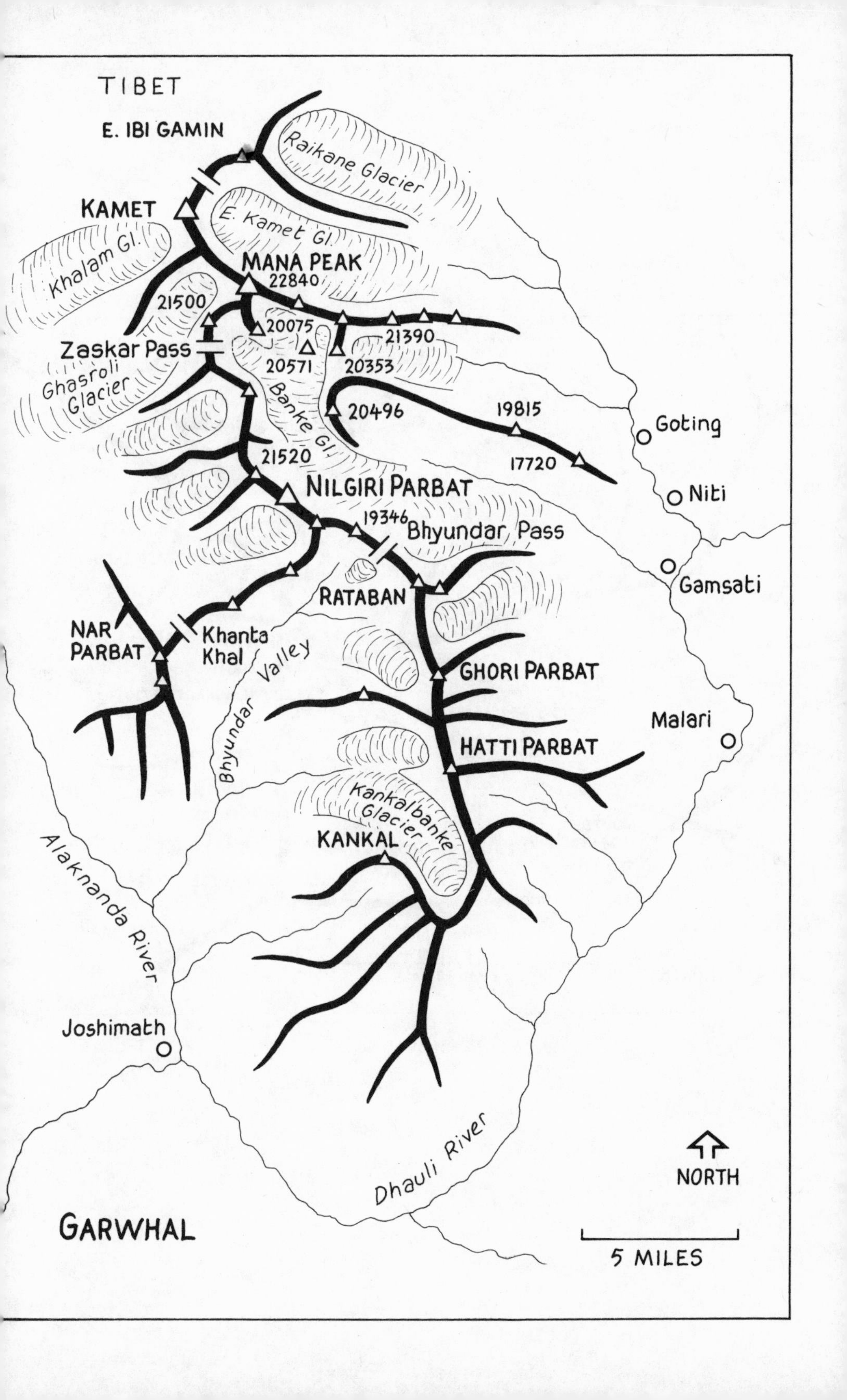
TIBET
E. IBI GAMIN
Raikane Glacier
KAMET
E. Kamet Gl.
Khalam Gl.
MANA PEAK
22840
21500
20075
21390
Zaskar Pass
20571
20353
Ghasroli Glacier
Banke Gl.
20496
19815
Goting
21520
17720
NILGIRI PARBAT
Niti
19346
Bhyundar Pass
Gamsati
RATABAN
NAR PARBAT
Khanta Khal
Bhyundar Valley
GHORI PARBAT
Malari
HATTI PARBAT
Kankalbanke Glacier
KANKAL
Alaknanda River
Joshimath
Dhauli River
NORTH
GARWHAL
5 MILES

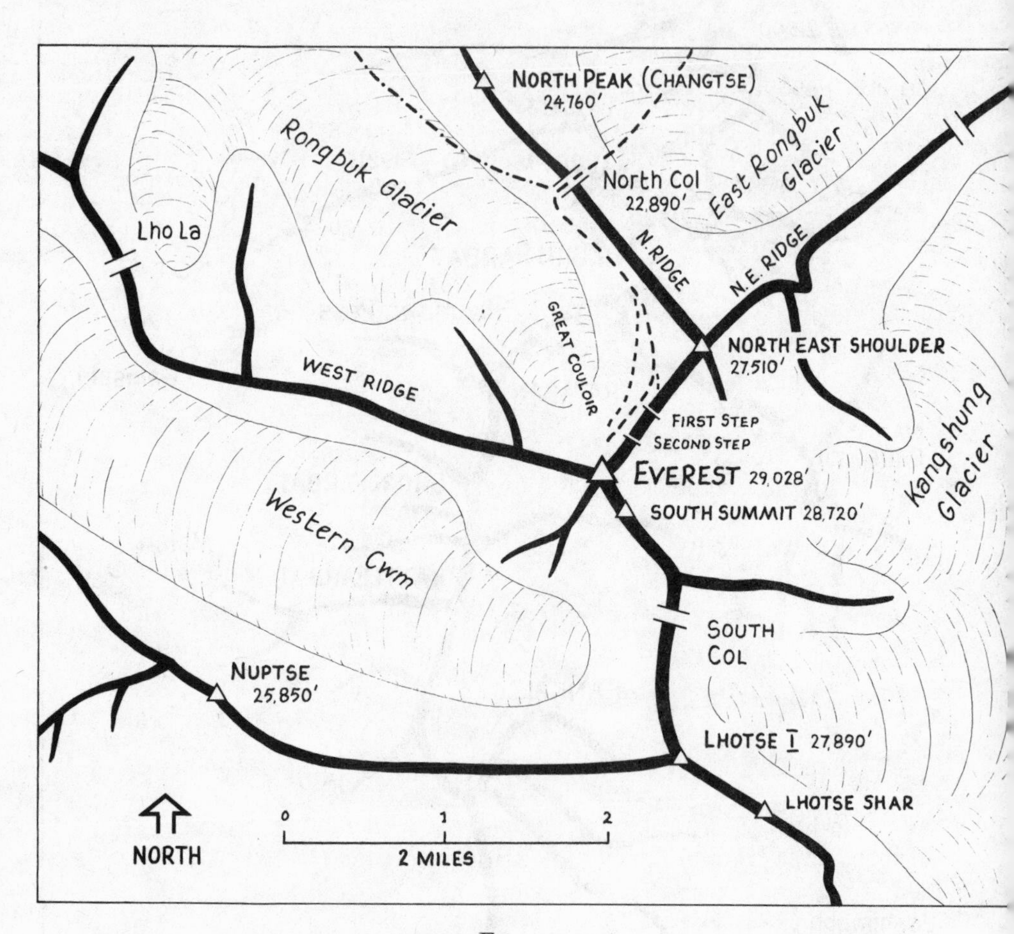
NORTH PEAK (CHANGTSE)
24,760'
Rongbuk Glacier
North Col
22,890'
East Rongbuk Glacier
Lho La
N. RIDGE
N.E. RIDGE
GREAT COULOIR
NORTH EAST SHOULDER
27,510'
WEST RIDGE
FIRST STEP
SECOND STEP
EVEREST 29,028'
SOUTH SUMMIT 28,720'
Kangshung Glacier
Western Cwm
SOUTH
COL
NUPTSE
25,850'
LHOTSE I 27,890'
LHOTSE SHAR
NORTH
0
1
2
2 MILES

Everest

BIBLIOGRAPHY

G. D. Abraham, *British Mountain Climbs*, London: Mills & Boon, 1909.
Alpine Club, *Alpine Journal*, London: 1853–date.
Alpine Club of Canada, *Canadian Alpine Journal*, Vancouver: 1907–date.
Ashenden, *The Mountains of My Life*, London: Blackwood, 1954.
P. Bauer, *Kanchenjunga Challenge*, London: Kimber, 1955.
J. H. B. Bell, *A Progress in Mountaineering*, London: Oliver & Boyd, 1950.
M. Boustead, *The Wind of Morning*, London: 1871.
British Ski Year Book.
T. Graham Brown, *Brenva*, London: Dent, 1944.
—— private papers, National Library of Scotland, Edinburgh.
D. L. Busk, *The Delectable Mountains*, London: Hodder & Stoughton, 1945.
Climbers' Club, *Climbers' Club Journal*, N. S., 1912–date.
Dictionary of National Biography, sub. nom. "Francis Sydney Smythe".
G. O. Dyhrenfurth, *To The Third Pole: the History of the High Himalaya,* London: Werner Laurie, 1955.
C. E. Engel, *A History of Mountaineering in the Alps*, London: Allen & Unwin, 1950, republished as:
—— *Mountaineering in the Alps: an Historical Survey*, London: Allen & Unwin, 1965.
R. C. S. Evans, *Kanchenjunga: the Untrodden Peak*, London: Hodder & Stoughton, 1955.
R. Greene, *Moments of Being*, London: Heinemann, 1974.
M. Herzog, *La Montagne*, Paris: Larousse, 1956.
Himalayan Club, *Himalayan Journal*, London: 1929–date.
H. C. J. Hunt, *The Ascent of Everest*, London: Hodder & Stoughton, 1953.
R. L. G. Irving, *The Romance of Mountaineering*, London: Dent, 1935.
—— *A History of British Mountaineering*, London: Batsford, 1955.
T. G. Longstaff, *This My Voyage*, London: Murray, 1950.
A. H. M. Lunn, *Zermatt and the Valais*, London: Hollis & Carter, 1955.
C. D. Milner, *Mont Blanc and the Aiguilles*, London: Hale, 1955.
A. Roch, *Climbs of My Youth*, London: Lindsay Drummond, 1949.
H. L. Ruttledge, *Everest 1933*, London: Hodder & Stoughton, 1934.
—— *Everest: The Unfinished Adventure*, London: Hodder & Stoughton, 1937.
C. Schuster, *Postscript to Adventure*, London: Eyre & Spottiswoode, 1950.
—— *Men, Women and Mountains*, London: Nicolson & Watson, 1931.

Scottish Mountaineering Club, *Scottish Mountaineering Club Journal*, Edinburgh: 1907–date.
E. E. Shipton, *Upon That Mountain*, London: Hodder & Stoughton, 1943.
—— *That Untravelled World*, London: Hodder & Stoughton, 1969.
F. S. Smythe, *Climbs and Ski Runs*, Edinburgh: Blackwood, 1929.
—— *The Kangchenjunga Adventure*, London: Gollancz, 1930.
—— *Kamet Conquered*, London: Gollancz, 1932.
—— *An Alpine Journey*, London: Gollancz, 1934.
—— *The Spirit of the Hills*, London: Hodder & Stoughton, 1935.
—— *Over Tyrolese Hills*, London: Hodder & Stoughton, 1936.
—— *The Mountain Scene*, London: A. & C. Black, 1937.
—— *Camp Six: An Account of the 1933 Mount Everest Expedition*, London: Hodder & Stoughton, 1937.
—— *Peaks and Valleys*, London: A. & C. Black, 1938.
—— *The Valley of Flowers*, London: Hodder & Stoughton, 1938.
—— *A Camera in the Hills*, London, A. & C. Black, 1939.
—— *My Alpine Album*, London: A. & C. Black, 1940.
—— *Mountaineering Holiday*, London: Hodder & Stoughton, 1940.
—— *Edward Whymper*, London: Hodder & Stoughton, 1940.
—— *The Adventures of a Mountaineer*, London: Dent, 1940.
—— *The Mountain Vision*, London: Hodder & Stoughton, 1941.
—— *Over Welsh Hills*, London: A. & C. Black, 1941.
—— *Alpine Ways*, London: A. & C. Black, 1942.
—— *British Mountaineers*, London: Collins, 1942.
—— *Snow on the Hills*, London: A. & C. Black, 1945.
—— *Again Switzerland*, London: Hodder & Stoughton, 1947.
—— *Swiss Winter*, London: A. & C. Black, 1948.
—— *Rocky Mountains*, London: A. & C. Black, 1948.
—— *Mountains in Colour*, London: Parrish, 1949.
—— *Climbs in the Canadian Rockies*, London: Hodder & Stoughton, 1950.
T. H. Somervell, *After Everest: The Experiences of a Mountaineer and Medical Missionary*, London: Hodder & Stoughton, 1935.
H. W. Tilman, *Snow on the Equator*, London: Bell, 1937.
—— *Mount Everest 1938*, London: Cambridge, 1948.
The Times newspaper.
J. R. Ullman, *Man of Everest*, London: Harrap, 1955.
W. Unsworth, *Because It Is There: Famous Mountaineers, 1840–1940*, London: Gollancz, 1968.
—— *Encyclopaedia of Mountaineering*, London: Hale, 1975.
—— *Everest*, London: Allen Lane, 1981.
C. Urech, *Bernese Oberland*, Thun: Schneider, 1925.
F. E. Younghusband, *Everest: The Challenge*, London: Nelson, 1935.

INDEX